WALKING THE HEXAGON

To Peter and Muriel, who first taught me to love the hills, and to Lizzie who accompanied me up many of them.

To Rob & Dave
Good luck !
Terry.

WALKING THE HEXAGON

AN ESCAPE AROUND FRANCE ON FOOT

TERRY CUDBIRD

Signal

SIGNAL BOOKS
OXFORD

First published in 2012 by
Signal Books Limited
36 Minster Road
Oxford
OX4 1LY
www.signalbooks.co.uk

ISBN 978-1-908493-03-3 Paper

Production: Tora Kelly
Cover Design: Tora Kelly
Cover Illustrations: Elizabeth Manson-Bahr
Photographs: Terry Cudbird; pp.9, 63, 69 Wikipedia Commons
Maps: www.hello-design.co.uk
Printed by Short Run Press Ltd, Exeter, UK

CONTENTS

INTRODUCTION
WHY WALK?

ON A COLD NOVEMBER day I was walking down a path of slippery cobbles and rain was falling. A grey sky covered me like a shroud. I was crossing the northern plain not far from Valenciennes in the Nord *département*. Slag heaps dotted the horizon near the large Citroën factory at Hordain. It was a scene reminiscent of Émile Zola's dark nineteenth-century novel *Germinal* about the mining communities of this region. And then suddenly I noticed three young men rolling towards me in a four by four. They wore hunting clothes and were obviously on their way back from a day's shooting. The driver stopped and lowered his window. "What are you doing?"

"Walking."

"Eh! Where have you walked from?"

"Beaudignies."

An incredulous smile spread across his face. "What nationality are you?" he asked, as if no Frenchman would be walking in the rain across the bleak plain on a cold afternoon in November.

"English."

"Do you do things like this in England?"

"Yes."

His expression suggested that my nationality explained everything. All the English, the French tend to believe, are eccentric.

I received a similar reaction on several occasions during my three hundred-day walk around France. English hikers never look the height of fashion, whereas in France it is important to appear smart even if you are trekking. Well-dressed ladies moved away from me in a tea shop in Brittany, probably because I looked like a bedraggled tramp. In a restaurant near Verdun my down and out appearance provoked pity and a free drink. A café owner in the north thought I was a poor St. Jacques pilgrim who had come in the wrong season. In the Vendée an hotelier politely showed me to the back entrance so as not to shock his diners.

My appearance and my plan to walk around France were not the only factors which struck the French as bizarre. They could not understand why I was walking alone. "The French are too sociable to do that," two ladies once said to me. French maps contain red lines for Grandes Randonnées stretching hundreds of miles, but few people walk a GR for long distances, except in the Pyrenees, the Alps and in Corsica.

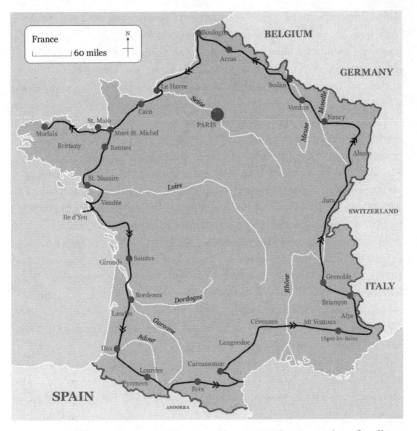

Why do third-agers seek adventures like mine? The crazy idea of walking around the circumference of France started with a conversation beside an Alpine lake just before my retirement. I told my wife Lizzie that I wanted to walk a lot of the Grandes Randonnées—the 38,000-mile network of long-distance footpaths that cover the French countryside—and write about my experiences. "Why don't you do it now?" she said, "before you become decrepit."

The best sound in the world for me became the clunk-click of the buckles when I put on my rucksack. It meant the freedom to go where I wanted, to dream my own dreams and escape the complications of everyday life. My project quickly became an obsession. I was never as happy as when I was poring over maps, calculating distances and making timetables. Having spent so much time creating detailed plans I had to carry them out. The timetable then took over.

When I first mentioned to friends what I had in mind some thought I was mad. Why wear out your sixty-year-old hips and knees walking around France when you could spend a comfortable retirement doing voluntary work in Oxford and going on cruises? Others were enthusiastic about the idea, looked wistfully at their walking boots and said they would love to join me for a stretch. The itinerary put most of them off when they realised what was involved. "How can you keep plodding along day after day?" was a common reaction. Why not just do the best bits and leave the rest out? I could not compromise. I had said I was going to walk the circumference of France and round I was going to go.

The idea of such a circular journey is nothing new. The tradition of *le compagnonnage*, artisans walking round France in search of opportunities to perfect their skills, was strong in the eighteenth and early nineteenth centuries. In 1877 a little book appeared which became a major publishing success, selling seven million copies by 1914. Augustine Fouillée's *Le Tour de la France par deux enfants* described the escape of two imaginary boys from German-occupied Lorraine and their journey around France, rediscovering its towns and villages, its industries, agriculture and historical sites. The famous cycle race, the Tour de France, started in 1903 and ever since has covered large parts of France, sometimes around its periphery. Yet as far as I know I am the only person to have attempted such a long circular tour on foot.

The French sometimes refer to their country as a hexagon, most frequently in the weather forecast. If you look at France on a map it has a six-sided symmetry, albeit with many lumps and bumps. My walk followed the shape of this hexagon more or less, hence the title (apologies to Corsica). I did, however, allow myself a bit of licence. For example, I did not complete the Pyrenean trail (GR10), preferring to visit the Cathar country in the east and the Béarn in the west. I stuck to the mountains behind the Mediterranean coastal resorts. I left the Alpine trail (GR5) at Briançon to take in the Écrins, Grenoble and the Chartreuse. I followed the crests of the Vosges rather than walk along the Rhine.

I completed my walk in a number of stages of around a month's duration. After each one I returned home for a rest and then resumed where I left off. Family demands prevented me completing my project as quickly as I would have liked. I covered half the total distance of 4,000 miles in one year and finished the remainder over the following two. My wife Lizzie accompanied me forty per cent of the way and friends joined us for a few days from time to time.

I wanted to have plenty of chances to talk to French people. This I certainly managed to do. I spent almost a year in France and the French I met came from every walk of life. I prefer hostels, refuges and guest houses where you eat with other walkers and can chat far into the night. I made a lot of French friends whom I have visited since I finished my walk. There are advantages to walking alone. I notice things around me more when I am not talking to a companion. I walk at my own pace and stop whenever I want. I talk to more strangers when I do not have ready-made company.

I have a secret desire to adopt a different identity in middle age, like a new suit of clothes. When I speak French I somehow take on a different personality: less inhibited, more expressive, less pragmatic. I am sloughing off my old skin and it is that sense of escape which is liberating. If I had spent some of my youth studying German, Spanish or Chinese, I might have disappeared to those countries instead. It is not France itself which is important, but rather the personal transformation brought about by immersion in a non-Anglo-Saxon culture.

I wanted to test myself physically and mentally as well. I covered four thousand miles and climbed one hundred thousand feet. Out of just under a year spent walking I was alone for six months. Gradually I found that walking long distances is a mechanical business. You quickly slip into a routine. Pack your rucksack in the morning, have breakfast, buy a snack for lunch, stride along for six hours, unpack your things in the evening, wash your clothes, have a glass or two of wine and a good meal. Life is stripped down to the essentials. You carry as few possessions as possible, you eat and sleep and leave the complications of modern life behind. There is no doubt walking is good for mental health. Recent research has confirmed this. If I want to think over a problem a good walk alone usually helps.

There is no doubt either that the regular rhythm of walking can induce a trance-like state of peace and contentment. Perhaps it is akin to repeating a Buddhist mantra or the Jesus prayer used by the "holy fools" who wandered across Russia. Very often you need a tune in your head to keep the rhythm going; something with a regular beat which is easy to hum. My own secret weapon in the battle to remain sane was to talk to myself; or at least to muse about my experiences into a voice recorder. Two machines were always zipped into my side pocket. I must have downloaded over one hundred hours of ramblings onto my PC at home.

Long distance walking also has its disadvantages—guard dogs, snorers, rain, heat, intense cold, man-eating insects, paths on the map which no longer exist, blisters, exhausted limbs, aching muscles, lack of water and a rucksack which is too heavy. Why is it I always carry things I don't need? Several times I had to go to the post office to send unwanted items home.

Perhaps the greatest attraction of walking long distances is that you are constantly exposed to the unexpected. However much you study the maps, the landscape is full of surprises and never quite as you imagined it. Nothing could have prepared me for the chasms of the Alps, the airy elevation of the Vosges above the busy world of the Rhine valley, the shifting light of sea and sky on the Somme estuary. If I had not walked I would never have found the old irrigation channels circling the heights of the Tinée valley or glimpsed the studded masses of primroses and violets in the shady banks of a green lane in Brittany.

Bridge and chasm, the Alps

Some readers might expect a book packed with heroic incidents and exotic adventures, in which case they may find my story disappointing. I am not a super-fit professional explorer trying to join the ranks of those who have crossed vast stretches of impossible terrain in record time. I did not fall off a cliff, join a hippy commune or walk from one hilarious incident to another. My adventure was lower-key than some but it was an adventure nevertheless. I proved that a sixty-year-old can still reinvent himself and have fun, without travelling to the ends of the earth and adding to global warming. If I excite other people to walk through France I will be more than satisfied.

*

Robert Louis Stevenson is one of my heroes. I fell in love with walking in France partly because of him. His acute powers of observation and his language turned a mundane walk into something magical. He also wove the history of his Protestant co-religionists into his story. This added to his appeal in my eyes, especially as I see myself as a historian manqué. I was always passionate about the subject, but never good enough to make the grade as an academic. Nor in truth was I suited to a life sitting in libraries and archives, consulting dusty books and old manuscripts. I do not quite know why I turned out this way. My interest in the subject predated school and university. I have embarrassing memories of being asked to do a party piece when I was eight, reciting the dates of the Kings and Queens of England. A family friend used to visit regularly in an outsize Chevrolet with an enormous chow on the back seat. But next to the dog was a pile of books for me, second-hand from Harrods Library. I remember C. V. Wedgwood's *The King's Peace* and *The King's War*, and Churchill's *English Speaking Peoples*. I was a bookish child, ragged mercilessly at school for being incapable of jumping over a horse in the gym.

March 1971 found me living in a flat in the Marais district of Paris and doing research in various historical archives. One of the key figures I studied was the Emperor Napoleon III. If you mentioned him to the French they usually laughed, as he ended his career a prisoner of the Germans after the catastrophic defeat at Sedan in 1870. If you used his name in Britain the normal response was Napoleon who? I had tracked down some of his letters in the hands of a ninety-year-old lady living in the middle of France, not far from Roanne in the Loire *département*. A letter in spidery handwriting arrived inviting me to come and see her. Château de la Grye was a modest eighteenth-century manor in the village of Ambierle. Guinea fowl strutted on the terrace outside the salon windows. I climbed the grand staircase past a formal portrait of the Emperor to see *madame* in her four-poster bed. She asked her servant to fetch a metal box and give me the contents, several bundles of letters in the Emperor's hand tied up with ribbon. I spent the next ten days by a log fire deciphering his correspondence and gazing across the overgrown garden at the hills in the distance. The local inn provided a room, five-course lunches and dinners for twenty-eight francs a day (four pounds). On Sunday afternoon another lady in the village showed me the fifteenth-century folding altar painting in the parish church. The charm of rural France started to exert its magic. Madame Duchon d'Espagny talked to me about her life and introduced me to some of her friends. I made an effort to string a few sentences together in French and was embarrassed at the results.

After four years struggling with a PhD on French history I escaped into the bracing fresh air of commercial life and never looked back. But history has always been the lens through which I have looked at the world. If you want to understand a person, or a country, then you had better know something about their past. I realised the truth of this once again as I walked around France. Geology affects landscape which in turn shapes agriculture, commerce, industry and communications. These factors have a major impact on language, religious belief and culture. I was fortunate enough to be introduced to a seminal work on the English landscape while I was still at school; W. G. Hoskins' *The Making of the English Landscape*. Hoskins concluded his book with the view from the window of his North Oxfordshire house: "Not every small view in England is so full of detail as this, upon the oolite of North Oxfordshire, for this was a rich and favoured countryside that was beloved of owners of Roman villas, even in places of Bronze Age men. The cultural humus of sixty generations or more lies upon it. But most of England is a thousand years old, and in a walk of a few miles one would touch nearly every century in that long stretch of time."

This reflection could equally well apply to France. The linkage of landscape and history has worked out differently in each region, producing variety which never ceases to astonish. As I walked around I uncovered the cultural humus with my eyes.

*

Another reason for walking around the periphery of France was to see the regions which differ most from each other. I saw many regional symbols, the Basque cross and flag, the Savoyard and Breton flags, and wondered what they meant in reality. How much genuine attachment to a region is there in the France of the early twenty-first century?

To the walker the distinctiveness of the regions is apparent in a number of ways: styles of architecture both religious and secular; regional cuisine; regional languages. I heard a number of the latter as I walked around: Alsatian in Alsace,

Breton to the west of St.-Brieuc, Occitan and Provençal in the south, Basque in the Basque Country. The number of people who speak them every day as a first language is in decline and they have no official status in France, unlike Welsh in Wales. French remains the only official language of the Republic, while UNESCO classifies Breton as a language in danger of becoming extinct. Even so, it is now possible to learn these regional languages in public schools if enough parents demand it. As I travelled around I also heard regional variations of standard French, both in accent and vocabulary. These are the remains of the thousands of local dialects or patois spoken all over France in the nineteenth century and before.

Linguistic complexity in the French Basque Country

I also encountered regional customs and folklore. Some regions have different political and religious traditions which reach far back into France's history. Alsace-Lorraine, the frontier country, has always voted to the right. Political support for the parties is far from evenly spread across France, even today. The same would be true of regular attendance at mass. Some regions near the frontier and far from Paris betray the influence of a neighbouring country. There are similarities between the Swiss and the French Juras, Baden-Württemberg and Alsace, the Spanish and French Basque provinces. Some of the regions near the frontiers were the last to be integrated into the old French kingdom and the differences from the rest of France still show: Alsace (1648-1918-1945); the Franche-Comté or the Jura (1678); the Pays de Montbéliard (1792); Lorraine (1765); the County of Nice (1860); Savoy (1860).

*

There is a very different thread running through my story which might strike a chord with many in early retirement or of my generation: the challenge of caring for and coping with ageing parents. I am an only child and my parents are divorced and on their own. Both of them started to develop dementia while I was away. Difficult phone calls punctuated my journey and I had to rush home to deal with crises. These domestic storms are a counterpoint to the slowly unfolding panoramas of the French countryside. They explain the sub-title of this book: an escape around France on foot.

*

If readers want more information and practical advice about my route I suggest they consult my website www.walkingaroundfrance.com

1

THE PYRENEES
THE START OF AN ADVENTURE

I FELT I WAS skiing like a dream; carving perfect turns through the soft snow and keeping up with younger and stronger men. It was the last run before lunch and I stood at the top of the Swiss Wall. The drop below my skis looked vertical. Some of the moguls were the size of a small car. My legs shook and I wished there was a way out, but I could not desert the group. I was determined to succeed, so I launched myself over the edge. It might have been a fatal error of judgement. At the third mogul I sought security in an awkward plough turn. Hopelessly off balance I dived head first down the mountain. I lost my skis and tried to brake by using my poles, but to no avail. I knew I would keep tumbling until the slope levelled out seven hundred feet down. I prayed that I could avoid the rocks and pylons, but I was out of control.

When I came to rest my right leg would not move and my knee was the size of a football. I spent the rest of the holiday resting on a couch with a bag of frozen peas strapped around the swelling. Later a surgeon told me I had ruptured a ligament in my knee; the anterior cruciate to be technical. A sadistic physio said, "listen to Mr. Cudbird's sound effects" as he bent my leg double and I yelled with pain. After an operation I spent six months in a gym with footballers and hockey players, running round bollards and balancing on wobble boards. It was a miracle of medical science. I could still do everything I used to do with only the occasional twinge of pain. Never a natural sportsman, I had gambled and lost. So I thought I would try a long hike instead, 4,000 miles to be exact; gruelling but unlikely to scare me to death. And here I was in the Pyrenees. Was I flying too close to the sun again?

Edwardian travellers in the Pyrenees came face to face with grizzly bears and packs of wolves. I passed one roadside chapel, "built in memory of an ancestor who had his throat ripped out by wolves". On my first day in the mountains another formidable adversary struck, swarms of man-eating flies: large spotted ones which bit hard and feasted on my blood until they were removed by force. I remembered Hilaire Belloc's line about "the fleas that tease in the Pyrenees". The valley was full of orchids and dog roses and the sky overcast, ideal conditions for these predators to multiply. A dead world of cloud enveloped me, echoing with the bells of invisible cattle. Just in time I saw the drop from a limestone ridge. As I wriggled down a chimney in the rock panic overtook. There seemed to be no way forward in the swirling mist. I tried several paths which turned out to be

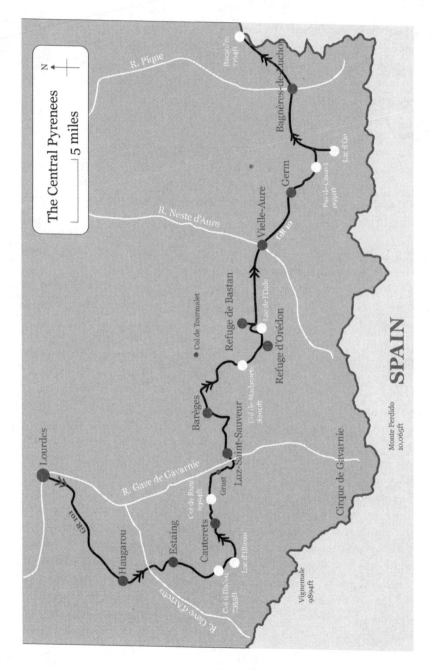

sheep tracks leading nowhere. I knew I was becoming quite irrational, for after all I had a map, a compass and a GPS. Yet somehow a spider's web of fear, like a childish nightmare, held me in its grasp. Suddenly I woke up to a wall of pine trees on a distant slope. The mist lifted from a remote valley. I was glad to reach the hostel at 6.30 p.m.

This dark cabin provided shelter but did not raise the spirits. Josette lived here on her own and enjoyed the quiet life. She had a rough red face, unkempt hair and obviously felt comfortable in baggy trousers. A woman of few words, she let slip that she had arrived in the Pyrenees from Normandy eighteen years ago. "I've always loved walking in the mountains. Here we're nine miles from the nearest village. My sister visits in August to help with the business. Friends drop in occasionally."

Then she confessed that she had lost heart. "Walkers come in July and August but the winter trade is important. There hasn't been enough snow recently. Business is right down. I'm trying to sell the property."

I felt ravenous after a hard day. "I can offer you sausages and lentils for supper," she said. The steaming plate arrived: one sausage. At least the lentils were plural.

Next morning a comfortable valley came into view with snow-flecked peaks in the distance. I picked out sights and sounds repeated throughout the Pyrenees: large barns built of black, grey and sandy-coloured stones with steep sloping roofs; a collie marshalling sheep across the pastures; the rustling of mountain streams rushing down hill. The next hostel was certainly out of the ordinary. I hammered on the door, but there was no one about. Eventually a couple turned up from Lyon to start their holiday and *madame* revealed that she was the sister of the owner. I had a small dormitory to myself, but the room was thick with farmyard dirt and the blankets smelt stale and unwashed. Outside flies hovered around the metal cover of a cesspit, which made me hold my nose. This seemed like a place where anything could happen, a set for the theatre of the absurd. A silver trout jumped out of a tank and flapped around the drive, until my acquaintance from Lyon rescued it. A shepherd ignored me when I asked if he was Serge, the owner. A young girl popped her head around the corner and promptly disappeared again. A moustachioed Frenchman drove up in a van and demanded to speak to Serge. *"Désolé"*, I said, and he shrugged his shoulders. I was beginning to think that Serge was a figment of the telephone book's imagination. When two men sauntered along I took no notice. One of them stared hard at me and I guessed that he might be the owner. The opening conversation was not promising.

"Are you Serge?"

"Yes."

I went to shake his hand and he seemed surprised.

"What time will you serve dinner?"

"We don't serve dinner," he said with a blank expression on his face.

At my evident look of alarm his companion laughed loudly. "Serge enjoys a joke at everyone's expense."

It appeared that Serge was running the *gîte* alone and he would be doing the cooking.

Outside the front door I met an endearing black and white fox terrier called Kali, who was in the habit of following walkers. After breakfast I made a fuss of him and, when the time came to leave, he followed me down the road. The surface of the Lac d'Estaing was calm and peaceful. I turned left to start climbing a dank path through a forest, with Kali still following on behind. Every time I threw a stone towards him he ducked behind a tree and then re-appeared five minutes later.

The ascent of 2,600 feet to the Col d'Ilhéou was the first real test of my fitness. At school I was the fattest boy in the class and came last in every known running race. In middle age I discovered exercise and so now I had a point to prove. The climb took three hours and I could hear my heart pumping faster as I laboured up the slope. A scooped-out glacial valley tumbled away behind me with protecting flanks of rocks and scree. Hawks circled emitting piercing shrieks. A few patches of snow covered the col and these caused Kali a good deal of excitement. He threw himself into them with great gusto, squirming around on his back and kicking his paws in the air.

Naively I assumed that Kali would now descend on his own back to Estaing. No such idea, however, had entered his head. He was in this walk for the long haul. He started chasing some sheep and only the severest tone in my voice, in French of course, could summon him back. When I reached Cauterets at last Kali refused to come any further. He resisted all attempts to grab hold of him and wandered off inside a dress shop sniffing around the racks. Once outside again he flopped down with exhaustion. I phoned Serge and an hour later Kali's owners arrived in a car from the other side of the mountain. After our eight-hour trek together I decided a fox terrier might be the perfect walking companion.

The Beau Soleil *gîte* in Cauterets is one of those stopping places where everyone on the Pyrenean trail meets to swap experiences. A tall house with several floors, it has been in the hands of Jean-Pierre's family for many years. His smiling face and helpful manner ensured that all the guests felt at home and mixed easily.

"My roots are deep," he said. "I do not have an old parchment to prove I own this building."

Jean-Pierre's maternal grandfather came from a village in the Ordesa, just the other side of the frontier. He escaped from Spain at the end of the Civil War, like a lot of his compatriots.

JACQUES AND HIS SAUCEPANS

Cauterets was also memorable because it was here that I met Jacques. He stepped softly into the dormitory and I turned round to meet the warm blue eyes of a gentle giant. "Will I be disturbing you?" he asked considerately.

His round face was very mobile and, when animated, the expression in his eyes changed rapidly from laughter to concern. Conversation came easily and he was very tolerant of my mistakes in his language. "I started at Arrens-Marsous and intend to follow the Pyrenean trail all the way to the Mediterranean," he said.

He was carrying everything he might need for the wilder stretches, including a tent and a cooking stove. Different items hung from his huge rucksack. "I need to buy some crampons," he continued. "I have just fallen six hundred feet in the snow."

I wondered where he would find a strap for them.

Jacques was a clinical psychologist from Paris. What he liked best was to travel without sticking to a timetable. "When Sylvie and I retire," he said, "we might give up on Paris and live in Bordeaux, a city of culture near the sea and the mountains. Provincial cities have so much more to offer now."

"I love technology," he exclaimed and pulled an iPod out of his sack with two miniature speakers. He had downloaded his favourite audio books, including a liberal dose of modern French philosophy.

There was a mixed cast of diners during the two evenings I stayed at the Beau Soleil and all of them had an adventurous spirit. As on many other occasions we seemed to concentrate on the French view of themselves and their place in the world. How much should we worry about Chinese competition? Why aren't we better at languages and more in the same vein? Inevitably we discussed Nicolas Sarkozy, the recently elected President of France. I knew that Jacques was not sympathetic, so I asked what he thought of Sarko.

"He is the garden gnome," was the reply, which produced gales of laughter.

Grust is a village on the edge of a deep valley with wide views of the mountains. Everywhere there are stone walls, wooden roofs and old barns. Some locals were making hay in the small fields, using hand rakes and scythes. Flowers exploded from small gardens and a stream ran singing down the main street in a stone conduit. My bed in the inn had a mattress with its own mountains and valleys. I last slept on one like this in Alençon in the 1970s. *Madame* served home cured ham and *garbure*, the vegetable soup typical of the region. She had been born in Australia and had started school there. "It's a shame the family put pressure on my parents to return home. I could have been happy in Australia. I had French friends out there who felt the same."

Luz-St.-Sauveur has a fortified church and elegant old houses with sculptured doorways hide behind iron gates. The castle stands just outside the town in the middle of hay meadows. A sign warns vandals that they will be prosecuted if caught. Only a French local authority could have written such a moral denunciation of mindless damage; it began: "vandalism is the most typical expression of immorality and stupidity!" The lady on the front desk of my hotel had bags under her eyes and a cigarette hanging out of her mouth. When I asked for a bill she rummaged among piles of paper and referred to a notebook where various items had been scribbled down. She then made out a handwritten note, which amazingly was accurate, but clearly the accounting system, like the décor, had not moved with the times. The *patron* told us that the race for amateurs over one stage of the Tour de France was due to pass through Luz shortly. Several thousand cyclists would be covering 106 miles including climbing the Col de Tourmalet at 6,939 feet. As I stood on a corner waiting for the competitors I was surprised and pleased to see Jacques walking into town. A few miserable cyclists came past in the rain and we sought shelter in a café while the worst of the weather passed.

The English and French find different things amusing, we both agreed. Jacques understood the English sense of humour very well and was a fan of the Goons and Monty Python. "I have now reached the age when I have to choose between sex and walking. I cannot indulge in both," he told me. He was whimsical on the subject of divorce. "Ladies with broken hearts can be very tedious. You find a lot of them in walking clubs. They carry their baggage with them." The expression he used was *traîner des casseroles,* literally dragging heavy saucepans around. It was evocative, I thought, the image of people walking through life with the sound of their pots and pans clattering behind them: things from their past they would rather forget, maybe that they were ashamed of or found embarrassing. We have a similar but less colourful expression in English when we describe someone as carrying baggage. This might seem an irrelevant piece of lexicography but it has a lot to do with why I embarked on a walk around France. I had some personal baggage which I hoped to escape by taking to the road.

*

In the Pyrenees I recalled the elation of wandering in the hills for the first time. My parents took me for walks along the Devon coast when I was ten years old: red cliffs, deep combes or valleys hidden from the outside world, yellow gorse, my father striding ahead in green linen shorts oblivious of my mother and me behind. Inevitably my thoughts wandered to the breakdown of my parents' marriage. The three of us were a close-knit nuclear family, or so I thought. It was therefore a shock to come home one day and find my mother sobbing in the kitchen. Looking out on our rectilinear suburban garden she tried to explain why she was having an affair with a married man from the church tennis club and could not live with my father any longer. It sounds banal and today it is such a common experience it hardly passes notice. In the less open world of a post-war middle-class community, where women were the homemakers and sermons in the Methodist chapel lasted forty minutes, it was almost an earthquake.

My father could not understand what the problem was. He was always kind and considerate but unaware of other people's emotions. It transpired that my parents had not been close for years and my mother, a highly emotional and needy person, cracked under the strain. While I was at university all this started to become clear. I have been living with divided loyalties ever since.

*

NO NEED FOR CRAMPONS

Barèges is trapped in a narrow defile and as we crossed the bridge it was shrouded in mist. I had heard that there might be bad weather in the mountains the next day, even snow on the Col de Madamète at 8,200 feet. I phoned the mountain *gendarmerie,* who told me there would be six feet of snow. I needed crampons. Not being an experienced Alpinist I wondered whether this was all a bit beyond

18

me, but Jacques was more philosophical. Although he had the air of an amateur, I was beginning to realise how intrepid he was. The Gîte l'Oasis was another tall building in a side street, with wooden floors and panelling scuffed by thousands of walkers. There was a crowd in that night enjoying the roaring log fire. The owner Philippe, an experienced mountain guide, laughed loudly when I relayed the gendarmes' advice. "You will have no trouble crossing the col. The gendarmes don't know what they are talking about," he said.

Others concurred and later that evening a Breton offered a bet. "If you meet any snow I will give you a case of champagne! I crossed the col today and it was clear."

I am not naturally brave but I felt I had no option but to go for it.

I lost sight of Jacques as I approached a long glacial valley submerged in cloud. After a chaos of rocks at the side of a waterfall, I reached a soft mountain pasture. This pattern of rocky lips followed by small meadows repeated itself until I scrambled over a moraine to a much larger Alpine prairie. I had emerged from the cloud to see a sky of pale lapis lazuli framing the peaks. To the right the route crossed a series of rocky barriers. Each of these moraines dammed a lake, which was a perfect mirror of sky, pastures and rocks. The pale blue trumpets of

Col de Madamète

gentians pushed up through tufts of rough grass in clusters. Snow had collected in the hollows and I had to step over a few patches with care. It was a pity I had not taken up the bet with the Breton. Scarves of ice covered the glassy surface of the last lake before the Col de Madamète. Suddenly there I was on the rocky base of a scree-lined funnel through the ridge. I could see three large lakes in the next valley, but no sign of Jacques.

The chalet hotel on the Lac d'Orédon was crowded and impersonal. I had almost finished my meal, when an exhausted looking Jacques staggered through the door. He claimed that he was not tired, but I did not believe him and instantly supplied a reviving carafe of red wine. Jacques never gave up, being resolutely *têtu* or stubborn. He confessed that he had got lost, fallen over and ripped his trousers and only reached the col at 5p.m. It then took him a further three hours to get down, making a walk of eleven hours in total. Even so, he was still as cheerful as ever. "Don't worry, I am still alive!" he exclaimed.

The Refuge de Bastan was perched on a moraine dividing two lakes. Cedric, a tall young man with his hair swept back in a ponytail, swung baby Noë on his knee while Stéphanie, pretty and petite, cooked supper for thirty-five guests in a kitchen no larger than a postage stamp. This small family lived in a hut up the hill with a donkey and a pig for company. The donkey carried supplies from below and the pig's job was to eat scraps so that nothing was wasted. Guests were expected to take their refuse away with them. The shower perched precariously on a pallet suspended over some rocks. A solar panel heated the water and we were asked not to use soap. "Heated" is perhaps an exaggeration, as I found out when I took the plunge at 6 a.m. the following morning and endured something like an electric shock. A shack concealed the long-drop loo. One external tap served for all other ablutions.

Inside the accommodation was not for those worried about their agility. To reach my bunk I had to climb a vertical plank with holes for hands and feet, which reminded me of humiliation in the school gym. There was no room for privacy. Fifteen of us dossed down in the small attic room and I played involuntary footsie all night with two French ladies. Those who had not booked, like Jacques, had to make do with a skimpy sleeping mat on the dining room floor. There was also a school party staying at the refuge. The girls slept on the bottom level of my room and the boys in a tent outside.

The dinner was a marvel, considering the conditions under which it was produced. *Confit de canard* was perhaps predictable, but after two days in the high mountains I would have eaten anything. I sat next to two men on holiday from Toulouse, one a Professor of Economics and one an aeronautical engineer. The economist said, "I do not know how the English economy survives. You do not make anything. All you do is pass pieces of paper around. How you have become so rich I cannot imagine."

I started to mount a defence but was cut off in mid-flow. "My sister in England lives off the rents from her properties," he added with a sneer of disapproval. I suspected he was an old-style French socialist.

After dinner I sat by the lakes. A gamelan of sheep's bells echoed off the rocks to the accompaniment of rushing water. Clouds covered the mountains in Spain, while the last rays of the sun disappeared in the west. Everything was utterly still. Perfect quiet still reigned when I got outside early in the morning, broken only by the pig honking at me in greeting. There was not a ripple on the surface of the lake and the sun was just beginning to creep down the far side of the valley. I traversed a ski bowl to a col, where a large group of walkers had huge sacks strapped to their rucksacks. This was the relief party for the Refuge de Bastan. Stéphanie was cooking for fifty-seven tonight!

The next lake had an extraordinary name, the Lac d'Ôo. This is probably a corruption of the Gascon word iu or eu meaning high mountain lake and therefore Lac d'Ôo means Lake Lake. The barrage towered above me with a gaunt refuge at one end, like a prison shut off from the world. I could just see water lapping the shore but very little of the steep sides and the cascade at the far end. Dense cloud muffled every sound, making the atmosphere close and mysterious. Just before I was due to eat, an English couple arrived. Anna was one of the thinnest women I have ever seen in the West, probably anorexic, with bony legs, protruding hip bones and an emaciated angular face. She admitted she had been feeling unwell. At dinner I discovered why. She munched a few vegetables; not enough calories to keep her going in the mountains. Despite her appearance she was a bundle of energy who never gave up. She did not speak much French, but was quite prepared to have a go in her English accent.

"I knew nothing much about the Pyrenean trail," she said," but I wanted to try it so I went to Stanfords in London, bought a map and here I am. We cover at least twenty miles a day and one day we walked for eleven hours."

I asked her which had been the most difficult sections.

"We left out the Chemin de la Mâture (a notorious path on the edge of a death drop with no protection) but we did the Hourquette d'Arre. I would not want to climb it in a gale," she added. "You would be blown into oblivion."

Anna did all the talking and Dennis followed her like a faithful Labrador. I asked him what he did. "I'm a librarian!" he explained.

A TASTE OF THE WILD

Under a blue sky the Pyrenees can seem like the gentlest mountains in the world. A typical Pyrenean ascent has four stages: the meadows of the valley floors; the woods above them; a band of pastures and barns with scattered trees; and then at the top level sparse vegetation, rocks and scree, the true *haute montagne*. The highest peaks are more accessible than in the Alps, the contours of the mountains seem softer and the tree cover is denser lower down. Rainfall is higher than average for France and thunderstorms are not uncommon. The resulting moisture supports a wide variety of plants. On one occasion I came across a large meadow by a cabin and every sort of wild flower imaginable. Particularly noticeable were the great yellow gentians six feet high with their large leaves and clusters of flowers. Suddenly a plump bottom protruded from the long grass next to a more slender one. They belonged to a French couple, botanists who had come up from the valley to photograph the flowers on this particular prairie. With their special lenses they were getting close up to the blooms, their large floppy hats making them look like intrepid nineteenth-century explorers. "This is a well-known spot for wild flowers. In fact it's like a botanical garden for the High Pyrenees. There are so many varieties here," they said.

Yet walkers should treat these approachable mountains with respect. I heard several tales of lone travellers freezing to death in April and late September, trapped by injury, bad weather and unexpected snow. Living on these slopes was tough in the past. The local museums are full of the little comforts which made life tolerable, from bed-warmers to roasting-spits designed for a dog to turn. They emphasise how hostile it could be outside, all alone in a portable shepherd's hut high up on the pastures. The piled-up stones of cottage walls recall backbreaking labour to find shelter from the climate. Balancing on the stepped gables to repair the roof required a head for heights.

Bears, wolves and lynx roamed the mountains until forty years ago. I told a refuge guardian about some unusual paw prints in the mud, definitely those of a big cat. "I have a friend who saw a wild lynx a year or so ago," she said.

She also told us about the bears which have been reintroduced into the French Pyrenees from Slovenia. My chances of coming face to face with a grizzly seemed remote, as each one needs a very large territory to survive. However, my host in Moncaup in the Ariège told me, "One walker came face to face with a bear outside his tent. He phoned the fire brigade. We had to respond! The sheep farmers object strongly to these bears. Hunters have killed them when they feel threatened by the female with her cubs."

It was the British who pioneered Alpinism in this region in the nineteenth century. The legendary Baron Russell still lives in the memory of many French who climb here. One said with a typically French flourish, "You are one of Baron Russell's countrymen. There is a cabin reserved for you."

Henry Russell owned a cave where he held candlelit dinners for his friends. The British also patronised spa towns like Cauterets and Bagnères-de-Luchon, where I rested after long days of effort. At the former I was pummelled by a rush of hot sulphurous water in the *thermes*, looking out at the wooded slopes of the narrow valley. In the past high society came to Pyrenean spa towns like Cauterets to be seen as well as to take a cure. The atmosphere now is altogether more clinical and quite a few people enjoy cures courtesy of the French national health service. While Cauterets is still a popular holiday centre for skiing and exploring the mountains, it does not have the prestige of a former age when writers, aristocrats and crowned heads were frequent visitors.

Most of the buildings in Cauterets date from the late nineteenth century. To get a feel for the Belle Époque I visited the old Hôtel d'Angleterre, with its four-storey façade of tall windows decorated with marble and wrought-iron balconies. George V of England patronised the Angleterre, where you can still see the dining room of his day and admire the clothes worn by well-dressed ladies and gentlemen: crinolines; ball gowns, top hats. The hotel was closed in the 1950s and turned into flats.

Bagnères-de-Luchon is another spa town whose splendour has faded. The Allées d'Étigny, which run in a straight line to the baths, are now full of cheap souvenir shops spilling out onto on the pavement. The casino looks like a run-down picture house with its crumbling red and cream bricks, busts of ancient worthies and stained-glass windows. Yet there are still hints of what Bagnères must once have been: the parterres of the formal gardens; the turreted villa where Edmond Rostand, the author of *Cyrano de Bergerac*, spent his youth; the imposing façade of the Hotel Majestic; the *mairie* with its grand stairs. Green hills and the snow-capped peaks of the Maladeta massif form an impressive backdrop.

Rostand was not the only well-known writer to come here. François Mauriac captured the atmosphere of Bagnères in the late nineteenth century in his 1932 novel *The Knot of Vipers*:

> I was at Luchon with my mother in 1883. The hotel Sacarron of that time was full of upholstered furniture, of pouffes and stuffed chamois. After so many years I can still smell the scent of the lime trees in the Allées d'Étigny. Each morning the trotting of the donkeys awakened me, the tinkling of their harnesses and the cracking of whips. The water of the mountains rushed into the streets. Sellers of croissants and milk loaves cried their wares. Guides went by on horseback and I watched their cavalcades.

From a peak at 7,194 feet near Bagnères Jacques and I had a clear view north onto the plain and west to the Pic du Midi, with its distinctive observatory, and Vignemale, a snowy hummock of black granite. All around us was rocky moorland, grazing country covered with heather. The track swung right up a slope and suddenly we were astride the Spanish border. Frontier stones marked the top of a ridge. Two giant vultures hovered over us, searching for prey. The tips of their massive wings were turned towards the heavens as they glided smoothly in perfect circles.

We charged along without a care in the world. The Pyrenees stretched out before us in perfect visibility. The Ariège hills in the east had been moulded into deep narrow valleys. After lunch I climbed up to a knife-edge summit and then down a trying descent over rough ground. I was ahead of Jacques but decided to wait for him at some cabins, as this would be our last opportunity to say good-bye before we went our separate ways. I planned to leave the Pyrenean trail shortly and take a forest road to St-Béat on the Garonne before traversing the hills of the Ariège to Foix. Jacques wanted to see how far he could get on the Pyrenean trail, so he needed to head further south. He came down the hill slowly, nursing his painful feet. I knew I would miss his warmth and sense of humour. He seemed to me not entirely French in his eccentricity. He loved to burst into song and was always easy-going and optimistic. We had said good-bye a number of times before, knowing we would meet up again, but this was for real. There is a special bond between people who have shared the ups and downs of the open road. We hugged each other several times. Then I was off on another tough scramble downhill to the next stage of my journey.

2 THE COUNTRY OF THE CATHARS
A SANCTUARY FOR HERETICS

THE UPPER REACHES of the Ariège are more remote than the great peaks of the Pyrenees because visited less frequently even today. It is not difficult to imagine the isolation of the communities who lived here before the age of the internet and fast roads. I encountered no towns of importance apart from Foix and St.-Girons. My host in Moncaup talked about life in his village. He said that seventy per cent of the houses were second homes and only twenty permanent residents lived there. He and his wife just enjoyed the village as a pleasant place to live. He worked in St.-Gaudens twenty miles away and had to get up at 5 a.m. to drive to work. His wife did all her shopping there. "You may have seen a large modern house being built as you came down. The owner is the last person still in the village who went to the school that closed in 1945."

Just outside St.-Girons I talked to a man who was tidying his cottage garden. He had a house in the town but also this *gîte* in the country, where he came to potter around. He was retired, so he had the time. I asked him about farming in the area. "Until 1960 there were few trees in this valley. Most of the land was cultivated for cereals and the farmers kept sheep and cows. Then everyone left for the towns to find better paid work and now there's virtually no one left. Farming is a hobby and trees are taking over the hillsides again. On the opposite side of the valley there used to be a lovely beech forest, but the Office National des Forêts came along and planted pines instead. They were intended to supply pulp for the cigarette factory near St.-Girons. Local people were upset. The factory employs three hundred people but it's facing hard times. Demand for wood is falling because the French are smoking less. Nowadays the factory's main customers are in China. The engineers have even been out there to install cigarette-making machines. The future for the employees is uncertain."

Prades in the Pays d'Aillou is a fortified town. Inside the walls I noticed two streets named after Senegal and Dakar in West Africa and wondered why. An old man with a bulbous nose and bloodshot eyes shuffled towards me in the sunshine. He had lived in the village for eighty years, although now he spent the harsh winters in Toulouse. "When my father was a boy there were about twelve hundred inhabitants in the village. Now there are only forty permanent residents throughout the year. It used to be a very poor village," he said, pointing to the deserted terraces on the hillsides above as evidence of his forebears' desperation to wring something from the thin soil. "The winter diet before 1940 was

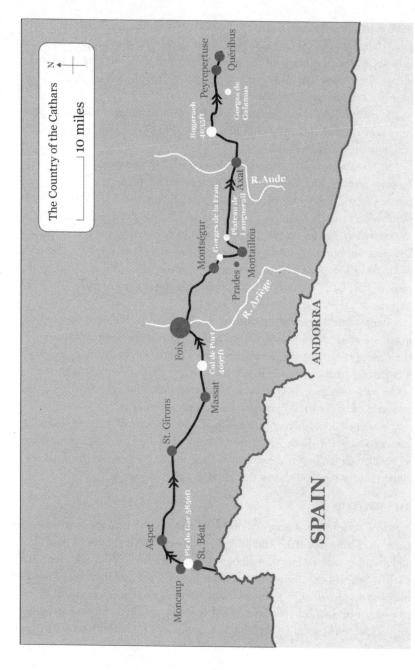

The Country of the Cathars

N

10 miles

Peyrepertuse
Quéribus
Gorges de Galamus
Bugarach 4095ft
R. Aude
Axat
Plateau de Languerail
Gorges de la Frau
Montségur
Prades
Montaillou
R. Ariège
Foix
ANDORRA
Col de Port 4097ft
Massat
St. Girons
Aspet
Pic du Gar 5850ft
St. Béat
Moncaup
SPAIN

monotonous and consisted mainly of potatoes. There was no electric light, only paraffin lamps. The village joke was that the crows flew over on their backs, as they knew there was no point in keeping an eye out for something to take! The village was so poor that many went to seek their fortune in colonies like Senegal, only to die of diseases like yellow fever."

I noticed that the poor terraces, which had once produced lentils and peas, were now covered with scrub and pine forests. Prades is dependent on visitors and outsiders to survive.

This remote country attracts people who want to find peace for their souls, far from modern life. They look after refuges and are prepared to live off their own resources. The Ferme de Soulan is an example, a hostel for horse riders in the Pyrenees run by a Breton and a German. This old farm looks like a hippy shelter with stables on the ground floor and a wooden balcony above. If you like antiseptic surroundings totally free of germs you should not stay here. Postcards of horses in Mongolia and the Camargue cover the walls. One summed up the spirit of the place: "My body is not a temple but an amusement park!" The smell of horse shit wafted up from the stables below.

Renate teaches movement both at the farm and in Toulouse. Her website manifesto suggests we should "dance with the earth, the wind and the sun in the natural theatre of the mountains." She believes in "body-mind centring". Her partner Jakez came here from Brittany in the 1970s, a minor manifestation of the back to nature movement which started after 1968. He cared about the preservation of the natural world: plants, birds and animals.

It seemed a rather chaotic household with all sorts of unusual characters coming and going. Both Renate and Jakez looked very tired. Yet as we dined by candlelight looking at the stars above and the snowy peaks in the distance, I could see why they had chosen this valley as a place to escape.

THE CATHARS

Heretical beliefs from the north found a sanctuary in this remote countryside, in particular Catharism in the Middle Ages. The word Cathar appears on road signs and tourist marketing literature all over this part of France. Who were they? The Cathars believed that the world was made by the Devil and that everything on the earth was irredeemably tainted. Man did not gain redemption through the sacraments of the Catholic Church, but by living an ascetic life and accepting the consolation of a Cathar Perfect (preacher) before death. Cathars were highly

28

critical of the greed of the established Church and its priests. Their movement was widespread and well-organised with its own bishops, and Cathars could be found among educated townsfolk as well as the peasantry. Nobles like the powerful Count of Toulouse and the Count of Foix were believed by the Church to be covert supporters. In fact they were not heretics themselves, but found it difficult to combat Catharism in their areas of influence.

The newly confident papacy which launched the crusades to the Holy Land was determined to stamp out this threat to its authority and revenues, as the Cathar faithful were not keen on paying their Church taxes. Innocent III appealed to the lords of northern France to help him and in 1209 a powerful army arrived in the south. Nobles who had turned a blind eye to heresy quickly saw the error of their ways. Amidst the rivalries between local and invading nobility, the Crown, the papacy, local bishops and Dominican Inquisitors many people used the opportunity to settle old scores. Influence with the winning side could produce all sorts of benefits: estates in the south or important positions in the courts and administration. Lawyers even fought lawyers for clients. What could possibly be more vicious?

In the end the Counts of the Languedoc were brought to heel. The clerks of the Inquisition pursued everyone who had contact with heretics. Men and women were burnt at the stake or imprisoned and their property confiscated. Cathar refuges were destroyed and Spanish lords lost their rights in southern France. The real winners were the French kings based in Paris. A revitalised monarchy saw the opportunity to make gains in the south adjacent to the English possessions in Aquitaine. Posing as a good son of the Church was clever policy, and over the next fifty years or so it worked. By the late thirteenth century the Count of Toulouse was the king's vassal and Languedoc was under royal control.

There has been a good deal of romanticising about the Cathars. For some they are new age mystics, more in touch with spiritual values than the established Church. This seems to be a message with contemporary appeal. The Cathars were also vegans, except that they did eat fish, which live in water outside Satan's realm on earth. Others have associated the Cathars with occult practices and the Knights Templar, always a fertile source for the modern conspiracy theorist.

In Montségur a middle-aged bookseller dressed in black and sporting a ponytail dragged me inside his shop to see his selection. Next to the usual crop of guide books and historical works was an impressive selection of Cathar-themed historical novels with lurid covers, not to mention cult books on the Holy Grail and the inevitable *Da Vinci Code*. A lot of the writing about the Cathars has strayed from an objective view of who they were and what they really believed. Now the word has become a convenient label to distinguish a tourist area, a piece of consumer branding to enhance a region's identity and appeal.

FROM GRANITE TO LIMESTONE

From the mountains and passes of the High Pyrenees I turned north to softer hills and valleys in the Ariège, from rugged granite to fragile limestone. As the sun set the Pic du Gar looked daunting, its limestone fangs pointing up at the sky. My eyes searched for a continuous line of grass and trees which might carry me around its shoulder. There was no obvious route and despite the comfort of a glass of wine I could feel the butterflies in the pit of my stomach. The next morning I climbed up a steep tree-lined spur with one or two exposed sections. Two hikers joked with me that things were "interesting" ahead. The path was not at all obvious as I headed for a gap between the evil-looking rock face on my right and more rocks on my left. One open slope was very steep indeed. On each hairpin bend I had to perform an outward-leaning turn, balancing on narrow ledges of rock and tufts of grass.

It took five days to cross the Haute-Garonne and the Ariège. At first I traversed a more homely countryside of wooded hills, pastures for sheep and cattle and apple orchards. The music of gentle streams was quite different from the rushing torrents in the mountains. The trees in the forests were more varied: hornbeams, dogwoods and cotoneasters as well as the everlasting pines. Some of the secluded valleys enjoyed a warm microclimate which encouraged even banana plants and bougainvilleas to flourish. In one village the gardens could have belonged to an English cottage. Wisterias grew around the eaves, daisies had gone to seed in the beds and roses covered the pergolas. Huge wooden barns, with open lofts protected by lattice work, towered above the village streets. The balconies of stone farmhouses were once used to dry grain and beans. I wandered between high grassy banks dotted with brambles, ferns and wild flowers. Perhaps the English like the Ariège so much because it reminds them of Devon or Somerset.

Beyond St.-Girons the landscape took on a different character. From a broad forest road along a coniferous ridge I enjoyed panoramic views of the black granite peaks near the Spanish frontier. Some were jagged like a printer's die and others smooth and rounded. I hacked my way through head-high ferns on a steep hillside and clambered over debris washed down by mountain streams. The inn on the Col de Port was covered in cloud. A large bull on the path was too wet to cause trouble. *Madame* offered me a bed for the night, even though she was about to close up for her day off. Her husband came mincing downstairs to derisive remarks from customers about his newly trimmed moustache. "My wife has threatened to come upstairs and cut it off," he said.

A hilltop trail five miles long led all the way to Foix. I misread the map in the fog and nearly fell over a cliff. Thank God for the GPS. Once the clouds had cleared I could see a moor which might have been in Wales or Scotland. One of the weathered rocks looked like a giant's crooked thumb pointing the way. It was not difficult to imagine scenes from the past: flocks of sheep being driven across the hills; Cathar Perfects moving from village to village in secrecy, but able in the distance to see Pamiers where their persecutors held the Inquisition.

Full of coffee and croissants I stood outside my hotel in Foix and sniffed the morning air. The castle with its three towers dominated the red Roman-tiled roofs below, so different from the flat grey stones used in the mountains. In the medieval streets the modern inhabitants were ambling back from the bakers, some with a newspaper under their arm. Older men in berets were walking their dogs and women in overalls washed their front steps, sweeping the dirty water into the street. Past the station I started looking for red and yellow waymarks on the side of the road. It was like being on a treasure hunt.

Beech trees and small green oaks predominate in this limestone country. A heat haze hovered over the mountains and the deep green of the pine trees was tinged with blue. I continued along a valley until the castle of Montségur appeared on my left. At this angle it looked like a pimple on top of a huge ziggurat of limestone. Later I emerged from a forest to see the massive triangular rock face blocking my path. Royal forces destroyed the original castle in 1244, when they burnt two hundred Cathars at the stake in one bonfire. I stood on the plateau where this savage event took place and pictured the scene: the smell of smoking flesh, the screams and the ghoulish crowd watching.

The deserted hamlet of Pelail was like a little Shangri-la, deep in the mountains and only linked to the outside world by a narrow road. Massive walls of limestone clothed in trees and bushes converged on a point a mile distant. I walked into the jaws of a nutcracker as the sides of the gorge soared above. These were the Gorges de la Frau, an apt corruption of Gorges de L'Effroi, gorges of fright. The sign on the side warned "Dangerous Path, Avalanche Risk in Bad Weather." The sun disappeared in the narrow funnel of the gorge as I had to crane my neck to scan the eight hundred feet of rock above. The course of the River Hers was dry, but after heavy rain this gorge would have been very dangerous with no means of escape from the water. A few stones clattered on the rocks above. In 1907 an attempt was made to build a road up this gorge for commercial traffic, which included charcoal makers with their mules. A storm washed the builders' work away and no one tried again. A long time ago smugglers used the gorge as a favourite route to and from Spain, where they could hide out in the caves dotted along the cliffs.

This was the first of three limestone gorges on this section of the walk. The third was the most awesome of all, the Gorges de Galamus. They were incredibly narrow, as if a giant had split the rock with a huge axe, the white limestone looking like crumbling pumice. The road clung to the side under a rocky overhang and I could see neither the river beneath nor the heights above. It seemed from the map that the chasm must be at least two thousand feet deep. Suddenly the Hermitage of St. Antoine appeared below, protruding from the face. Hermits have used this precarious place since the seventh century, and the faithful of Languedoc and Catalonia flock here on pilgrimage at Easter and Whitsun.

MONTAILLOU

Above the Gorges de la Frau a plateau stretched for several miles, the small and distinct Pays d'Aillou, an expanse of pastures surrounded by mountains with one or two small villages. Here I found Montaillou, the last stronghold of Catharism and the most famous Cathar village. I decided to stop and do some historical detective work.

In 1975 the French historian Emmanuel Le Roy Ladurie created a literary sensation with his book *Montaillou, village occitan*. In 1320 the Bishop of Pamiers, Jacques Fournier, who later became Pope Benedict XII and built the Palais des Papes in Avignon, started an inquiry into a few remaining Cathars. Le Roy Ladurie dissected the Inquisition's records, which describe in absorbing detail the way of life and personal rivalries of the village in the early fourteenth century: who was sleeping with whom, who was fighting whom, and how they earned a living. We learn about the voracious sexual appetite of Pierre Clergue, who played a double game as vicar and Cathar, and the secret nocturnal journeys of the Authie brothers, two Cathar Perfects. The châtelaine of Montaillou,

Béatrice de Planissoles, played a prominent role in this story. Pierre Clergue first propositioned her during confession in the village church. After being raped she became Clergue's lover, before moving to nearby Prades where she continued her liaison with him in the parish church. Her past caught up with her, however, and she was imprisoned in 1320. This book brought readers face to face with life in a fourteenth-century Pyrenean village and made it as vivid as a TV soap opera. I had to discover where these events actually happened.

Wandering around the churchyard in Montaillou I was astonished to see familiar names from the fourteenth century on several gravestones: not only Clergue but also Baille (the Bailles had a house in medieval Montaillou). Soon I had another surprise. On inquiring who held the keys to the church, I was advised to contact M. Georges Clergue who lived in the village. Later he was kind enough to show me around.

A track led up towards the ruined keep of the castle. The remains of the medieval village lay on the slopes underneath. In the sixteenth century a new village was built even lower down, using the stones from the older settlement. All that remains of the original village are a few foundations. Armed with a map and photographs from a recent history, I plunged down a slope of scrub, anxiously

Modern Montaillou

33

searching for the lines of streets and houses. I saw some dips in the ground and a few stones. Was this the Clergue house? Was this line in the grass the main street? After an hour's search I found a level area which had been the main square of medieval Montaillou. If I felt disappointed that there was so little left of the former village, the enclosed plateau in the mountains was exactly the setting my imagination sought.

Since Foix I had been following a former Cathar escape route into Spain. I was very tempted to take off over the Pyrenees, but instead turned north then east towards the sea. I made up my own route to Axat on the River Aude, where I rejoined the Sentier des Cathares. I am not a person who easily leaves things to chance. I planned my route in advance down to the last detail, every twist and turn on local tracks described as "of uncertain continuity." Spreading out large sheet maps and looking for a way, where no official footpath exists, is my idea of fun. In most cases the route worked out well, with the added interest of finding the landscape not quite as I imagined it. Just occasionally "uncertain continuity" was an accurate description of my chosen path. I remember plenty of barbed wire fences and dense clumps of vegetation barring the way. Sometimes the unwillingness of the landscape to fit my preconceived ideas sorely tested my patience.

The Plateau de Languerail is a mountain pasture stretching for five miles. There are few sources of water and the ground is dry. I came across two deserted villages, Serre sec d'en haut and Serre sec d'en bas. Their names, which roughly translate as Upper and Lower Dry Mountain, show just how precarious living up here used to be. A flock of some three hundred sheep, both rams and ewes, appeared over the horizon. They looked strong and healthy, with fine curved horns and large bells supported by red collars. A shepherdess and a sheep dog with a very loud bark were driving them along. The word shepherdess immediately conjures up the image of Little Bo Beep, but this one was a young woman of around thirty-five wearing a fleece, faded jeans and walking boots and carrying a crook. Years ago shepherds used to drive their flocks very long distances from summer to winter pastures in what was called the *transhumance*. This practice has almost faded out and my shepherdess was only walking from the nearby village of Belcaire to Comus, a distance of a few miles.

AN OLD FRONTIER

The so-called Cathar castles are all romantic ruins in picturesque locations. The

Cathars themselves did not build the castles, although some became refuges for a brief period. The French kings took over several as frontier fortresses and later had them dismantled. The most famous are Peyrepertuse and Quéribus. The approach to the former is awe-inspiring as the curtain wall appears to grow out of the cliff at the top of a thousand-foot slope. To an attacker this fortress would have looked impregnable, the complex occupying the entire plateau on top of the mountain. It is shaped like a dagger with a large grip and a short blade. Guarding this place must have been miserable in the winter and ordinary soldiers would have struggled with the grinding boredom of their isolation. A grand open staircase leads to the large keep known as San Jordi. One might imagine it as part of the Dark Tower in *The Lord of the Rings*. I was curious to know who San Jordi was but then remembered that this had been a Catalan castle until 1240. San Jordi is our own St. George but also the patron saint of Catalonia. An observation platform on the site of the former chapel afforded a spectacular bird's eye view of the lower complex. It seemed to hover in the air over the valley floor far below. In the distance Quéribus appeared quite clearly, while the Pyrenees rippled away on the horizon. This felt like border country. Peyrepertuse had belonged to the Counts of Barcelona. The lord of the castle

The Pyrenees from Quéribus

refused to submit to French forces during the crusade against the Cathars. Later he had to surrender to the French king and Peyrepertuse became a royal fortress on a new frontier with the Kingdom of Aragon a short distance away. In 1659 the French finally wrested what is now the *département* of Pyrénées-Orientales from Spain and pushed the border back to the high mountains further south.

Quéribus was a turning point in my journey around France. To the north the *garrigue*, a dry Mediterranean heath of bushes and wild flowers, covered the limestone hills of the Corbières. Below was the route I had taken along a glacial valley, where ice had worn the sides into a smooth curve long ago. The vines pushed right up these slopes like soldiers on parade. The Pyrenees stretched from Andorra on my right to the bulk of Canigou directly opposite. To the south-east the plains of Roussillon rolled towards the Mediterranean. In the far distance the last mountains of the Pyrenees tumbled into the sea.

3

THE LANGUEDOC
WINE AND WIND

THE LANGUEDOC IS THE southern third of France where the inhabitants used to speak different dialects of a Latin language called Occitan. This language struggled to survive against the onslaught of French. After the occupation of the south following the defeat of the Cathars the French spoken by the court and the government gradually took over as the language of the educated élite. In 1539 French was made the one and only language of the law. Occitan almost died out. Today it is spoken as a second language by a limited number of people in the countryside. It is also studied in a literary form. The distinctive twang with which southerners speak French is one of its legacies. Occitan words also survive in place names and street signs.

One of my hostesses said, "I feel there is something of an identity crisis in the south and now people want to keep it going." A schoolmaster I met was attached to his native *département* of the Corrèze further north. He and a number of older people still spoke Limousin, one of the Occitan dialects. He claimed that these dialects were still widely used. But Martine, a *vigneronne* in the Corbières, was more pessimistic about the language's future. "Yes I speak Occitan" she said, "as did my parents and grandparents. The language is dying out, though children have an opportunity to learn it in some schools. You know they even speak it in front of teachers so they won't understand!"

Today we use the term Languedoc to describe a smaller crescent-shaped slice of territory running from Toulouse to the Rhône Valley. Many visitors think of it as a land of sun-drenched vineyards, crumbling castles, sandy beaches and rocky hills. Most of the population is concentrated on the coast and in one or two major conurbations like Carcassonne. Before the Second World War more people worked the land and there were many industries in the countryside. Most of them have now disappeared, but I saw evidence everywhere of their remains. In the Corbières several hundred people used to mine barite, a mineral which stabilises sugar. One of my hosts had taken his son to explore a valley full of caves created by miners. The barite, he said, sparkled like diamonds.

The story of Mazamet is typical. Here I saw a number of ruined industrial buildings. Some of them had evidently used water power judging by the dilapidated wheels left by the river. In the nineteenth century the Tarn was the most industrialised *département* in the south. Small-scale industries developed in many towns, with textiles and tanning the speciality at Mazamet. By 1900

Languedoc, Cévennes and Ardèche

N

20 miles

MEDITERRANEAN

R. Rhône

Pont St. Esprit

Vallon Pont d'Arc

Balazuc

Tanargue

Thines

Les Vans

Gorges de l'Ardèche

Alès

Nîmes

Notre Dame des Neiges

Montagne du Goulet

Mt. Lozère 5574ft

Cassagnas

Pont-de-Montvert

Mt. Aigonal 5141ft

Le Vigan

Cirque de Navacelles

Montpellier

Barre-des-Cévennes

Lodève

Le Bousquet-d'Orb

Sahetan-sur-Agout

Béziers

Port-la-Nouvelle

Espinouse 3688ft

Parc du Haut-Languedoc

Narbonne

Roquefort-des-Corbières

Anglès

Montagne D'Alaric

Corbières

Pic de Nore 3996ft

Carcassonne

Mazamet

Conques-sur-Orbiel

Villerouge-Termenès

some 7,000 people were employed locally in these industries. Then they declined in the face of more efficient competition at home and overseas and Mazamet's firms were too big to depend purely on local markets. Eighty tanneries closed, although specialised leather-making factories still exist in the town. The pollution of the river and the smell must have been very unpleasant. Today's ageing population of 10,000 has declined in recent years, but unemployment has dropped substantially as well. Mazamet was not the spectacle of industrial decay I had expected. The town has developed some new industries, based on traditional skills in metalworking and textiles, and is an important commercial centre for the surrounding countryside. It is well-maintained with smart boutiques, a modern cultural centre and an elegant park.

THE SCENT OF THE GARRIGUE

I started on the coast and my first experience was not of sand but of a small dockyard. A light breeze disturbed the evening air and ruffled the surface of the grey water in Port-la-Nouvelle. Pontoons rattled against the stone quay and yacht masts bobbed away from the vertical. A chiffon scarf of cirrus decorated the sky, which was turning from pale blue to grey as the pink light of the setting sun disappeared in the west. Commercial buildings stretched along the side of the canal, which joined the distant sea to a lagoon, the Étang de Bages et de Sigean. Under the Roman Empire this lagoon was a gulf on the Mediterranean coast. From time to time a car clattering over the harbour bridge broke the silence. Two trains rumbled into the station. The sky promised fine weather for walking the next day.

Inside the Hôtel du Port the conversation of forty French at dinner was rising to a crescendo. I had bumped into the Club Nautique Nouvellois and been plied with the *kir* which they could not drink. *Le club* catered for sailors and also enthusiasts who built radio-controlled model ships. In the corner of the dining room was a large-scale replica of a local fishing boat. The president was folding his paper napkin in a complicated origami pattern to demonstrate a point about model building. The club was about to launch an exhibition in the *lycée* including replicas of the *Bounty* and the *Queen Mary*.

I had been surprised to learn that Port-la-Nouvelle is the third largest port on France's Mediterranean coast. Leaning over the bar I listened to the *patron* talking about the local fishing fleet. "It consists of about twenty-five ships," he said, "and the price of fish like cod is rising all the time. Those Italian and

Spanish fishermen take all the young fish."

It seems that English fishermen are not the only ones to complain about their competitors. Next we got onto the subject of rugby which interested him much more. Of course, many of the best French teams come from this region.

The neat roads of the town came to an end in the Rue des Anciens Chantiers, full of potholes and former dock buildings. Eventually two breakwaters met the sea near a red and white striped lighthouse which looked like a seaman's pullover. A promenade lined with ugly hotels and neon signs held back the perfectly raked sand. In the distance cargo boats plied a vast expanse of grey and blue. Seagulls wheeled overhead attracted by the smell of landed fish. Now it was time to escape to the hills through a wilderness of railway lines, quarries and storage tanks. A short climb up a dusty track and I was on a chalky plateau of *garrigue*.

Bright yellow broom mingled with mauve rock roses and the serrated leaves of the miniature Kermes oak native to the Mediterranean. A beetle with a brilliant blue, orange and green back scuttled across the path. Fat lizards with lurid green skins sunned themselves. Further on the deep pink of valerian contrasted with yellow euphorbia. Every so often the scent of thyme reached me on the breeze. The first man-made landmark on the morning's trail was a group of modern

Terry and nine French friends

windmills. The Languedoc experiences strong winds about half the year, usually from the mountains to the north. I saw several wind farms on my journey.

Three older windmills overlook Roquefort-des-Corbières and there are rows of vines everywhere. Martine's dark eyes welcomed me into the house built by her great grandfather, the first of four generations of *vignerons*. She had raven-black hair and burnished golden skin, which carried the scents of the *garrigue*. The next day a fierce sun bounced off the shale of mountain roads. I slaked my thirst at village standpipes before retreating to the shade of plane trees for a rest. The evening provided plenty of entertainment in the shape of nine French women getting away from their husbands on a walking tour. "They will survive," they said. "We have left them plenty of food in *le frigo*."

The heart of the Corbières is a deserted region of limestone crags and deep wooded valleys. The roads wind a long way round the hills but my path cut straight across country. A scramble down a dried-up waterfall led to a lake trapped between limestone cliffs. There are many water courses subject to flash floods in the autumn when over one-third of the annual rainfall arrives. I passed two more "Cathar" castles. At Termes the owner changed sides to join the king at the right moment, while at Villerouge-Termenès the Inquisition burnt the last Cathar Perfect at the stake. The village takes its name from the arid slopes of red soil which once contained bauxite.

The top of the hill above the village is a dividing line between the impenetrable valleys of the central Corbières and the plain running inland from Narbonne. A shepherd was driving a flock of sheep and goats down the hill in front of me. His white Pyrenean dog and a Collie were having difficulty persuading their charges to leave the grass either side of the path. They turned their attention to me as if to keep me under control instead. "It is their first day out on the hills," the shepherd said. "The sheep are all over the place." He stared at my walking poles as if he had seen nothing like them before. "Ah! You have four legs like my animals!"

The Montagne d'Alaric to the north dominates the view for miles around. It looked like the back of a giant whale rising out of the plain, a sinister primitive beast which might awake from its slumber. The Montagne forms the eastern end of a long ridge which runs alongside the Autoroute des Deux-Mers as far as Carcassonne. Approaching from the south only the head of this beast was visible; a layer cake of limestone interspersed with dark green foliage. What had this mountain got to do with Alaric I, the leader of the Visigoths who sacked Rome in 410 and carried off a lot of booty, including the jewels of King Solomon? After looting Rome the Visigoths established a kingdom in the Languedoc with a capital in Toulouse. Alaric II was killed by Clovis, the first King of the Franks, in 507. Some contemporary historians claimed that he took the wise precaution of sending his treasure to Spain; others that he buried it somewhere near what is now the Montagne d'Alaric and yet others that it was taken by Clovis. Some myth-makers have speculated that the lost treasure even belonged to the Templars.

Approaching Alaric's lair I did not waste time searching for a hoard of jewels because a steep climb lay ahead. The path skirted a bare cliff which dropped sharply to the plain below. Villages started to disappear as small dots on a patterned carpet of fields. A group of windmills in the far distance marked my next high point, the Pic de Nore on the Languedoc ridge north of Carcassonne. A dry cold wind, known as the Tramontane, was gusting at gale force from the north.

*

As my feet scraped away the crumbling limestone I heard the call of my mobile phone in my pocket.

"Hello! Are you all right? You sound a long way away!"

It was my mother. I explained I was halfway up a mountain in a howling gale.

"What are you doing there? Is it dangerous?"

"No, just hard work."

My mother has always wanted to know where I am and what I am doing every day. A few years after my parents split up I bought a country cottage and used my mother's London house during the week. Gradually we slipped into a routine of moving together between the two. We always had a lot to talk about and would sit around half the day discussing the meaning of life. We went to the theatre together and occasionally on holiday. When my mother realised there was another woman in my life it was a real shock. She would never say so but in her eyes I could see she thought I had betrayed her. I remember her waving good-bye after a celebratory meal, a wounded bird that needed a nest but did not know how to find one.

For years emotional crises punctuated her life. Sometimes she was upset because of a slight, real or imagined. To escape her demons of loneliness and insecurity she moved house once every four years after leaving my father. She made a successful career as a tour guide with American Express. She had been a talented dancer in amateur theatricals and loved to be the life and soul of the party. Ebullient groups of American visitors provided her with a natural audience and yet she found dealing with their demands a strain. I spent many evenings on the phone as a counsellor. When she gave up her job I provided more and more emotional and practical support in her everyday life. Aged eighty, she came to rest in the tourist bubble of Stratford-upon-Avon: ducks and swans, pleasure boats, ice-creams and cameras.

My father made fewer demands. After the divorce he moved away but we met regularly. Our talk covered history and politics but skirted around more personal issues. Eventually he settled in suburban Essex near my aunt and uncle. His house was typical of the 1930s Roseland semi-detached in which I had grown up. He had hopes of a permanent relationship but several mature women backed off. I suspected they found it was all give and no take emotionally, but I never talked to him about such matters. He preferred the company of young girls and found solace from time to time in the arms of dyed blonds with leopard skin leggings and thigh length boots.

Lizzie got on fine with my father but was everything my mother was not: robust and emotionally self-sufficient. They prowled around each other like cats but never opened formal hostilities. Lizzie came from a family who had travelled the globe from China to America and most places in between. My mother always thought she would encourage me to travel to dangerous places: but across the Channel, for heaven's sake?

*

CARCASSONNE

As the ridge ran west towards Carcassonne it became a featureless plateau. There were few signs of agriculture except for some ruined sheep pens. Alaric's ridge gradually slid into the valley and the trail turned through a new estate of villas, some of which looked like pastiche models of Mexican haciendas. Then suddenly, the mother of all fortresses appeared dramatically at the last minute, rising above rows of vines. Soon I was standing in the middle of crowds of tourists outside the Porte Narbonnaise, with a merry-go-round clanking out its mechanical music.

In the Middle Ages the view of Carcassonne would have struck terror into the heart of a Cathar heretic approaching under guard. Many of them were interrogated in the palace overlooking the river. At that time the mighty fortress with its double walls and huge towers was a statement of raw military power. The French Crown wrested Carcassonne from Cathar rebels and it became the key to a defensive system for south-east France. Now it is one of the capitals of the heritage industry.

Fortress of Carcassonne

The old city is completely dedicated today to satisfying the needs of tourists. The stonework of the walls was in perfect repair and the pointed slate roofs on the towers shone brightly in the sun. The shops were selling plastic swords and all manner of cheap souvenirs. Cafés turned out dishes of *cassoulet* by the dozen. A densely packed horde of tourists thronged the narrow streets, while a procession dressed in garish costumes enacted some ancient ritual. How did "Carca", as it is known locally, change from a decaying fortress and provincial capital of the wine industry into a tourist hot spot? Why did Georges Brassens sing the ironic ditty called "Carcassonne" originally written by Gustave Nadaud in the nineteenth century?

I understand that no one enjoys complete happiness on this earth.
My wish will never be granted.
I have never seen Carcassonne!

And

They say that you can see castles there as big as in Babylon.
A bishop and two generals!
I don't know Carcassonne.

The responsibility lies mainly with a nineteenth-century architect who recreated many of France's best known medieval buildings: Eugène Viollet-le-Duc, who restored this fortress from 1849 to his death thirty years later. Viollet-le-Duc tried to return Carcassonne to its original state as a royal stronghold, but some have criticised him for imposing his own conception of what a medieval building should look like. If he stopped many fine monuments—Mont-St.-Michel, Notre-Dame in Paris, the abbey at Vézelay—from falling down, his methods arguably created an idealised version of the Middle Ages. Carcassonne now is a Disneyland fantasy for visitors.

St. Louis had already ensured that some old buildings would escape the attentions of the restorers. He decided to move the inhabitants away from the fortress to a new settlement below: the area of Carcassonne now known as the Bastide St.-Louis, which lies between the River Aude and the Canal du Midi. Enclosed by boulevards it still retains the character of a fortified township with its bastions and gates. In the grid of narrow streets cars jostle with pedestrians. Here people live, work and buy meat and groceries rather than tourist souvenirs. To my mind the Bastide has far more life than the UNESCO world heritage site on the hill.

I visited one small museum which made a deep impression, explaining the psychological damage inflicted on France by the horrors of the First World War. The House of Memories was occupied after the war by a remarkable soldier and poet called Joë Bousquet. Joë grew up in Carcassonne, and there is a photograph of his *baccalauréat* class from 1914, a tragic image of so many young lives wasted. Joë joined the army in January 1916 and in April 1917 was awarded the *médaille militaire* for bravery. He took part in a desperate counter-attack near Château-Thierry in May 1918 and at 7p.m. on 27 May his spine was shattered by enemy fire. Sick and bedridden for the rest of his life, he lived in the house on the Rue du Verdun. You can still see the study-bedroom where he spent most of his days. Suffering was the impetus for a second career as a writer, both of war memoirs and poetry. He counted as friends and visitors many distinguished writers and artists of his generation. Within his broken body and from his darkened room Joë Bousquet celebrated the joy of being alive. He finally died in 1950.

The Place Carnot with its fountain lies at the heart of the Bastide. The sky was like a crisp blue sheet and the Tramontane not cold enough to deter restaurant customers from enjoying the sun. Leaves scuttled across the paving stones. A waiter with a line of chat kissed his female regulars on the cheek. Settling into a chair, I ordered the *plat du jour* with a carafe of local rosé and opened *Le Monde*. The pace was unhurried as locals came and went on their errands. I got out my map to study the next stage of my journey. I had to reach the great curve of hills stretching from Carcassonne to the valleys of the Cévennes. The south bank of the Canal du Midi seemed to provide a convenient escape from the city. I packed up my rucksack and was soon striding along the tree-lined towpath.

Françoise and Pascal had converted some old farm buildings at Conques-sur-Orbiel into an unusual guest house. Tired of life in Paris with the stresses of commuting to work and arranging child care, they had decided to drop out near Carcassonne which was Pascal's home town. Françoise admitted it was a big change from Clichy inside the capital. Using the ambiguous French adjective *tranquille* (both calm and boring), she raised her eyebrows: "The valley of Carcassonne is like a funnel for the wind. The winters are long and cold. There's not much going on in the town, apart from making wine and tourism."

Pascal had been an architect and interior designer for FNAC, the chain of superstores selling books, DVDs and electronic goods. This showed in the décor of his new home and not just because the shelves were lined with books on modern architecture. The living room was a converted stable with CDs and magazines installed in the former hay trough. The original brick floor and plaster walls had been cleaned up but not changed much: a long way from the philosophy of Viollet-le-Duc. The bedroom looked like a modern warehouse conversion. Clearly Pascal believed in minimalism.

As I ground my way up the southern slopes of the Montagne Noire the *garrigue* gave way to moorland. On the summit of the Pic de Nore an icy blast rushed at me and I had difficulty battling forward in the swirling mist. When I reached the woods on the far side the tempest ceased and all was suddenly calm. The Refuge du Trilby brought a pleasant surprise. A group of horse riders had stopped for lunch and a log fire was roaring in the hearth. To one side of the clearing were a large Land Rover full of food and eight horses. Spirits were already high.

"Come and share a bottle with us!"

Someone poured me a glass of red wine and then another. Eventually they left the bottle and said "help yourself." The group came from Toulouse and were spending a long weekend riding in the hills. The men's flushed faces betrayed the effects of fresh air, exercise and copious glasses of wine. There was much shouting and laughter and although city dwellers with the aura of affluence they spoke with a slight Midi twang.

"What is an Englishman doing walking around France on his own? We will have to find you a French woman for company."

I declined their bibulous offer.

Ahead I could see Mazamet and a wide vista of hilly country to the east, the Parc du Haut-Languedoc. For the next two days I crossed a different landscape from the dry *garrigue* further south. Friesian cattle grazed in fields of lush grass and the crops included wheat. Large oaks grew alongside beech and chestnut, and buttercups and cow parsley carpeted the meadows. In the woods I heard the familiar tapping of the woodpecker.

It was a pleasant surprise to arrive at a farmhouse and slump down in the shade. Marten was pottering in his sheds and spraying his vegetables, a seemingly idyllic life. With his wife he had dropped out of the rat race in Eindhoven to run this hostel. "I was a courier for a Dutch coach company before the bottom fell out of the market. Now we enjoy growing fresh vegetables, making jam, yoghourt and cheese and raising lambs in the hills of the Languedoc. But it is hard making a living from camping and the *gîte*."

His teenage son must have found it boring. He shut out this rural world by listening to the TV with headphones. A weekly border at a school in Mazamet he rose at 5.30 on Monday mornings to catch the bus. I suspected the family's roots were still in Holland. Their establishment appealed to Dutch holidaymakers like the young couple from Eindhoven who shared the dinner table with me.

Next day spines of jagged rocks crumbled away from a ridge to invisible valley floors. The Mediterranean reflected the sun's light like a cloudy mirror. Espinouse at 3,688 feet turned out to be a tree-covered hummock with no defined peak. The ridge ahead running all the way to my next destination, Le

Bousquet-d'Orb, looked tempting. Mont Aigoual in the Cévennes beckoned from the far distance.

I found a hostel deep in a beech wood. Christophe, who lived alone with his huskies and twenty-eight cats, was an eccentric character. He immediately took me on a tour of the house, stopping in front of an old metal barrel with a chicken inside. "This is my special one," he said.

"Why?" I asked.

"Because he scratches forwards rather than backwards."

He then introduced me to his cockerel Albert. Christophe had an amazingly mobile face, his sing-song voice recounting each story in a stream of slurred Midi French, moustache twitching as he spoke. He delivered the punch line with a deadpan expression and waited for a reaction from the listener. Then his face creased into a smile and he would start laughing at himself. He lived alone and obviously liked an audience, but I was not surprised to learn that he had been in *le showbiz* in Paris for twenty-five years. I could imagine him in a revue in some smoke-filled night club. He had a passing resemblance to Georges Brassens, who grew up in nearby Sète on the Mediterranean.

I dumped my rucksack in the attic dormitory, rustic but clean: seventeen beds on a wooden floor, a high ceiling festooned with cobwebs and a small window. A concrete step led down to three shower cubicles partitioned by waterproof sheets flapping in the breeze. An ingenious system of hoses distributed hot water, but I noticed that only one had a shower rose on the end. Christophe told me the house had been in his family since 1820. He had come back to live here after his time away in Paris. He said he was happy with his lot. "I am a free spirit. There's always nature to enjoy."

The ridge ahead seemed to march on for ever. I had to reach Bousquet by nightfall, a distance of twenty miles. This was essential if I was to rendezvous with Lizzie in Lodève the following day. Eventually the trail plunged downhill through chestnut woods. Exhausted, I tripped on several rocks and at one point twisted awkwardly, pulling the muscles in my left leg. This descent continued forever but eventually I staggered into Le Bousquet, where the phone box was like a furnace after a day in the sun. My hostess for the night, Christine, answered the phone: "Good evening, Mr. Pilgrim!"

At first perplexed, I explained that I was not doing the St. Jacques, the pilgrim route to Santiago de Compostela, like many of her guests. Her husband was the local hairdresser and his salon was just along the main street. When he had finished with his clients he would bring me home up the hill. I was much relieved and hurried along to the salon next to the baker's shop. Thierry, clippers in hand, greeted me warmly, his chubby face breaking into a friendly smile. I must have looked dishevelled and in need of a haircut myself. "I know it is the end of the day but I can give you a tidy up if you like."

He set to and soon I looked fit for a city street.

The meal with the family was not exactly a modest affair. After two *pastis* and some wine Thierry started to speak with the passion and speed of a true Frenchman. Christine, tall and slim with red hair in frizzy ringlets, let him have his head. Thierry had a number of *bêtes noires*: unsatisfactory tenants, people who wasted water, factory closures and the mismanagement of private forests. The next morning he ran me down to Le Bousquet. We stopped in front of the salon and he jumped out to shake hands with several friends, smiles all round. Thierry was a real mover and shaker in his local community.

When I set off my left leg started to give me trouble. After an hour I stopped for a shot of strong black coffee before carrying on further. Walking along a busy road with a stabbing pain after every step is not a lot of fun and I was glad to escape onto an ordinary footpath. As I approached Lodève there was a sting in the tail, in this case a scramble down a dried-up waterfall full of rocks and tree roots. I lost my way among apartment blocks before limping down steep steps to an ancient bridge. An old lady sitting on a bench could not give me directions to the hotel. With a beatific smile she said she was Spanish and could not speak French. Eventually I flopped onto my bed as the rush hour traffic rumbled past outside.

I spent some time tending my injured leg at the doctor's, discovering the streets of the old town and shopping for food. Lodève has a significant Muslim population, with women in traditional dress and shops run by North Africans. I walked into a smart butcher's shop and asked for slices of ham. The owner politely suggested I go over the street to the "other" butcher's shop and I retreated, embarrassed at my mistake. Eventually I was ready to climb past the steep wooded limestone slopes on the far side of the river. A statue of the Virgin watched over me as I stepped towards the Cévennes.

4 THE CÉVENNES AND THE ARDÈCHE
IN THE STEPS OF A DONKEY

MY FASCINATION WITH THE Cévennes started in 1995 when I completed the Stevenson trail, the itinerary followed and described by Robert Louis in his 1879 book *Travels with a Donkey*. The region has a special character derived from an evocative combination of landscape and history. The word Cévennes provides an important clue; it means *sept veines* or seven veins, because seven rivers flowing east to the Rhône cut deep into the mountains.

From the top of Mont Aigoual I made a 360 degree sweep of the horizon. To the east mountain ridges crumbled into the Rhône Valley. On the far side the distinctive pyramid of Mont Ventoux was clearly visible. Further away I could see the foothills of the Alps and the faint outline of Mont Blanc. The long undulating crest of Mont Lozère dominated the view to the north. Further west cliffs protected a plateau beyond which lay the Gorges du Tarn. The hills of the Languedoc ran away to the south-west horizon, while the valleys due south of Aigoual were deep and the ridges craggy. Small hamlets filled the valley bottoms and isolated farms populated scattered clearings on the upper slopes. Sun and shade dappled this landscape, moulding the peaks and troughs into a vast relief map.

Apart from the scale of the landscape the sheer variety is also impressive: limestone gorges, mountains of schist (consisting of rocks like mica, quartz and graphite) with acid-loving plants, forests, open moorland, chalk downs and lush meadows for cattle. Approaching the Cévennes from Lodève I had to cross two of the arid plateaus known as *causses*, either side of the Gorges de la Vis. The grass in the fields is coarse and sparse, purple-headed thistles flourish and there are a few stunted trees. A prehistoric circle of stone molars had been worn down to the level of the surrounding bushes. The parched topsoil lies above a thick layer of porous limestone. Rain permeates the rock very easily, leaving little moisture on the surface.

Gorges de la Vis is an apt name in view of its many twists and turns, *vis* meaning a screw. The Vis river rises in the Cévennes Mountains further north and tunnels its way underground before gushing out of the hillside at the top of the gorge. It then flows in a series of meanders cut over three million years ago in the soft limestone. The most famous of these is the Cirque de Navacelles.

The white limestone scree which covers the sides of the gorge was dazzling in the midday light. Some of the slopes reach sixty degrees and the top cliff is

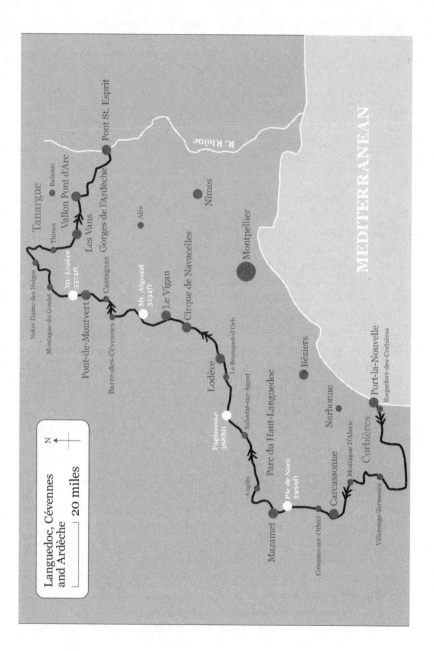

Languedoc, Cévennes and Ardèche

N

20 miles

MEDITERRANEAN

R. Rhône

Pont St. Esprit

Vallon Pont d'Arc

Balazuc

Thines

Tanargue

Les Vans

Gorges de l'Ardèche

Alès

Nîmes

Notre Dame des Neiges

Montagne du Goulet

Mt. Lozère 5574ft

Pont-de-Montvert

Cassagnas

Mt. Aigoual 5141ft

Le Vigan

Cirque de Navacelles

Barre-des-Cévennes

Montpellier

Le Bousquet-d'Orb

Lodève

Béziers

Port-la-Nouvelle

Salvetat-sur-Agout

Roquefort-des-Corbières

Espinouse 3688ft

Parc du Haut-Languedoc

Anglès

Narbonne

Pic de Noire 3699ft

Montagne d'Alaric

Corbières

Mazamet

Carcassonne

Conques-sur-Orbiel

Villerouge-Termenès

53

vertical. Box grows in abundance, interspersed with small oaks. After walking carefully down a zigzag path I reached a forest track one hundred feet above the river. It took my eyes a few seconds to adjust to the deep shade. Ruined cottages hid next to crude shelters in the rocks. A three-storey house called the Mas du Pont, its pink paint now fading, stood in a dark grove. The walls and roof looked solid but it had been abandoned many years ago. Walking at the bottom of these massive rock walls was a claustrophobic experience, my heart missing a beat when the path ahead seemed to cross a wall of vertical rock. In fact the ledge was wide enough to pass, with the worst of the drop obscured by bushes growing out of the fissures.

Two modern eyesores spoil the *cirque* itself. The road makes an ugly scar right across the face, and just over the lip of the cliff is an intrusive yellow building. My host in Navacelles told me that this restaurant was formerly an old farmhouse. Normally the *mairie* would require a more discreet finish for such a prominent building, but in this case the authorities let the owners do what they wanted. The locals suspect shady dealing and call it the verruca. Despite these blemishes the horseshoe-shaped wall of rock is still an impressive feature. A small island stands in the middle of an amphitheatre of grass at the bottom. The river used to flow across this meadow until about six thousand years ago when it broke through the neck of the meander. Now it thunders over a waterfall past the modern village. The mule track wound up the face opposite in a series of hairpin bends. From the top Navacelles looked small and vulnerable shut in by the cliffs. To the south a series of ribs cut into the gorge, as the river twisted its way through the limestone. I could see layers of rock like gigantic *millefeuilles* of pastry.

At the end of the second *cause* near Le Vigan the rocks changed from limestone to flaky schist and the trees from small oaks to lush green chestnut. This schist dictated the character of the country ahead all the way up the other side of the valley to Aigoual. My boots kicked up a fine grey and red powder among clumps of yellow broom. As elsewhere in the Cévennes you can gauge your height on the southern slopes of Aigoual by the type of trees. Up to 1,500 feet you find small evergreen Mediterranean oaks; between 1,500 and 3,000 feet chestnuts as well as deciduous oaks; between 3,000 and 4,500 feet beech; and over that height no trees at all.

Areas of open moorland followed; an unforgiving landscape with no shelter from summer sun and winter storms. Clusters of calcareous rocks lie across the high plateau south of Le Pont-de-Montvert, as if they had been scattered at random from a plane. The prairies here are the stage in a vast amphitheatre of mountains, with the slopes of Mont Lozère as the upper rows. The highest point is the Sommet des Finiels at 5,574 feet. As I puffed to the top a strong wind chilled the bones. Hundreds of sheep grazed on grass growing out of a thin layer of topsoil above the chalk. It was a treat to walk on springy turf after so many stony tracks.

North of Lozère a higher percentage of the land is cultivated. The trail enters the forest covering the Montagne du Goulet where the source of the River Lot lies. There were few trees here in Stevenson's day. In the next few miles I crossed the watershed between the Mediterranean and the Atlantic. The River Allier flows north to join the Loire. The source of the Chassezac, which flows east to the Rhone, is a few miles away. The Lot flows west to the Gironde.

Crossing into the Ardèche I entered a zone of transition. The deep valleys of the Cévennes had disappeared. Approaching Loubaresse the plateau of the Tanargue was bleak and forbidding. The climate is not a Mediterranean one and plenty of snow falls in winter. Loubaresse at 4,000 feet consists of a few stone-tiled houses huddled together around an open space with a fountain. All the walls are built of blocks of rough-cut granite and basalt, strong enough to resist storms, and a crenellated watchtower transforms the church into a fortress. Five of us crowded into one dormitory at the hostel, like kids going back to school. I had to fight for a shower in the morning, but the menu and local wine plus accommodation cost only €30. I asked for an extra carafe of wine and the hostess exclaimed, "I would never have believed it!"

Later that night we woke up suddenly when bats flew around the bedroom. I jumped off my bunk flapping a towel in vain at the unwelcome intruders while startled heads retreated further into sleeping bags. *Madame* downstairs came to investigate. With a disdainful look at so many pathetic townies she shooed the bats to safety out of the window.

Plateaus with poor soil, or *chams* in local dialect, are typical of the landscape in the hill country of the Ardèche. They are unsuitable for mixed agriculture, scrub has invaded the cultivated fields and clusters of granite boulders litter them. The mule track continued in a straight line down a plateau's edge known as the Corniche du Vivarais Cévenol. The tree-covered folds of the hills plunged down to the river below and the village of Thines. This seemed like a forgotten valley untouched by modern life. The houses huddle together on the very edge of the gorge. Built of large blocks of schist, several have outside staircases to the upper floor, a feature characteristic of the Ardèche. The Romanesque church is huge with a high barrel vault and semicircular apse. Why was it so big for such a small village? The answer to the mystery is that Thines was the best-known stopping place on the major pilgrimage route from Le-Puy-en-Velay to the monastery of St.-Gilles in Provence, whose seventh-century Athens-born patron was thought to protect believers from fire and nervous diseases and also to watch over children. The church's architecture, like the local climate, is a mixture of southern and northern, the multi-coloured façade of sandstone, granite and limestone coming from the Velay to the north with the different colours alternating to highlight decorative features. The sculptures, like the Last Supper over the main door, come from the south.

The lush vegetation in the valley was a change after the bleak plateaus near Loubaresse. Facing south to the Mediterranean, Thines enjoys a warm climate with plenty of rain. I bathed in some rock pools, an experience repeated several times in the Ardèche. The rivers here are reputed to be the warmest in France for swimming. A climb down into the Gorges de l'Ardèche involved forcing my way through thickets of willows and uprooted trees cast aside by the river in flood. I emerged on a deserted beach of large pebbles right on the gorge itself, alone in a sunlit paradise. Despite its placid appearance the river had a strong current and I had to swim hard to reach the opposite bank.

*

As I changed back into my walking clothes the sound of synthesised rock music echoed around the gorge. I pulled my mobile out of my rucksack.

"Terence?"

It was my mother again.

"It's all dark here. The lights have gone off. I don't know what to do."

"Have you looked at the fuse box? I told you that if a light bulb blows it trips the switch controlling the circuit. You have to use that stick I gave you to poke it back into position."

"What stick?"

"We left it in the hall next to the cupboard."

"Yes, what do I do with it?"

"You find the switch in the fuse box, the one pointing in a different direction from all the others. Then poke it up again. Have you got the torch?"

"Where's that?"

"Next to your bedside table. Please try. I will phone back in five minutes."

I counted up to ten to retain my composure. The limestone cliffs opposite were one thousand feet high and honeycombed with caves. The river had eroded the rock, creating several different terraces or undercliffs. I called back.

"Have you managed it?"

"No. What do I do now?"

"There's nothing much I can do from here. You will have to ring John the electrician in the morning. His number's on the list by the fridge."

She did not call again. I learnt subsequently that she got the lights to work. I knew she was lonely and wanted an excuse to talk to someone. I was also concerned that her short-term memory was failing.

I would have found it impossible to manage the situation at home and to keep walking without a mobile phone. However, the interruptions broke the spell of being in a different world. As my journey progressed I was torn between anxiety for my parents and the desire to escape such responsibilities, at least for a time.

A STRUGGLE FOR SURVIVAL

The signs of economic and social change over the centuries were obvious everywhere. I found terraces created to sustain agriculture on inhospitable slopes, but now fallen into disrepair and covered in vegetation: these were conspicuous either side of Le Vigan, outside Le Pont-de-Montvert and below Thines. These terraces are witness to the population pressure in the years before 1850 and the determination to bring every possible acre of land into cultivation. The ubiquitous chestnut trees provided the Cévenol peasants with their monotonous staple diet of bread and soup, and the inhabitants of the region were some of the poorest in France.

Some writers have idealised life in the Cévennes before modern times, but Jean Carrière gained the Prix Goncourt in 1972 with a much starker description of the landscape and the harsh life of the peasantry, in his novel *L'épervier de Maheux*. He describes "the shadows of the clouds prowling around the giant rocks, throwing immense tracks of countryside into darkness, only for them to light up again with the bubbling of insects, a light both raw and voracious" and also the barbarity of the area with its climatic extremes: "Even the finest seasons have something convulsive and unhealthy about them."

He then talks about the struggle which was the peasants' daily life:

"He is alone facing a mountain which has to be rebuilt into terraces, alone at the bottom of a well he is digging, alone trapping thrushes on the plateau or shooting a hare for a special meal, alone cutting down trees in a wood or grubbing out the ubiquitous yellow broom, alone with the demon which drives him to struggle on, when it would be so easy to pick up his belongings and to turn his back on this land which offers no future, on this existence without any pleasures, as many do."

Two villages which I visited illustrate the struggle for survival very well: Le Pont-de-Montvert in the Cévennes and Balazuc in the Ardèche. Le Pont-de-Montvert is a gaunt town in a naked valley with old houses clustered around the Tarn. The four separate medieval suburbs are clearly visible, the old bridge with its clock tower and the promenade by the river protected by high embankments. Before modern times it must have been isolated and desperately poor. Today the slopes around the town look barren with rocks everywhere; not the best land for growing cereals. In the eighteenth century agriculture just about produced enough to keep body and soul together, with incomes supplemented by the cottage textile industry. When troops were conscripted to fight in the French army of 1792, only one in seven of the adult males were over 5 ft 4 inches in height. After 1815 conditions gradually changed. The poor agricultural labourers, as well as many members of the local bourgeoisie, drifted off to seek an easier life in the local town of Alès or further afield in Marseille and Paris. The farmers made more money from keeping cattle. The population has declined from a peak of 1,400 in 1887 to only 270 today, and the self-contained community is now a thing of the distant past. Seventy per cent of houses are second homes and tourism is a major source of income for Le Pont-de-Montvert.

Balazuc overlooks the River Ardèche. This is a village where the buildings seem to grow out of the rock on which they stand. From the top of the old church tower a cascade of oddly shaped roofs tumbles down the hill, as in a cubist painting. The recent history of Balazuc is similar to Le Pont-de-Montvert's: the struggle for existence, depopulation, the growth of tourism, second homes. Paulette runs the oldest café in Balazuc. I met a spry slightly-built old lady who kept a sharp eye on local life. *Chez Paulette* was quiet in the afternoon as she was off-pitch for the tourist trade serviced by competitors near the river. We chatted about the village. Yes, the school was still in existence, although shared with another village. It was lonely in the winter but terrible in August. One sensed

Le Pont-de-Montvert

that when Paulette did eventually shut up shop, it would be another nail in the coffin of old Balazuc.

Raising sheep played a very important part in the old rural economy and the drove ways used by shepherds are a boon to the walker. The Draille de la Margeride is typical. From Mont Aigoual it follows a long mountain ridge and offers some of the finest views in the Cévennes. It was used to drive flocks of up to 2,000 sheep from the plains to the high summer pastures. Even today the National Park of the Cévennes receives about 20,000 sheep each summer, and their grazing maintains the traditional appearance of the grasslands. The *draille* was clearly marked out and the flocks were meant to stay within its boundaries. I set off through the forest and found the former drove way in the trees, a few yards from the forest track. It was about twenty yards wide, the regulation width, and from time to time a few boundary stones ran along its edge. I also made use of ancient mule tracks to cross the bare plateaus around Loubaresse. Mule trains carried wine, spices, salt, oil and cheese up from the coast, as well as books and seditious religious tracts. Cereals came down from further north.

At one time it was thought that the silk worm would provide the answer to the region's problems. In the first half of the nineteenth century it produced the golden product which provided much extra income to peasant households and transformed lives. On the slopes surrounding Thines a few mulberry trees remain, but nothing like the number when the silk industry was in its heyday. Locally produced silk was severely affected by disease and declined rapidly after 1855, but some weaving of the fabric continued. On the edge of the valley at Le Vigan I saw a long factory with high windows by a shady stream. It was empty, a ghostly reminder of a great industry.

"Stockings are packaged in Le Vigan but made in Morocco!" a local shopkeeper told me.

The town and its hinterland have undergone huge economic changes in the last hundred years. At one time there were 570 establishments spinning and weaving silk and making hosiery around Le Vigan. In the twentieth century the introduction of artificial fibres had a huge impact on traditional materials. Small family firms closed and larger groups saw their profits collapse. Today there is only one firm left. Around one in five is out of a job.

The crisis in the silk industry also brought major changes to the forests of Mont Aigoual, the impact of which is still evident. The forests were extensive until well into the eighteenth century, but then population pressure, grazing by sheep and the search for fuel took their toll. The crisis in the silk industry meant that peasants were looking for extra pastures to make up for their loss of income. Most of the forest was felled and the consequences for the environment were disastrous. Heavy storms, which are frequent in this region, washed huge quantities of rocks and soil down the mountain because the tree roots were no longer there to bind them together. Towns in the lowlands suffered badly. A law was passed in 1882 providing for the restoration of mountain environments, a far-sighted piece of legislation. By 1925 the Administration des Eaux et Forêts had organised the planting of millions of trees on Mont Aigoual. Local peasants carried out the work, lured away from their hard life as farmers by the regular wages on offer, while some of them sold their smallholdings to make room for more trees. Eventually the massive work of planting dried up and the Administration only required a handful of workers to maintain the new woodlands. As a result many agriculturalists moved away from the Cévennes for good to seek work elsewhere. Returning to the land was not a viable option.

Despite the variety of culture, the upland areas of the southern half of

France have all suffered the same fate as the Cévennes in the last hundred years: the growth of modern communications, the decline of local agriculture, the collapse of locally-based industries, the flight of population to the large towns, the dependence on tourism and second home owners. The Languedoc was haunted by its industrial ghosts: the abandoned barite mines in the Corbières, the windowless tanning and textile factories in Mazamet, the closed coal mines at Le Bousquet-d'Orb. There have been sporadic outbursts of anger about the deindustrialisation of the Languedoc, and since the 1970s a number of radical political groups have demanded more self-management for the south. Resentment at decisions being taken in Paris and ecological concerns have fuelled their militancy as they denounce the Languedoc's "colonial" economy based on tourism, wine and oil refineries. In recent years, however, their appeal has declined with the decentralisation measures initiated by the Socialists, despite the efforts to keep the language going.

The Languedoc has never really forged an identity, certainly not politically or culturally like Brittany and Alsace. I saw the Languedoc cross and the word Occitania scrawled on the side of a cistern in the hills. This was perhaps just a cry of despair at the decline of an old culture in an age of mass communication. As I moved on to the Alps, the Jura and even parts of northern France I witnessed the same story and heard the same cry.

Two characters crossed my path who saw the Cévennes as an escape from Marseille. Georges was a France Télécom employee who was planning to retire soon. "I have had a holiday home here for twenty-one years and now I am on my own. My son and his wife live here. The owners of a local hostel are very good friends. I have my dog. I can't wait to get out of Marseille. It is crowded, polluted and full of undesirable foreigners from all over the world. Some of them mug you for your money at red traffic lights."

Everything was *dingue*, a forceful French expression meaning "nuts." What chance was there of any change for the better when all the politicians were corrupt? "Every politician is trying to get a slice of the cake. When they have done that they argue about the crumbs!"

Georges was clearly a man with traditional French tastes. American hamburgers were also *dingue*. "People must eat proper food," he said.

North of the Montagne du Goulet I asked an old man chopping logs for directions. One of his daughters had married a local peasant farmer. He had worked in a laboratory in Marseille with psychologists who were all *fada* or mad. He wanted me to know he was an educated man who read a lot, and that some of his grandchildren had attended the *lycée* in Mende, twenty miles away. He said all this to contrast himself with the local peasants. "They only think about meat and milk," he said, "*les sous et la terre* (money and land). That is the peasant spirit!" He continued: "One peasant woman kept boasting to my wife how much land she had. My wife said to her, 'you only need two metres long, one metre wide and one metre deep for a grave.' That shut her up!"

I asked him what the winters were like. "They can be bitterly cold," he said, "because of the wind. When snow falls the wind drives it in drifts right up against my house. But I can gather logs for free in the woods. I do DIY and read to keep myself going. Remember, *la parole c'est la connaissance!* Speaking imparts knowledge." He was fond of aphorisms about life.

ENTER ROBERT LOUIS STEVENSON

The influx of visitors is partly due to the Stevenson trail. I came across this success story as I crossed the River Mimente to the former railway station of Cassagnas, now a small hotel. It is remarkable that this station is only kept going because of a writer who passed through before the railway was built. Robert Louis Stevenson came to Cassagnas on 2 October 1878 with his donkey Modestine. He described "a cluster of black roofs upon the hillside, in this wild valley, among chestnut gardens, and looked upon in the clear air by many rocky peaks." The village, two miles from the station, still climbs up the hillside on a series of terraces. Woods surround the Mimente in the valley and open slopes lead to the Montagne du Bouguès. The track of the old railway, which was open from 1909 to 1968, still weaves its way either side of the river. The main differences are that the population is now only 134 (600 in 1878), two-thirds of the houses are second homes and the Route Nationale from Alès to Florac is a dual carriageway. Despite this it is not difficult to imagine how remote this place must have been when Stevenson arrived.

Robert Louis travelled through the Cévennes for a variety of reasons: to think about his relationship with Fanny Osborne whom he subsequently married, to discover the history of his Protestant co-religionists and to find adventure and write about it. "For my part, I travel not to go anywhere, but to go. I travel for travel's sake. The great affair is to move and to write about it afterwards."

In doing so he made a walk in the country into a romantic adventure that has a particular appeal to city dwellers today. The Chemin Stevenson was created in 1978 to celebrate the hundredth anniversary of Stevenson's journey. When I completed it in 1995 there were only a few walkers. Today 10,000 people a year make the journey, many accompanied by donkeys. They come not only from France but from all over Europe, and most of them are fit and healthy sixty-year-olds as a new market has opened up for middle-aged hiking in comfort. Now there are Stevenson stickers on every hotel door and a well-organised system for carrying bags. On top of the Montagne du Bouguès fourteen German walkers accompanied by five donkeys laden with luggage disturbed my sleep after lunch. As the owner of a small hotel told me, "without this business we would be in dire straits." The *ancienne gare de Cassagnas*, or Espace Stevenson, offered camping and some guest rooms, and the hotel itself was full. Two large French groups were staying, there were piles of bags at the door waiting to be collected and donkeys tethered outside. A young couple had recently taken it over and were working flat out.

Walter Crane's frontispiece for *Travels with a Donkey*, 1879

Stevenson liked sleeping *à la belle étoile*, but I had accepted accommodation in a caravan with two friends who had joined Lizzie and me. In reality, however, the caravan was a tent on a trailer with two small air beds. This might have been fine, except that at 2,300 feet the thermometer hovered at freezing point all night and we had no sleeping bags or warm bedding. The cold air crept in from every side. In the end we all went to bed fully clothed, but for Lizzie the sight of her husband in a woolly hat, Japanese dressing gown and striped thermal leggings was too much. Sleep did not come easily but unlike Stevenson we could revive ourselves with a hot shower at 6 a.m. and coffee.

HEARING GOD'S WORDS

The religious conflicts which wracked France in the sixteenth and seventeenth centuries had a particularly tragic outcome in the Cévennes and to a lesser extent the Ardèche. It was this story which so fascinated Stevenson and I first stumbled across it in Barre-des-Cévennes. The Protestant *temple* here was an austere building with a single bell. It was finished in 1826, the third to be built in the village. The first was erected early in the seventeenth century and its successor was destroyed on the orders of Louis XIV after he decided to end the toleration of Protestants. On the wall was a plaque which recalled the great Protestant revolt which followed this decision, *la guerre des camisards*—the word *camisards* meant men in shirts, a soubriquet which referred to their humble origins. It read:

Élie Marion
Born at Barre in 1678
Camisard, prophet and missionary
Died at Livorno in 1713
He that is of God heareth God's words
John 8.47

The Protestant Church had been strong in the Cévennes and the Ardèche since the Reformation. Itinerant preachers spread the new ideas across much of southern France and they became well-established in the mountain valleys. The result was bitter fighting with Catholic neighbours which lasted throughout the second half of the sixteenth century. Wherever you go in the Languedoc you find references to towns, fortresses and churches destroyed. Peace finally came with Henry IV's Edict of Nantes in 1598, but this interlude was brief. Louis XIII and Cardinal Richelieu moved against the Protestants in the 1620s and it was in 1629 that towns like Les Vans in the Ardèche reverted to their Catholic allegiance. Later the French monarchy regarded the Protestants as a threat, at a time when France was constantly fighting against Reformed countries like Holland and England. In 1685 Louis XIV revoked the Edict of Nantes, thus outlawing the practice of the Reformed religion. Persecution and the destruction of Protestant churches followed.

Protestant *temple*, Barre-des-Cévennes

The spark which ignited the War of the Camisards originated in Barre. The Abbé Chayla, who was responsible for harrying the Protestants, was attending the fair of Ste.-Madeleine in the town when local Protestant leaders demanded the release of some co-religionists who had been imprisoned. When Chayla refused the news spread quickly and outraged Protestants swore revenge. The story moves on to Le Pont-de-Montvert. On 24 July 1702 the Abbé was hiding in the clock tower. Outside fifty psalm singers were calling for vengeance. A struggle ensued and the Camisards decided to smoke him out of the upper floor. His guards were either shot or escaped, but he lowered himself on a sheet and fell with a bullet in his thigh. The Protestants stabbed him over twenty times and he died of his wounds. The leader of the Camisards, Esprit Séguier, was later caught and burnt alive.

The government then sent its crack troops and the Protestants waged a guerrilla campaign against them from their mountain hideouts. Near Le Vigan I saw an old *bastide* with tunnels which allowed the occupants to escape by a secret route. Eventually the revolt was crushed and the leaders killed or imprisoned. Élie Marion negotiated the surrender and then went into exile. Most of the Camisards were poor labourers and artisans, but the Protestant middle class also suffered in the subsequent repression. Throughout the eighteenth century Protestants were deprived of their civil rights. Yet although many outwardly conformed to Catholic practice, the Reformed spirit survived in clandestine meetings. On the path from Barre to Cassagnas I passed a remote farm with some graves nearby. After 1685 Protestants could not be buried in church graveyards, so their bodies were often laid to rest near their own homes. Protestant rights were restored in 1787, just before the Revolution.

The spirit of revolt did not die. The Protestant tradition, which was buried for almost one hundred years, adapted very easily to the ideology of 1789. The Catholics found themselves on the losing royalist side. I crossed a bleak plateau in the valley near Les Vans where a bloody massacre took place. In 1792 the townsfolk surrounded a camp of royalists conspiring to overthrow the revolutionary government, and butchered them.

The remoteness of this region makes it an ideal place for anyone seeking to retreat from the world. The Cistercian monastery of Notre-Dame des Neiges is buried in a secluded valley where the quiet is absolute. It was refounded in 1850 on the site of an earlier house. Luckily it survived a republican attempt to close it down and a disastrous fire in 1912. I stayed in the retreat house and the rules of silence were:

> No talking at meals
> No talking in the corridors
> No baths to be taken after 9.30 p.m.
> Talk quietly in the guest rooms

At Notre-Dame des Neiges the monks follow the rules of the order very strictly, surrendering themselves to the will of God. This devotion is illustrated by the prayer of Charles de Foucauld, who entered the monastery in 1890 and was later martyred in the Sahara: "Father I abandon myself into Your hands. Do with me what You will, whatever You do, I will thank You, I am ready for all, I accept all. Let only Your will be done in me, as in all Your creatures, and I'll ask nothing else, my Lord."

Robert Louis Stevenson stopped here for three days in 1878. He had many observations about the vow of silence, the frugal diet and the regular schedule of work and worship. He noted with amusement the regulations in his room for MM. les *retraitants*: "What services they should attend, when they were to tell their beads or meditate, and when they were to rise and go to rest. At the foot was a notable N.B.: *Le temps libre est employé à l'examen de conscience, à la confession, à faire de bonnes résolutions*, etc. To make good resolutions indeed! You might talk as fruitfully of making the hair grow on your head."

Occasionally the silence could seem oppressive but it had a comical side, particularly at supper. I sat at a long refectory table with various church members on retreat and one or two nuns. The *père hôtelier* read a short passage from the Bible and then put on some suitable music; in this case the universal Vivaldi. As we could not talk there was a lot of gesticulating when someone wanted salt or another potato. I motioned for an extra glass of the abbey's excellent red wine and received a frosty stare from one of the nuns. The meal was simple and afterwards we were expected to help with the washing up. In the kitchen a bit of light-hearted banter seemed to be acceptable. I had been asked to respect the privacy of all the individuals on retreat. Some looked troubled and I could only speculate on their motives for coming.

After supper I attended Compline in the church. Like many Cistercian buildings this one was stripped to the essentials. Dressed in white habits the monks glided out of a side door with very little light to guide them. Some were stooped and bony faced, and only one novice had a fresh complexion. The chanting of the psalms was ethereal and less accented than the settings traditional in the Anglican Communion. At the end the monks turned to the statue of the Virgin and sang the Salve Regina. It was not yet ten o'clock, but retiring to bed was the only option. It looked as if I would get a long night's sleep, but the hooting of an owl broke the total silence. After that I tossed and turned for several hours.

The remoteness of the mountains meant that the Cévennes and the Ardèche were a favourite safe haven during the Second World War. Aire de Côte is an old farm in a forest clearing near Aigoual, which has been tastefully converted by the Cévennes National Park into a hostel. A plaque on the wall of the house recalls that this was an important centre for Resistance operations during the war: "Paul Cabouat, Surgeon in the *Maquis*, Mayor of Nîmes after the Liberation, and Pioneer of the Grandes Randonnées, 1888-1983." The Cévennes became a place of refuge for thousands, including Jews and especially Frenchmen who refused to work for the Germans through the infamous Service du Travail Obligatoire. It was difficult to hide all these people in remote farms and many joined the first *maquis* organisations in the region, including one formed at Aire de Côte in

January 1943. The Germans destroyed this group in one of their first operations against the Resistance.

*

The path near the Gorges of the Ardèche crossed a wooded plateau with few signs of habitation except a forester's hut and some prehistoric remains. As I neared the medieval village of Aiguèze there was a rumble of thunder and rain started to fall hard. I charged full tilt down the slope ahead, stumbling over rocks and nearly tumbling into the gorge below. The first building housed an excellent restaurant, so I dived inside. The owner relieved me of my soaking clothes and instantly supplied a reviving glass of Côtes du Rhône. Peering through the curtain of water I realised I had left the hills which had been my companions for several weeks. Ahead lay the broad valley of the Rhône, the busy highway which joins Paris to the south, and on the far bank the challenge of Mont Ventoux.

5 THE RHÔNE AND THE ALPS OF UPPER PROVENCE
A LANDSCAPE FOR HERMITS

I COULD NOT AVOID the challenge of climbing the 6,273 feet of Mont Ventoux which can be seen from miles away, its summit cone a brooding presence above the vineyards of the Côtes du Rhône. At close quarters the northern face looked forbidding, often in shade and covered in pine trees. My climb started at Malaucène, a working town which was refreshingly ordinary after the tourist delights of the Rhône villages. The wind blew litter and leaves across a drab boulevard. Dog shit covered dimly lit back streets lined with run-down tenements. The flock wallpaper, varnished panelling and white paper tablecloths in my hotel provided a stark contrast with the elegance of a restaurant in Séguret the night before.

The ascent started with a 1,300-foot climb, followed by a steep descent to a horseshoe valley covered with vines, cherry and apricot trees. The deep red berries and orange fruits of arbutus and mountain ash injected a welcome touch of colour into the dark green backdrop of pines. After a testing ascent the trail traversed le Grand Vallat, a V-shaped gash in the north face, covered entirely in scree and boulders. Darkness fell as I turned down the road through a ski resort to find my chalet. A further 1,600 feet remained to be climbed in the morning. The sun was setting over the centre of France in a furnace of pink and vermilion. Later the stars stood out like halogen lamps in the night sky. There was no light pollution up here.

The dispiriting Mistral wind from the north howled on a cold grey dawn; hardly the best conditions to go up Mont Ventoux. On the summit ridge it was determined to knock me down if it could. The large communications station is an ugly building with massive walls of stark cream plaster and a forest of bristling antennae like a military bunker; a real blot on the highest peak in France outside the Alps and the Pyrenees. Mont Blanc and the Alps were visible to the north and east. When I looked down the slopes immediately beneath, the contrast with the north side of the mountain stopped me in my tracks. For more than six hundred feet there was no vegetation in sight—just a vast expanse of sun-bleached shale, a complete desert. I had not seen such a well-scoured landscape since crossing the Tibetan plateau some years before.

I found a shelter to make some notes and reread what I had written about the Rhône Valley: "Old bridge with twenty-five arches across Rhône at Pont-St.-Esprit. Well-preserved medieval house belonging to local grain merchants.

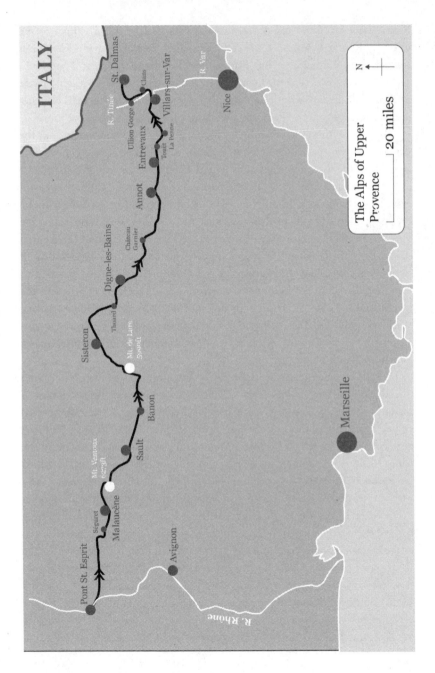

ITALY

St. Dalmas
R. Tinée
Clans
Ulhon Gorge
Villars-sur-Var
Entrevaux
Toult
La Penne
R. Var
Nice
Annot
Château Garnier
Digne-les-Bains
Thoard
Sisteron
Mt. de Lure
Sisteron
Banon
Sault
Mt. Ventoux
6273ft
Siguret
Malaucène
Pont St. Esprit
Avignon
R. Rhône
Marseille

The Alps of Upper Provence
N
20 miles

Romanesque windows and delicate ceiling paintings. Fortified villages of the Côtes du Rhône: Cairanne, Rasteau. Heady wines. Fierce summer heat. Séguret snuggles into a limestone cliff. Narrow cobbled streets, irregular stone walls, shuttered windows, concealed courtyards. A film set. Townsfolk might appear in medieval costume. Old fountains splashing into large basins. Bells clanging in ancient clock towers. No longer a working village but preserved for tourists."

The fury of the Mistral lashing the mountain interrupted my memories. The Col des Tempêtes is a notch in the ridge to the east of the summit. Some cyclists coming up the road from the south were dismounting for fear of being blown over. I descended a few yards tacking backwards and forwards like an awkward crab. It was hard work. In order to make better progress I escaped the wind by dropping down onto the road on the south side. A line of sheep was crossing the scree, and I might almost have expected to see a robed tribesman from Central Asia driving them along. The ascent for cyclists starts at the village of Bédoin to the south-west and then turns in a great loop near the Chalet Reynard to complete the climb across the lunar landscape. It is twelve miles long and the height gain is 5,250 feet. During my descent I met a horde of amateurs puffing their way to the top. Their coloured vests and pants stood out, garish and bright, against the rocky background. None of them had enough breath to exchange even a few words of greeting.

A stele commemorates the death of Tommy Simpson, the British rider who died during the Tour de France in 1967. Tommy was the first Briton to make a major impact in the European world of professional cycling, to wear the coveted yellow jersey during the Tour de France and to finish in the top ten. In 1967, at twenty-nine, he fell off his bike in the searing heat during the ascent of the Mont Ventoux. He shouted for help to remount but fell off again and collapsed unconscious. Rushed to hospital in an ambulance he died a few hours later. There was an even darker side to the story; the autopsy showed he had amphetamines in his body. In the aftermath of his death the International Union of Cycling banned the use of any performance-enhancing drugs in the sport. The stele was erected by friends in 1997 and is still garlanded with flowers and photos.

I traversed back to the ridge. As is often the case during the Mistral the air was crisp and clear. High cirrus cloud streaked the blue sky. The path crossed a surreal landscape of stunted pine trees growing straight out of the shale. A glass of Côtes du Ventoux would certainly have improved my baguette. This is one of my favourite French country wines, unpretentious with a slightly spicy flavour.

Most of the wine is made on the southern slopes, but also further north around Malaucène.

LE GRAND PAYS BLEU

Sault stands on a rocky outcrop above a broad fertile valley. From the terrace on the western side there is a remarkable view of Mont Ventoux behind its lower buttresses. It looks like a pimple trying to attract the traveller's attention. From the north the mountain presents its massif bulk to the walker and the ascent offers a challenge, but the gradient on the southern slopes is much easier altogether. Sault seemed to have all the elements of an ideal Provençal town: a cluster of old buildings in a mixture of styles from the Middle Ages through the Renaissance to the eighteenth century; an uncluttered Romanesque church with tall powerful arches; a square with cafés shaded by plane trees and old town walls. The next morning a market brought life to the streets. The nougat in M. André Boyer's shop was too great a temptation. He is a fourth generation *maître nougatier* in an area well-known for nougat. He mixes lavender honey gathered from the slopes of Mont Ventoux with whipped egg whites and cooks them in vats. Later he adds syrup and locally grown almonds. The resulting paste is poured into moulds lined with unleavened bread.

The plateau of the Pays de Sault is famous for its lavender, one of the most distinctive products of Provence. Jean Giono described it as a *grand pays bleu* in the growing season. This was a secluded landscape of oak and pine forests, shuttered farmhouses and small fields, the preserve of hunters. I saw few people all day and only disturbed two guard dogs. Some perfume lingered in the immaculate rows of lavender bushes, even though the harvest was long since over. A village shopkeeper told me about the local obsession with pregnancy. "Many of the villages are desperate to keep their schools open in order to attract young families. Every young woman who puts on weight is assumed to be pregnant! We urge them to register a new arrival with the authorities in order to demonstrate the continuing need for a school." It was at Contadour, not far from my route, that Giono gathered with his disciples after the First World War to discuss world peace and the way forward to a better life. In his novel *Le Grand Troupeau* he had described the horrors of that conflict which turned him into a pacifist. Subsequently he became famous for a number of books which celebrated the virtues of a simple life close to nature. His best known novel in England is probably *Le Hussard sur le toit* (*The Horseman on the Roof*), which was made into a film.

*

My host Henri easily spotted me in the main square of Banon. With long frizzy hair and a pointed beard he looked like a revolutionary from the nineteenth century. He should have been wearing a tattered frock coat with a large cravat and carrying subversive tracts. In fact he was a businessman, working partly at home in Banon and the rest of the time in Lyon. I had only just settled into my room when my mother called again from Stratford-upon-Avon.

"I'm afraid I've had a nasty fall in the street. I had just been to a poetry reading. I tripped over the kerb and knocked myself out for a few seconds on the pavement. The next thing I knew two ambulance men were looking down at me. It was rather funny actually. They wanted to take me to the hospital for a check up. I told them I was on my way to a wine tasting which I would not miss for the world. Eventually they persuaded me. I'm all right; no bones broken, just a few bruises. But I do feel a bit shaky, so I shall rest for a few days."

"This isn't the first time you have fallen over recently," I reminded her. "There was that time you collapsed into a bush outside your flat. Didn't the doctor suggest you attend a falls clinic? You ought to go. You might find out if there is anything seriously wrong."

I might have known what the answer would be. I suppose children should suppress their natural concern and let their elderly parents run their own lives.

"Don't tell me what to do. I'm fine and I'm not going."

I suspected she might have had some minor strokes. Arthritis was also getting the better of her and she was struggling to get up and down the stairs to her flat. There was no lift. After a couple of faints she had been banned from driving for six months. Now she used her car infrequently, so the battery kept running down in the garage. I started to wonder how much longer she could live independently, but knew she would hate the idea of moving.

*

Monique, Olivier and their daughter Élodie occupied a remote farmhouse and enjoyed the peace and quiet of living deep in the country surrounded by the natural world. Olivier had a sad story about two baby boars. A hunter had shot their mother in error. The two babies were very distressed and Olivier took them in and cared for them. They accompanied him to his garden where they enjoyed rooting around for vegetables. In France, however, it is forbidden to keep wild animals at home. Olivier gave the two young boars to an animal charity where one of them died of stress. Olivier and Monique kept goats and two hunting dogs who greeted me playfully. Tibetan prayer flags decorated the entrance along with pieces of driftwood and other natural artefacts.

Next morning Monique asked me if I would deliver a letter to their friend the hermit with an offer of help. What sort of assistance they had in mind I had no idea. Even so, I could hardly turn down such an intriguing assignment. The sanctuary of Notre-Dame de Lure nestled in a shady grove near a sacred spring. On the other side of the clearing a row of cottages stood next to a vegetable garden. I knocked on one of the doors to meet Lucien. He looked every inch a hermit with unkempt hair and a knee-length beard. I tried to engage him in conversation, but he played his role and adamantly refused to talk. When I persisted he waved me away impatiently. I was forced to nod politely, hand him the letter and leave. What an anti-climax! I had walked a long way for an interesting encounter and found out nothing. Another visitor in the clearing came up to me when he saw Lucien turn away.

"Everyone around here knows M. Lucien," he said. "He's not religious. He just wants to live a quiet life surrounded by nature. The local council let him live in the cottage free provided he looks after the site. He's a difficult character. He chases visitors away. The council are loosing patience with him. He's looking for alternative accommodation."

On the summit crest of the Montagne de Lure I crossed a plateau of loose rock shattered into slabs by the snow and ice. Behind was the shadowy outline of the Montagne du Luberon, protecting the plains of Provence and the Rhône delta. The steppe lands of the curving ridge stretched for six miles, rising up and down just above the tree line. The path down tumbled through a beech forest. Within an hour I was on the road, just a mile distant but 2,000 feet lower. From there I could see the rocks above had been compressed over many years into linenfold panelling, the top edge as sharp as a pastry cutter.

A FORETASTE OF THE ALPS

After the Montagne de Lure I reached Sisteron and embarked on the Grande Traversée des Préalpes to Entrevaux on the Var. This trail across the mountains of Upper Provence passes through some of the remotest countryside in France and is unknown to most walkers. Even here, however, chance encounters happened from time to time. A Swiss of African origin, who was teaching in France, engaged me in a passionate discussion on the Middle East near a deserted hamlet. He was full of prejudice against the Algerians he had to teach. When he discovered I was English he started to extol the virtues of the British monarchy: "I am very happy to meet one of Queen Elizabeth's subjects!" I wondered how long the conversation might last, so I suggested standing under the shade of a nearby tree rather than in the heat of the sun.

One strenuous twenty-mile hike sticks in my memory. First stop was a chapel, formerly a staging post for the *transhumance* and an important place of pilgrimage. The trail crossed a river in an idyllic valley, with saplings creating shady pools in the shallow water. I set off on an ascent through the trees. After reaching a long crest 1,600 feet later I threw off my pack, desperate to ease my aching shoulders. Past the Sommet du Corbeau the track downhill was long, stony and wearisome. At the bottom I was not in the mood to appreciate the picturesque village of Thoard and flopped down for a drink in the café. It was about 7 p.m.

Some old men from a nearby retirement home were enjoying an evening *pastis* and they looked on in amusement at my obvious exhaustion. I asked for a juice with plenty of *flocons*. My new companions laughed out loud at this turn of phrase; *flocons* are snowflakes and I had meant to say *glaçons* or ice cubes. I enquired whether my *chambre d'hôte* was far from the village. Only a mile or so I was told: "that will get you in shape!" I phoned my host and said I would be about half an hour. At the end of a long day the hill up to La Bannette proved to be steeper than expected and my pace was pathetic. Imagine my relief when my host came round the corner in a people carrier.

Often dog tired at the end of a long day, I always had one job before dinner which could not be shirked: the washing. I tried to carry as few clothes as possible so this chore was unavoidable. The smell of stale sweat reminded me if I felt lazy. French wash basins have a curious mechanism to stop the water flowing out. It consists of a lever attached to a long rod, which pulls a cross piece in the waste pipe up and down, thus moving the metal plug into position. If it sounds complicated, it is, and it frequently failed to work. French hotels also provide miniscule bars of soap; not enough to give woollen walking socks a good rub. Once the clothes had been washed the next challenge was to find somewhere to hang them. Proprietors do not like their rooms being turned into laundries full of damp garments creating puddles on the floor, while festooning the shutters was unthinkable. The obvious place was the shower but sometimes it was tricky to attach soaking wet clothes to bars and pipes. Shirts had a nasty habit of falling into my dirty water, which refused to flow away because of the French plumbing. There are no purpose-built hooks in French showers; let alone a washing line. Ingenuity was called for. A bent metal coat hanger worked wonders. Sometimes I was lucky enough to find a hot radiator. The most suitable was the old fashioned cast-iron variety. I used to close the bedroom door to the gentle sound of dripping with a sigh of relief.

Digne-les-Bains is a quiet town which, like many towns in the south, is a refuge for people fleeing the industrial cities of the north. Napoleon marched through Digne in 1815 but the most fascinating person associated with the town is the intrepid explorer of Tibet, Alexandra David-Néel (1868-1969). The persistence of the early travellers who were determined to reach Lhasa was amazing. Alexandra spent years studying Sanskrit and Tibetan and travelling all over Asia. She reached The Forbidden City in 1924, dressed as an old beggar woman, with her companion Yongden who wore a monk's habit and did most of the talking. Her book *Voyage d'une Parisienne à Lhassa* is a travel classic, although she is less well-known in the English-speaking world than Heinrich Harrer and his *Seven Years in Tibet*. After her travels Alexandra settled in Digne in 1928 and built her own house called Samten Dzong, where she lived to the age of one hundred and one. Now the house is a Tibetan cultural centre and museum about Alexandra. It helps Tibetan refugees, teaches Buddhism and stages cultural events.

The hostel at nearby Château Garnier was designed for large numbers of young people to spend their summer holidays. The dining room was like a barn with concrete floors and a huge fireplace, and the bunk rooms spartan. Suzanne, the guardian, gave me a key to visit the Chapelle St.-Thomas with its twelfth-century apse. Murals showing Christ in glory with the four evangelists cover the ceiling. Their seventeenth-century restorers were probably illiterate, as the words in the paintings have been copied with a mirror and therefore they appear back to front and some of the letters are incorrect. While the restorers probably altered the pictures of the apostles, the figure of Christ is thought to be original and has a touching naivety. The Saviour stares ahead, his right hand raised in blessing and his left hand grasping an orb surmounted by a large cross. It is relatively unusual to find a Christ in Glory in a Catholic church in France, and while the image is common enough in Byzantine churches it was supplanted in

St. Mark "copied with a mirror"
Chapelle St.-Thomas

Western Europe by the more familiar image of Christ on the cross. St. Thomas' chapel was a little jewel and also blessed with remarkable acoustics. I ended my visit by breaking into song.

Not long after my return Suzanne came down on her bicycle laden with food. She lit a large log fire which was soon roaring away, creating a cocoon of warmth in an otherwise freezing cold room. Out of her basket came a very wholesome meal: homemade vegetable soup, pork chops with *ratatouille*, cheese, baked custard with nutmeg and a bottle of wine. Suzanne chatted freely about her life. "I grew up in Marseille and went to a Catholic school. I still remember my white blouse with a frill. After getting married my husband and I moved to Château Garnier and he works for the Office National des Forêts. He is creating an arboretum which will tell young people about the different trees and plants to be found in the region."

Then she expressed her concerns about the village. "I don't know how a remote rural community like this can survive in the twenty-first century. The village school is under threat and it serves a huge area. Drugs are a scourge among the young people, even here."

When I woke the next morning cold air slid under the rough blankets and made me shiver. Through the window I could see a lowering sky and thick clouds covering the mountain tops. Some of the hills also had a dusting of snow. Suzanne said that this weather was unusual for late September. In a hamlet I stopped to talk to a widow sweeping her front drive. She carried her eighty years well and had been a teacher in nearby Annot for thirty years. "I lost my husband forty years ago. Recently my brother died of cancer. Now I am on my own and very quiet," she said.

In each hamlet are streets like hers, in every street houses like hers; dignified, but painfully lonely.

If you want to enjoy the views without walking you could use the Train des Pignes, small carriages in cream and blue rattling along a single track over brilliantly engineered viaducts. Some say that in the old days of locomotives one train ran out of coal. Pine nuts (*pignes*) fell in the fender and kept the boiler burning. The railway runs from Digne to Annot, Entrevaux and the valley of the Var, ending up in Nice. Its origins lie in the transfer of Savoy and Nice from Italy to France in 1860. The idea was to link Nice with Grenoble and enable the military to rush troops to the Italian border in case of need. The line was given to the Compagnie des Chemins de Fer du Midi and not the great Paris-Lyon-

Méditerranée company. This is why there are still two train stations in Digne with different gauges of track.

Above Annot I looked up at jagged pinnacles of rock where the adventurous practise their climbing skills. At some time in the past a mountain ridge collapsed, creating a cliff where there are some particularly unusual rocks, the so called sandstones of Annot. Consisting of quartz and feldspar, they are thought to have been transported from further south just before the creation of the Alps. The oil industry is particularly interested in these rocks, because they contain some valuable lessons for prospecting elsewhere. Annot is renowned as a summer resort in the hills. The ramparts were finished in 1382 and the oldest houses date from the fifteenth century. Narrow streets climb the hill in steps, passing under Gothic arches and twisting round the tall houses.

THE VALLEY OF THE VAR

After the Grande Traversée des Préalpes I tackled the valley of the River Var which squeezes through a narrow defile at Entrevaux. It is rarely more than half a mile wide, surrounded by steep mountain slopes crossed by deep ravines. The underlying bedrock is friable, constantly eroded by the heavy autumn and spring

Touët-sur-Var

rains. The valley provided a walking challenge as I scrambled up and down its mountain walls. Touët-sur-Var, pronounced Touette in the Provençal dialect, clung to a steep rock face. The old houses had open attics which used to be employed for drying figs. The path wound up a narrow crack above the village— not a place to look down!

Ghosts of empty settlements also appeared in these foothills of the Alps. Brilliant red butterflies flitted around my feet. Tinted smoke bushes lined the way to a rocky promontory and the remains of the Chapelle Ste.-Elisabeth. Further along I came across the ruined walls of cottages scattered across the hillside among unpruned fruit trees. I pushed open the door of the Chapelle St.-Antoine. Paint was flaking off the walls and cobwebs hung from the ornaments on the altar. A frayed copy of the Bible in Latin was open at the beginning of St. John's Gospel: "In the beginning was the word." I looked at the Var below and wondered how long this village had been deserted. Perhaps the inhabitants had given up the struggle to maintain a few terraces, once the road and railway provided an easy escape.

The medieval village of La Penne is cut off from the main thoroughfare. At 7a.m. the valley was full of milk white mist, with just a few hills poking up their tops like islands in the sea. I might have been looking at a stage setting for Swan Lake, with smoke being pumped on from the wings. A chapel with a tall tower looked like a fairy castle. The village square provided a small platform for the *mairie* and the miniature thirteenth-century Romanesque church. I noticed the war memorial from the First World War with twelve names, two of which were Italian. Although it is over 150 years since France absorbed Nice and its hinterland, there are still quite a few local people with Italian origins. My hostess commented, "The local people are fiery but warm-hearted. I used to live in Bordeaux where they were much more placid."

The square in Villars-sur-Var was full of people: children and mothers coming home from primary school, a cycling team in blue outfits drinking beer in the café. The plane trees provided ample shade for everyone. The houses either side of the narrow medieval streets nearly touched each other, and many alleys looked like impasses until I discovered a crack in a wall or a tunnel under an adjacent building. The château once belonged to the Grimaldi family who used to be leading nobles in mercantile Genoa and now rule Monaco.

The River Tinée is one of the many tributaries of the Var which drain the Alps. A house at Clans, above the river, allegedly belonged to Queen Jeanne of

Provence who led a colourful life in the fourteenth century. She indulged in intrigue and assassination, loved luxury and had four husbands and many lovers. Unfortunately she lost her possessions and ended up being suffocated by her heir. An unguarded path along a cliff led to a pocket-sized bridge over a narrow chasm. The Ullion gorge turned out to be one of the most exhilarating walks in the area, a paved mule track winding 1,500 feet up a precipitous face. Serrated fangs of unstable rock plunged downwards like forked lightening. I was pleased to reach overgrown terraces, ruined farm buildings and eventually the alpine meadows on a col. I had now walked over a thousand miles and the Alps proper beckoned.

THE ALPS
PASTURES AND PASSES

IN THE COURSE OF a month in the Alps I climbed 66,000 feet, ate huge meals and still lost fourteen pounds. I started by leading a group of friends and some of them found the walking tough from day one as there was no gradual build up. Alan suffered from blisters, but kept his spirits up with a supply of Mars bars. Others abandoned the challenge and took a taxi. At one point my insubordinate party went their separate ways. I was left alone on the mountain at 7 p.m., engaged in a fruitless search for them.

We scrambled over a pass to look down on the Zone des Merveilles and the first of its many lakes. A high mountain landscape unfolded; scree and massive boulders at the bottom of a glacial valley. The Refuge des Merveilles was a new experience for some of my group and one they were not anxious to repeat. We slept in a large dormitory with over thirty people. The highlights of the night included stumbling around in the dark without lights, listening to snoring bodies, the overpowering fug, cold showers, watery soup and dry bread for breakfast. I kept thinking of the great mountain views I would see in the morning, until thunder started crashing overhead around 4 a.m.

At 8 a.m. heavy clouds covered the valley and the rain was hard and continuous. I headed straight up a slope to the Pas de l'Arpette and the Gordolasque Valley. My party was strung out in a bedraggled line, as a large bank of cloud rolled up the mountain from the lake below. Mercifully it did not stay long. Once over the pass the steps down the *arête* were clearly visible on the other side. Five chamois leapt across the bowl of rock below, moving gracefully off their back legs and making arcs in the air.

The route descended a series of steps down a former glacier. We slithered across slopes of grey shale to the second level and then through a steeper barrier of rocks. The path across muddy pools and around trees was very slippery and I concentrated on the slope immediately ahead, trying to ignore the vertiginous drop to a waterfall below. There was some comfort as the zigzag descent drew close to the rock walls on our right, but then we were forced out onto exposed slopes, stumbling through clumps of soaking bushes. The slope looked much steeper from the bridge over the Gordolasque than it appeared further up. After this test of stamina some of the group took a day off at a fair in St.-Martin-Vésubie. Refuges were definitely off the menu.

Luc and Christiane at St.-Dalmas could not have been more welcoming.

Geneva

SWITZERLAND

R. Rhône

SAVOIE

Culoz

Lac du Bourget

Aix-les-Bains

Chambéry

St-Christophe
-la-Grotte

Mt. Granier

St. Pierre-en-Chartreuse

Grenoble

La Grave
Col d'Arsine

Bourg d'Oisans   Écrins

Briançon

Queyras

Château Queyras

Col de Girardin

Fouillouse

ITALY

Larche

Bousiéyas

St. Étienne-
de-Tinée

Mercantour

St Martin-
Vésubie

Mt. Mounier

Le Beuil   Roure

Vallée des
Merveilles

Sospel

The Alps

N

20 miles

Nice

Our dinner companions included a woman who worked in security at Nice airport. She told us about the number of smart young Russian women entering France with their male minders. "They are clearly prostitutes working the Côte d'Azur, but the police can't prove it. There's no reason to refuse entry." She also agreed that the Alpes Maritimes locals are not on the whole particularly friendly, unlike most people in the Midi. The deep narrow valleys seem to have conditioned their attitude to outsiders.

Beyond St.-Dalmas the valley floor dissolved into a maze of bottomless gorges and the whole landscape looked very brittle. Soaring mountain walls increased my feeling of claustrophobia and red rocks swept to the bottom of the hillside opposite in a frozen waterfall of scree. It was as if you could see the erosion happening before your eyes.

I heard a high pitched shriek warning of predators and turned round to look for a bird. A furry mammal, like an overfed squirrel, twitched its whiskers and scampered to a burrow. This was a marmot, which some large birds of prey will attack. I thought back to when I purchased children's toys for a living and felt sure that fluffy marmots, complete with button eyes, would have been bestsellers. The valley narrowed to pass through the Portes du Lognon where huge walls of limestone looked like sea-foam frozen in motion. The path crossed a pink scree slope with a few wisps of vegetation. Erosion had moulded the sandy brown rock ahead into holes, caves and pinnacles. A posse of cowboys would not have looked out of place.

Le Beuil, in contrast, seemed a rather unexciting ski resort. The food in the chalet-style hotel was all show and no substance. The salad was decorated with a cocktail stick covered in tinsel, the trout smothered in basil sauce from a bottle and the pastries buried in cream.

*

I lay on the bed and phoned my mother to check she was OK.

"I know it's silly but I can't remember how to use the microwave. What do I do?"

I gave her some simple instructions, repeating them several times, but alarm bells rang in my head. My mother had been a brilliant cook all her life, turning out sophisticated dinner party food and elaborate buffets without turning a hair. When I was young she baked Victoria sponges oozing with strawberry jam and cream, and lemon meringue pies. I struggled to keep my weight down. She took a course at a well-known London catering school and emerged successfully from the hell's kitchen test at the end. Now she found it difficult to cook for herself. The last time I visited her, I ended up preparing the meal. Having seen my mother-in-law suffer from dementia some years before, I was frightened that my mother would go the same way.

*

Next day an astonishing variety of flowers dotted unrelenting slopes of grey shale: brilliant yellow rock roses, small white daisies and iridescent blue gentians. Eventually I rejoined the Alpine trail winding its way upwards to the Col de Crousette. The mountain slopes had been scoured clean of vegetation. Large white clouds started to boil up a cliff to my left and surge over the ridge ahead. The upper slopes of Mount Mounier were completely submerged in mist. Dropping down over the ridge I faced a difficult traverse across sloping slabs of black rock in very poor visibility. The mountain face to my left dropped away quickly, but I had no idea how far it went. I crept along slowly on the slippery ground and reached the col, only to be assaulted by a gale and torrents of rain. Now the challenge was to keep my feet while descending a steep rocky gully. The boulders were as big as houses, cascading down from Mounier.

The mountain slopes reduced the valley floor to a mere crack for a stream. Under the pall of cloud it looked as if I was entering a tunnel. The river started to plunge towards a gorge and suddenly I found myself on a rocky ledge, where one false step to the left would have been fatal. As I manoeuvred over a gap, with a void between my legs, I could hear the roar of a waterfall below. Opposite was a wall of perhaps five hundred feet, fissured into a thousand tiny blocks. It is hard to concentrate at the end of a long day, but soon I was scrambling over the Torrent de Roya to the hostel called *Ma Vieille École*.

I was exhausted and the modern *gîte*, with hot showers and home-cooked food, seemed like heaven. Matthieu and Melanie were a very engaging couple. Matthieu was a local boy, but Melanie came from Montreal and he joked about differences between French and Québécois, which can cause acute embarrassment—for example, *gosses*, the French slang for kids or brats, refer to a man's testicles in Québécois. A large flock of sheep pushed its way around the back of the hostel, led by a shepherd with a scythe and filling the entire road way. Some fell into the garden to escape the crush and ate the geraniums. The atmosphere and excitement was the same as in the great days of the *transhumance*:

the whistling of the shepherd, the barking of dogs and the ringing of bells.

From the valleys of the Mercantour onwards I also got used to the sound of cow bells. In summer the Alpine pastures provide rich grass for dairy cattle and the local cuisine depends heavily on dairy products. *Tartiflette* is a popular dish of potatoes covered in cheese, so popular that if I ate it once I ate it a dozen times. Even when a meal was well-prepared it was very high in calories and fat. Once I was offered blue St.-Marcellin cheese in filo pastry followed by rabbit and potatoes in a cream and cheese sauce. Tome de Savoie cheese and peach tart concluded the meal. There was nothing green in sight. If you do not like cheese, bacon and cream, then do not visit the Alps.

In the inn at Roure one young couple were determined to bring higher culinary standards to the Alpes Maritimes, and the cuisine was lighter than some of the meals I had been served. The chef told me he did not use much cream and avoided high fat meats like *charcuterie*. He liked to bring out the natural flavours of good local ingredients.

All along the Alpine trail the buildings told me I was not far from Italy: pink and yellow walls in Sospel, and now vibrant terracotta, sea green and peach in St.-Étienne-de-Tinée. One of the Penitents' chapels in St.-Martin-Vésubie is full of grandiose baroque altars in the Italian style, the tower culminating in a Genoese bulb. The west front of the church in Roure looks like a set for an Italian movie, with its classical pilasters and flaking paint. An iconic picture of the Assumption under stucco cherubs dominates the mouldy walls of the nave.

St-Étienne-de-Tinée was enclosed in a deep valley, far from the big wide world. The height of the houses in the old streets meant there was very little light on the pavements, even on a hot day. Forty British cyclists had taken over the ground floor of the hotel, blocking the corridors and even sitting on the receptionist's chair. They were attempting eighteen cols between Geneva and Nice in eight days to raise money for leukaemia research. However, bad weather had forced them to take refuge. *Madame* and her mother seemed completely flustered as they searched a chaotic ledger for a sign of my booking. Would I be sleeping on the floor? Eventually they found a scribbled note in the margin of a dog-eared diary. The name looked a bit like Cudbird.

The room hardly merited the one-star rating of this Gallic Fawlty Towers. I started by moving the bed so I could shut the door to the toilet. In the absence of a shower-curtain water flooded the bathroom floor. Damp green stains covered the walls, the hair dryer was broken and there was no bath plug. A wardrobe concealed the only external window in the bedroom. I placed something on a shelf which promptly collapsed on the floor. A murky light filtered through the grimy net curtain over the glass-panelled door. Only one light worked and I complained to *madame*. "I do not know where the spare bulbs are. You will have to ask my husband!"

The portly owner of the hotel ran hither and thither while his plump wife and daughter sat in the office watching TV. They were as sedentary as an obese black Labrador called Tommy. The sense of disorder was undiminished by the time I went down for dinner, but now groups of motorbikers had replaced the cyclists. Dust covered the furniture in the lounge, cartons blocked the doorways and laundry spilled out of plastic baskets.

THE HIGH ALPS

There was only one place to stay in Bousiéyas, the hostel unnervingly described in the *Topo-Guide* as offering *confort sommaire*, summary comforts. The dormitory consisted of one room with eight narrow bunks on the lower level and eight on top: stone floor, stone walls and a very narrow corridor for everyone to pile their luggage; in short, a small cattle-shed. It had one old-fashioned French loo with two foot rests, a washing-trough and a shower with hot water as long as the kitchen-tap was not in use upstairs. A French acquaintance later ironically described the *gîte* as *folklorique*, which might translate as rustic or authentic but implied dirt. I sat in the sun watching more and more people arrive. In the end thirteen of us slept there that night. Every time I turned over I hit my neighbour in the face. During the night several men relieved themselves in the long grass across the road, rather than face the loo which groaned whenever you flushed it. Someone always comes in late and wakes everyone else up. A man clambered over me in the dark, pushing my belongings onto the floor. In the morning he sat on the end of my bunk, cutting his toe nails and eating breakfast out of his rucksack while refusing to acknowledge my presence.

I met a mountain guide called René and his wife. He described the approach to the Pas de la Cavale from the north, which was on my route. "I was up there at about 9.30 a.m. and found some hollows full of snow running across a 40-degree slope. One was very hard and slippery. I crossed it by fixing a rope between two poles," he warned.

This sounded slightly beyond my technical expertise until I met two Englishmen called John, aged 78, and Brian, a mere spring chicken at 71. John was one of the most robust and phlegmatic men I have met, with the Englishman's gift for understatement. "Don't worry about the snow," he said. "Just look ahead, lean on your poles and keep shuffling across; you'll be fine! Oh and watch the steep scree this side of the *Pas*; quite tricky."

Later René reassured me that the snow would be soft and easy in the afternoon. If I fell, he said comfortingly, I would probably get away with a broken leg. John was incredibly fit for his age. This was his second trip on the Alpine trail, covering twenty miles a day and 4,000 feet of up and down with no problem. In recent years he had walked the Pyrenean trail, again with Brian. How had he found it? "OK, but sleeping was a bit rough in the Ariège; some of those shepherd's *cabanes* you know…"

"What was wrong with them?"

"When you wake up and see rats' eyes looking at you, you feel a bit uncomfortable."

I approached Fouillouse through a Garden of Eden with alpine flowers in full bloom. Clusters of white anemones bathed their roots in the clear water of a mountain stream. The pink flowers of mountain rhododendrons were just starting to emerge, a month later than their lowland cousins. Long grass sheltered sinuous purple geraniums and orange daisies. Tall and delicate larch held their fronds with the poise of a ballerina. Fouillouse stood high on a bare hillside, a single street of gaunt houses including the inn built with solid stone. A notice pinned to the church door stated that the prefect had closed it because of an imminent danger of collapse. The Abbé Pierre, who founded the Emmaus organisation for homeless people and was regularly voted the most popular man in France, was born in Fouillouse and used to return to the church to celebrate mass. His father was an itinerant merchant who sold rough Alpine cloth, but the family left to live in Lyon. In 1875 overpopulation and deforestation led to terrible floods, which persuaded many to leave remote Alpine settlements like Fouillouse. For a period the family joined others from the region who tried their luck in Mexico. Now Fouillouse only has five residents and one elderly couple during the winter.

The village of Roure and its surrounding landscape had already shown me how tough life was before tourists flooded the mountain valleys. The castle rock recalled the violence of the late Middle Ages, when the rapacious Grimaldi family murdered their way to the feudal lordship. It was a remote spot before the road was built in 1933 to replace the mule track I had used. A cable running up from St.-Sauveur-sur-Tinée was used to bring in supplies. The rusting winding gear can still be seen below the *mairie*. The village lost two-thirds of its population of 500 souls in the twentieth century. The communal *lavoir* no longer echoes to the chatter of women doing their washing and the terraces above the village are uncultivated. "Roure is too quiet in the winter," said the hotelier's wife. "I miss my girlfriends. There's no snow, but the weather is cold and sad."

In the past men went to extraordinary lengths to make the mountain slopes suitable for crops to sustain the local community. Just outside St.-Étienne-de-Tinée I found the Canal d'Ublan, one of many irrigation channels built in the late nineteenth century. The canal encased in a concrete conduit runs on one level around the mountain slopes. Peering into a tunnel through the rock I could just make out a pinprick of light at the other end. The exit seemed to be half a mile away. I put on a head torch and waded along the canal bed. The tunnel was no more than six feet high, so I could just stand up. It was lucky I do not suffer from claustrophobia. Desperation to feed a growing population caused hunger for land. This was the only explanation for such an extraordinary piece of engineering.

"Another 3,000 feet up and down," I thought as I set off from Maljasset. The first section of the ascent to the Col de Girardin was extremely steep. The ground looked like ash, grey tinged with pink, and there was not a blade of grass to relieve the monotony of the rock. The Alps are often bald and bleak like this; more scree and fewer trees than the Pyrenees. In the distance was the pointed peak of Monte Viso in Italy; to the left the snow-covered Massif des Écrins; further down I could see a vicious peak and a perfect glacial lake with a steely metallic sheen. Then some friends from Newcastle popped up from behind a rock. "We thought we might find you here," they said. "Some Swedish lads on the col said an older Brit was ahead of us."

They had already come from Fouillouse that day and were clearly fast and sturdy walkers. John Hussey had adventure in his genes. His great uncle Len Hussey went on the famous *Endurance* expedition to the Antarctic with Shackleton. He kept his colleagues cheerful by playing the banjo.

In this frontier region life used to be insecure and it was therefore no surprise to find the remains of old fortifications. Château Queyras, south of Briançon, is perched on a rocky outcrop dominating a narrow gorge. A massacre occurred here in 1692 when English and Savoyard troops tried to take the castle during one of the long wars with Louis XIV. The commander of the fortress drove the besiegers away from the walls by setting fire to the village below. Thirty-four houses were destroyed but the assailants departed. The great military architect Vauban came here in the same year to strengthen the fortifications with a new wall. Arguably he made a greater impact on the French landscape than any other architect before or since. His defensive works to strengthen the new frontiers established by the Sun King stretch right around France. At Briançon Vauban created a whole complex of fortresses, now a living museum of military architecture.

The fortress building did not stop with the Sun King. In an isolated clearing above Sospel I had found the rusting remains of a pre-First World War cannon. The Italians fortified the massif of the Mercantour, where the frontier ran in those days, and the French responded in kind. After 1918 the search for security became even more desperate. North of Larche I looked down on a horseshoe valley denuded of vegetation, a hostile environment littered with old military fortifications. To the right a fort topped a steep wall of rock. The broken wires of telegraph poles flapped eerily in the breeze. On the valley floor below four ruined barracks stood around a square, some still with their roofs on. Several hundred soldiers used to sleep here, but now it is only used by tramps like me. These barracks were part of the Maginot line, built to defend France against Italy and Germany.

LES ÉCRINS

After Briançon I turned west away from the Alps proper. My objective was to join up with the Tour des Écrins trail at Le Monêtier-les-Bains some eleven miles away. Les Écrins form an outlying Alpine massif, black granitic mountains less fragile than their eastern neighbours, but equally demanding to climb. During the evening meal at Le Monêtier I sat next to four French walkers and two Belgians, all around sixty and looking very fit. In their view the only proper walking was traversing mountains with a big pack; everything else was for weaklings. They were all on the Tour des Écrins, one of the toughest walks in the Alps.

The trail threaded its way towards the Col d'Arsine, past a large hanging glacier. The blocks of ice on the upper slopes looked like whipped cream. After crossing an ice-blue lake on a row of boulders and panting up a steep gully, I came face to face with an awesome amphitheatre of granite. Another glacier swept down in a curve from the left. It had deposited a huge moraine of grey rubble which held in the Lac du Glacier d'Arsine. On one of the peaks I could just see the Refuge de l'Aigle, the highest in Europe at over 11,000 feet. Only experienced Alpinists can reach it.

The suspended ice falls of La Meije were to be my constant companions for the next three days. This mountain is a huge hummock of black rock moulded into bumps, troughs and gullies by the ice. One glacier spreads itself across a gentle plateau and then stops in its tracks, as if a King Canute had cried halt. La Meije's massive bulk dominates the village and ski resort of La Grave, a threatening presence which seems to shut out thoughts of anything else. When the sun shone directly over the peak at midday the locals used to say in patois, "*il est meidjou*", *midi* in French, which was corrupted into *meije*.

Above La Grave I found a featureless landscape of unlimited pastures and small streams, with no shelter in sight. Shepherds from the surrounding villages have used this communal land since the Middle Ages, and for hundreds of years legal disputes raged between neighbours over where flocks could graze and drink. One *commune* accused another of moving boundary stones. These hostilities were known as the sheep wars and gave rise to the local saying: "whoever has a flock also has a war on his hands."

The refuge looked straight across an intervening chasm towards Meije. I could almost have reached out and touched it. Céline was a plump lively lady with a mass of frizzy hair. Her husband had risked his life every day guiding strangers up mountains, but met his death prematurely in a car crash. The only paying guest that night, I felt like an intruder at a private event. Various members of the family, young and old, wandered in and out. Preparations for a party were in hand, for the next day they were due to celebrate Céline's parents' golden wedding anniversary. I was shown a space on one of the long bunks in the dormitory over the bar. Family members would be discreetly placed behind a curtain. A separate hut on the open slope towards Meije housed the shower. Hot water cost €2 extra and a chill wind was blowing. The young men and women lolling around outside hooted with laughter as I ran across the Alpine meadow in a dressing gown to wash away the day's sweat. "*Bon courage!*" they cried.

As the evening progressed the temperature dropped inside the refuge. The small stove in the bar was ineffective and I put on all my thermal underwear. It might have been midsummer, but we were at 7,369 feet. At about 10p.m. all the family members ate in the large dining room next door. In between the laughter I could hear the calls of their bilingual squawking parrot.

At 8.45a.m. I sat with a friend of Céline's from Grenoble and watched the sun flooding the plateau. "The glaciers on Meije are definitely receding," he said. "Another resort near La Grave has closed down recently because there's never enough snow."

The tempo of preparations for the big party accelerated. Céline had assembled a team around a large trestle table, tying up sheaves of dyed corn to decorate the house. Balloons bounced around a signpost on the road. I asked myself what had been peculiarly French about this gathering. The family members were attached to their second home. They valued living simply for a weekend in the country. The banter and repartee never stopped. They were constantly fencing with each other, emphasising points with the jab of a cigarette. There was also a good deal of displacement activity; people rushing about in an uncoordinated way. The company vibrated like the taut strings of a violin—*nerveux* would be the French word.

Le Bourg-d'Oisans lies deep in a valley surrounded by sheer cliffs of Jurassic rock. The three thousand-foot climb up the mountain wall was steep and arduous. On the pastures of the col a flock of sheep grazed peacefully. Suddenly a large white Pyrenean sheep dog came bounding up, barking fiercely. He stopped, barked again and then approached even closer, eventually facing me from a few feet away with bared teeth. I stared him straight in the eyes and we both stood still for a few minutes, until he slunk away to sit by a tree ten yards distant. Every few seconds he turned his head to look at me, and then back to keep watch on his flock. I remained standing for a quarter of an hour until the sheep moved on with their guardian following. He was a big beast clearly trained to do a job. I am sure he would have attacked me if I had moved nearer. This was an isolated spot with no help at hand.

It was on the reverse slope that I faced my moment of truth, the only time in 4,000 miles when I had to take my courage in my hands. The path projected left across a rock face to the next hairpin. Beyond some trees the mountain side disappeared over a cliff. I had to edge down an eight-inch ledge under an overhang and then jump around to make the 180-degree turn. Slipping on wet earth under my feet, I moved with extreme care one step at a time and eventually made it to the corner, sweating profusely. My mobile was out of range. I was foolish to be there alone, but luckily I escaped without a mishap. Once at the bottom of the gorge I looked back to see a ribbon of trees snaking between vertical slabs of granite.

Having escaped one danger to life and limb I promptly encountered another. A yapping sausage dog ambushed me on the road and made a determined attempt to bite my ankles. I am a coward where fierce dogs, even sausage dogs, are concerned and I waved my sticks, but sensing victory he renewed his attack with more determination. Eventually he grabbed my trousers. Only a direct hit with one stick stopped him sinking his teeth into my flesh. He continued to bark from a safe distance as I retreated swiftly from his territory, looking every bit the underdog. The hostel that night provided plenty of creature comforts: a roaring log fire, a soft sofa and plenty of books. I chatted to Marie-Odile while she cooked supper. According to her no one ever uses the trail I had taken as it is difficult to find and considered too dangerous.

Next morning I struggled up yet another pass in apparent isolation. Suddenly three dogs rushed round a corner barking, followed by their master and two asses. He wore a peaked cap, baggy trousers and a stud through his left eyebrow. A painted patch surrounded one eye, which made him look like a pirate. The two asses were laden with large plastic bags containing empty tin cans, which seemed an extraordinary cargo high in the mountains. I saw him as a modern holy man, with a mission to save the planet by cleaning the countryside of debris. After a speedy *bonjour* and an assurance that his dogs were not dangerous, he disappeared.

GRENOBLE

The centre of the city sits in a great bowl surrounded by mountains: the walls of the Chartreuse, the wilderness of the Vercors and les Écrins. Blanched limestone cliffs threaten to engulf this outpost of modern civilisation. From the Bastille high above the River Isère I enjoyed a helicopter view of Grenoble. The red and ochre roofs of the old city hug the left bank of the river in a tight semi-circle. Grandiose public buildings and bourgeois houses constructed after 1850 surround this ancient burgh. The commercial middle class regarded the medieval city as dark and unsanitary and wanted light, space and wide avenues. Now Grenoble is a thriving industrial city, one of the poles of the prosperous Rhône-Alpes region. Concrete towers, the pipes of chemical works, the Winter Olympic village from 1968 and the distinctive annulus of the Syncotron nuclear research facility reach up to the mountain walls. On a hot day a heat haze covers everything, a cocktail of urban pollution for which the conurbation is well-known.

Grenoble is a city with a lively cultural life. Old buildings in the narrow winding streets have been restored and crowds throng open-air cafés and markets. The novelist Stendhal was born in Grenoble, but could not wait to leave the city. In his autobiography *La Vie de Henri Brulard* he wrote, "Grenoble is for me like the memory of some abominable indigestion; no danger but a frightful disgust." He found the town provincial and small-minded, unlike today, yet he used to enjoy the social life in the *Table Ronde Café,* which still exists, and also browsing in the only *cabinet littéraire*. There would be even more bookshops for him to rummage in today. On a hot evening I joined the crowds in the Place St.-André and sat looking up at the statue of a local hero posing against the tower of the church. Stendhal did not like the statue, but I found the quirky pose arresting in an alcoholic haze induced by Green Chartreuse liqueur. I ordered another and started musing about this classic novelist whose dissection of the human heart and the great themes of history has always captured my imagination.

It was in Grenoble that I first came face to face with one item of baggage which France has dragged into the twenty-first century: the memory of defeat in 1940, the Occupation and the role of the French Resistance. Coming to terms with these events has been one of the most difficult challenges France has faced in her history. De Gaulle and his followers did everything they could to play up the role of the Resistance and French regular forces in the Liberation of France, and he singled out Grenoble for the honour of being named a Resistance city. Now there is a museum to commemorate the Resistance networks and people maltreated and murdered by the Nazis.

It has taken two generations to recognise all those who suffered in France between 1940 and 1944, many at the hands of the collaborationist French state. Unifying the country behind the story of *la France résistante* made it very difficult to admit to the evil deeds of the war years. The first step came with Marcel Ophuls' film *Le Chagrin et la Pitié*, first shown in France in 1971. I can still remember the shocked silence of the audience in a Left Bank cinema in Paris. Thirty-three years elapsed before President Chirac officially accepted the role of the French state in the Holocaust. Now it has become almost an obsession to commemorate all the Jews, gypsies, homosexuals, communists and deported workers who perished. I first encountered this renewed sense of memory on a remote col in the Languedoc National Park where a monument commemorated those sent to the Auschwitz and Sachsenhausen concentration camps. An urn contained the ashes of some deportees and remnants of electrified barbed wire. Underneath I read the following: "Whoever wants to ignore his past is condemned to relive it."

Recently the National Assembly has passed laws which take a stance on how history should be remembered. Historians must not write about past events in ways which encourage racism, or with lack of respect for human rights, or question the occurrence of known acts of genocide. For example, they should not question the massacres in Armenia before 1914, the Holocaust or the wickedness of slavery. At Grenoble the museum was staging a special exhibition about the Armenian massacres. There are about 500,000 Armenians living in France. Some eminent French historians oppose what they see as the stifling of historical debate and enquiry in the name of political correctness.

One name I had not expected to see among the pantheon of Resistance heroes in Grenoble was that of the Abbé Pierre. On the wall of the Resistance Museum hangs the portrait of a young priest, with an enigmatic smile, short moustache, beard and prominent ears. In July 1942 he was appointed a vicar at the Cathedral of Notre-Dame in Grenoble, where his first act was to hide a number of Jews being pursued by the Vichy police after the round-up of August 1942. He forged papers and arranged the conduct of some escapees to the Swiss border. When the Germans introduced forced labour for young Frenchmen in 1943, he encouraged his compatriots to join the *maquis* and organised a camp in the Chartreuse. In January 1944 the Abbé Pierre was threatened with arrest in Grenoble, so he moved to Paris and subsequently escaped to Spain and from there to Algeria.

THE CHARTREUSE

To reach the Jura I had to cross the Chartreuse, a region of limestone peaks and plateaus north of Grenoble. It is one of the most unusual landscapes I have seen anywhere in France: multiple fissures in the fragile rocks, deep chasms, sheer cliffs and parched fields.

I followed the crest parallel to the Isère far below. The hum of the city reached me even two thousand feet up. A very old notice warned walkers against falling stones and advised another route. Graffiti displayed contempt for the edicts of the French bureaucracy: "I am a big boy and the state is not my mummy" and "In my beautiful country everything is forbidden."

The path was perilously near the edge at times and the view downwards vertiginous. Waves of limestone crests surged out of the pine forests, like naked giants reaching for the sky. Some of them showed their strata, human skeletons stripped to the bone. Gaps in the foliage revealed the streets of Grenoble spread out like an aerial photograph far below.

A path in this limestone wilderness leads through a gap in the mountains to a hidden valley. Here St. Bruno first settled with his monks in 1084 to found the monastery of the Grande Chartreuse, the mother house of an order which once counted two hundred monasteries. Now it is reduced to twenty (plus five nunneries), including one at Parkminster in England. The Carthusians in France lost everything during the Revolution and were expelled from the valley. They returned in 1816 after the Bourbon restoration, but were expelled once more in 1903 as a result of the anti-clerical campaign of the Radical government. They returned again in 1940 as the German armies advanced into France and Vichy France saw a renaissance of Catholicism.

I listened in silence to the wind, the bird song and the sound of running water. The gnarled cliffs were the buttresses of a Gothic cathedral. The Carthusians are the strictest of all orders, their life one of contemplation, a ministry of prayer and study. This austere existence might appeal to me for a few days, but not for a whole lifetime even though I would enjoy their outstanding library and they are allowed to go for country walks (I met two fathers in their brilliant white robes in the sunshine). However, the continual silence would probably drive me away in the end.

The walk from St.-Pierre-de-Chartreuse was one of the toughest I undertook while traversing the Alps. I climbed 4,000 feet and descended 2,400 over difficult ground. The distance of fourteen miles was modest, but at the end of a long day I felt I had covered twenty. The temperature soared, and there was little shade on the desiccated limestone plateau which I reached after lunch. Two litres of water proved to be totally inadequate. I should have been carrying four.

The first frightening section was a traverse above the chasm at Mollard, where a few feet of sloping scrub separated me from a crumbling limestone cliff. At one point the path crept along a ledge. A rope fixed to the inside rock wall steadied my nerves. I was learning never to take these mountains for granted and I knew that at any moment I might find a hidden crevasse. A long open path across rocks followed. Hazardous cliffs closed in from the right. Peaks aptly named the Lances de Malissard towered above as the gradient of the slope increased suddenly. If one stone was dislodged the whole lot could come tumbling down.

Large rocks and stunted fir trees littered the plateau beyond the Col de Bellefont. To my left the hillside swept upwards in a perfect curve, while to my right another cliff overlooked the Isère valley. Any rainfall percolated far down into the porous rock, leaving the grass devoid of moisture. Trees grew on top of the bigger rocks. Walking under them felt like navigating an ocean floor.

The going became more difficult. It was late in the afternoon and I was nothing like as far forward as I had hoped. Would my legs hold out? The path started up a canyon with large boulders barring the way. I tried to get into a rhythm; haul myself up a rock cursing the weight of my rucksack, have a rest and then make another effort. But worse was yet to come. I turned left up a crack in the canyon's side and the gradient became even steeper. As I pulled myself up over each rock step I could only see the sky between my legs. I was pointing on my toes and hoping my calf muscles were up to the task.

It was 5.15 p.m. when I reached the plateau above. I had at least an hour's walk to a col before making a steep descent to the hostel. When I could get a drink of water was the only issue that mattered. I reached the col on time and slumped to the ground to drain the last drop from my flask. I could have drunk a bucket full. The massive south face of Mont Granier kept watch from above. Experienced climbers have tried to climb the northern face and found the rock difficult and unstable. Rubble covered my path which fell away sharply through the trees. My leg muscles were too tired to cope and I hobbled into the hostel just after 7 p.m., having left St.-Pierre before 9 a.m.

I immediately asked for water and downed three large tankards. Jumping into a hot shower was nothing short of ecstatic. A farmer called Didier ran the *gîte* with his son. He was tall for a mountain man and heavily built, with a long face and moustache. His swarthy complexion and dark eyes suggested Italian descent. The food was basic, but I was so hungry I could have eaten anything. After the ritual green salad he served great mounds of pasta with huge slabs of beef, followed by a hunk of local cheese. The red wine soon had an effect and I was half asleep.

At breakfast Didier offered me rye bread, traditional in Savoy because wheat cannot be grown at high altitudes. Father and son chatted to me about the village. "There are only ten houses, mainly occupied by locals; sixteen inhabitants in all," said Didier.

The village seemed a place cut off from the outside world below the semi-circle of cliffs. Didier was a typical *montagnard*, not a great talker and not that interested in what outsiders were doing.

I entered a zone of transition between the Chartreuse and the Jura. The Alps are younger than the Jurassic mountains and here pushed up over the latter, leaving the Jurassic rocks about half a mile below the surface. Looking towards the plain, it seemed as if I could walk straight down into it, but in fact steep cliffs barred the way. Suddenly the path turned a corner and there in front of me was a deep chasm where an invisible river flowed through a narrow crack into the plain. The descent started while still on the edge of the gorge, and from time to time I experienced a frisson of fear. Eventually a Roman bridge appeared, marking the frontier of Savoy. As I strolled along an even road among fields of wheat fearsome cliffs rose above my right shoulder, the last bastions of the Chartreuse.

Near the centre of St.-Christophe-la-Grotte is the entrance to the Voie Sarde, a track up another gorge built by Charles Emmanuel II of Savoy in the seventeenth century. It used to be one of the most important roads linking the Kingdom of France to his duchy. On the borders of Savoy I came across some of the pride which Savoyards feel in being different from other Frenchmen.

Savoy was united with France one hundred and fifty years ago, but the feeling of distinctiveness has not entirely died out. Didier said to me, "We are now on the edge of Savoy. The western boundary of the old duchy runs through the col above. Our local town is Chambéry, which is in Savoy. My son is studying metallurgy at a *collège* there. I am proud to be a Savoyard."

I saw many representations of the *croix savoyarde*, the cross of Savoy, in my bed and breakfast at St.-Christophe and on several village signs. Someone had left a sticker on one signpost with the slogan "Savoie Libre". The mountain biker I met later in the hostel at Culoz found these dreams of independence rather ridiculous. He told me that the Savoyards were notoriously attached to their territory and did not like outsiders, despite the large sums of money they had made from tourism and skiing. Marc, whom we will meet in the Jura, told me about the insular inhabitants of Seyssel in the upper Rhône Valley. The town spreads out on both banks of the river and is therefore partly in Savoy, and partly in the *département* of the Ain. There are two *mairies* and indeed two of almost everything. When the inhabitants in the Savoyard half cross the Rhône they say, "now we are in France", as if Savoy was still not French.

Next morning I tried a short cut back to the main footpath, ripped my trousers on some barbed wire and fell in a cow pat within reach of a snarling Alsatian straining at his chain. Making a hasty exit from the farmyard it seemed prudent to consult the map again. Fortunately it showed a neat red line for the trail towards the Rhône and the Jura. I calculated three days walking to reach the next mountain chain.

7

THE JURA
FORESTS AND FRONTIERS

NOW I WAS IN very different country, the rolling hills beside the Rhône as it pours out of Lake Geneva into France. I had already spoken to Pierre on the phone. When he discovered that I lived in Oxford he warned me that he wanted to talk about the crisis in France's universities. I expected an interesting evening and I was not disappointed. He had the avuncular air of a retired school master and his sympathetic expression immediately put me at my ease. Sitting on the terrace he introduced me to a friend as his *ami d'Oxford*. At first I thought that they were two intellectuals who had opted for the rustic life. They seemed to distrust all politicians, both their own and those abroad. Pierre was evasive about his past. "I came for the view," he said. "I have wandered the globe. I have followed different paths, but I cannot remember how many."

The Swiss pilgrimage route to Santiago de Compostela runs past the hostel. A Swiss couple, the only other guests that night, had taken a whole month off work to walk as far as Le-Puy-en-Velay. Duni was about forty and Denise a few years younger, with huge tattoos on her arms. Pierre accommodated many pilgrims. His hostel was untidy and the building half-finished. The windows in the top storeys lacked glass and the breeze blocks remained unplastered. On my floor light bulbs hung from the ceiling on wires without proper insulation. Maps and notes covered one large room and washing was piled up in another.

Another friend, who had spent 27 years in the French Army, joined us for dinner. The meal which Pierre produced was simple, but highly enjoyable when eaten outside on a hot summer evening. We washed a delicious peach tart down with Muscat de Rivesaltes, a sweet wine from the region of Perpignan. After clearing the dishes he said there were two more things we had to do. "First you must look at my exhibition on the Santiago de Compostela pilgrimage. Secondly we need a few minutes to bring a fitting closure to the day; to reflect on what we have all done."

To my surprise, what looked like a garage on the outside turned out to be a chapel with plain stone walls and three stained-glass windows. One contained a picture of a raven giving food to the Prophet Elijah in the desert with the motto "long is the route which climbs". A cross made out of a vine branch stood behind the altar. Pierre announced somewhat epigrammatically that there were "several

104

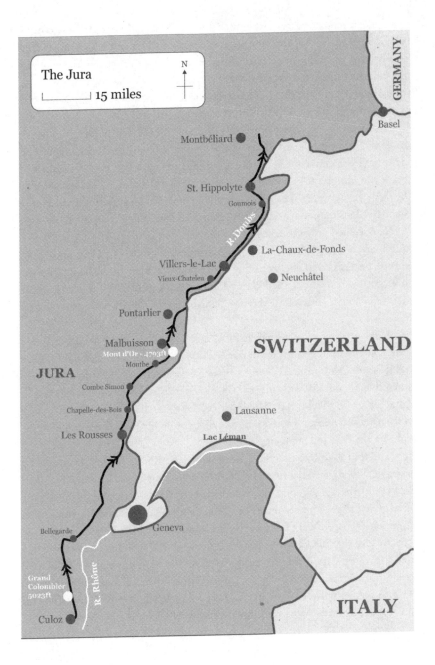

The Jura

15 miles

N

GERMANY

Basel

Montbéliard

St. Hippolyte

Goumois

R. Doubs

La-Chaux-de-Fonds

Villers-le-Lac

Vieux-Chateleu

Neuchâtel

Pontarlier

SWITZERLAND

Malbuisson

Mont d'Or - 4703ft

Mouthe

JURA

Combe Simon

Chapelle-des-Bois

Lausanne

Les Rousses

Lac Léman

Bellegarde

Geneva

Grand
Colombier
5023ft

R. Rhône

Culoz

ITALY

ships", i.e. several ways forward in the Christian faith, although this was not the belief of Benedict XVI, the new pope. He made this remark with some feeling as if he were a disillusioned Catholic or even a lapsed priest. He then told us the story of Elijah who experienced the presence of God neither in the wind, the earthquake nor the fire, but as a still, small voice. Suddenly I was aware of a presence not of this world when I had least expected it.

So we sat on benches giving our reflections on the day, holding candles in the dark. Our ex-soldier asked me why people walked long distances. I replied on the spur of the moment, "It's a way of paying homage to the earth." I explained that it was important to do this if you were a believer, because God has given us the earth. If you were a non-believer, walking provided an opportunity to admire the marvellous natural world we have inherited and to reflect on man's abuse of it. Pierre seemed rather touched by my phrase about homage. He clearly felt that an important part of his life was ministering to pilgrims, but I did not like to intrude on his private life by asking about his past. After breakfast he gave me three postcards of the stained-glass windows in his chapel. On the back of the picture of Elijah he wrote, "May the light breeze of Elijah accompany you on life's road."

Later versions of our English Bible talk about the sound of silence, but I rather like the still, small voice of the Authorised Version, or as a French version has it "a soft light murmur". Some people have a special insight into others even when they do not know them well. I have experienced this with the religious in other places, and Pierre certainly understood my search for faith. The still, small voice has always meant more to me as a description of God's revelation than the light on the road to Damascus.

The trail followed a wooded ridge along the Rhône, which dropped in a series of cliffs right to the river's bank. After labouring up a steep slope I reached a statue of the Virgin and three wooden figures of modern pilgrims marching towards Santiago. Vines covered the valley ahead and a cross bore the inscription from John's gospel, "I am the way, the truth and the life." Medieval pilgrims lived out the idea that the Christian life was a way, and a very tough one without any maps in those days. I met several Swiss plodding up hill, young and old, and could not help wondering why they were putting themselves through so much pain. A golden retriever was carrying his own rucksack. Maybe it contained his dog food. His owner wore the Christian fish symbol around her neck.

UNCONVENTIONAL ENCOUNTERS

The Rhône forms the border between Savoy and pre-Revolutionary France. I had arrived in the rural *département* of the Ain, most of which was annexed in the early sixteenth century. My first impressions of Culoz were not favourable as it looked very much like a town that the world had passed by. I trudged up a forlorn road past a huge factory owned by CIAT, France's leading air-conditioning equipment company and still in the hands of a wealthy local family. The town seemed drained of life, a through-route for cars and trains. The *mairie* made its presence felt, but there were few shops and only one café open. The owner had a sallow complexion and was smoking behind the bar. Cigarette ends and sugar lump wrappers littered the dirty floor. "No," he said, "I told you on the phone. There is no accommodation in Culoz except the hostel at the top of town. You have to look after yourself there. And you had better get to the shops soon or you will have nothing to eat."

I loaded myself up with everything I could conceivably need for the night: food, toilet rolls, cooking oil, matches. I knew that a self-service hostel does not always have essential supplies. Laden like a packhorse with three shopping bags as well as my rucksack, I lumbered up the hill to a housing estate on the edge of the mountain to collect the key. M. Marion had left it in an envelope on his front step. A gaunt two-storey building, which had once been an electricity generating station, housed the hostel. I rattled around making myself comfortable while it rained heavily outside.

It was dark at 9p.m. when I heard a bang on the front door. A man with a well-trimmed beard, short greying hair and glasses pushed his way in with a mountain bike. He lived in Neuilly, a smart suburb of Paris, and was taking a few days holiday biking around the Jura. His appearance suggested he was very sporty. "I took up cycling because of an injury to my right knee. Other sports became too painful," he explained. "You will find this part of the Jura almost deserted. Do watch out for the ticks! There are lots of them." He told me about his life: "My wife is a high-powered banker. At the moment she is doing business in Mexico City. Life in Paris can be stressful. I have thought of moving out, but my wife will not hear of it! She feels there is not enough to do outside the capital, even in Lyon. Paris is still the heart of French business."

We talked into the small hours about different parts of France. "The Ain and the Jura have a reputation for not liking outsiders. They are very attached to the soil; their world is very closed up. The people in some valleys in the Alpes-

Maritimes have similar characteristics."

We discussed whether the French have a strong feeling for the region in which they had been born. He said that some people felt like this and wanted to make their life in their *pays*. He knew Perpignan well. Quite a few people there thought of themselves as Catalan rather than French. Others ended up in Paris, or another city, because they were ambitious and wanted to develop their professional skills. It was a matter of personal preference rather than education or economics.

I mentioned the Savoie Libre stickers I had seen and asked what he thought about this movement. "These children of the 1970s are rather stupid," he said. "I have no time for Free Savoy, Free Corsica or Free Brittany. However life in the provinces is certainly looking up. Take Rennes for example, a city with a fast growing population and a lively cultural life. Before the war Brittany was an agricultural backwater. Now industrial development and opportunities for recreation in beautiful countryside are attracting young people. Toulouse is another example of a regional centre which is thriving."

The path wound upwards in a series of never ending hairpin bends, each one a balcony with a stupendous view. Above the tree line the summit ridge of the Grand-Colombier climbed into the clouds. Either side of the limestone plateau I enjoyed bird's eye views, east to Savoy and west to France. In a soft evening light I found my lodging overlooking the Rhône Valley.

Marc told me that he had only just been appointed manager by the *commune* that owns the building. "A private group have taken over the refuge down the hill to have a party. Techno music! Boom! Boom! Boom! All night! You are welcome to stay here in the hostel. You will be on your own."

I found the only hot water tap upstairs in a kitchen next to the freezing cold dormitory, but no shower. I had to content myself with a strip wash on the tiled floor. It was a long hike downstairs to the toilets next to the bar. The niggardly *commune* was obviously reluctant to pay out for better facilities. Next year Marc hoped to install showers and develop the hostel as a restaurant. He wanted to run his own business.

Marc was another free spirit who had turned his bank on society and decided to seek a new life in the mountains. We embarked on one of those passionate discussions about the future of the world which the French seem to enjoy. Marc was very articulate. Sometimes his ideas were confused and a little naive, but he expressed himself colourfully and with conviction. Marc suspected anyone in authority: the governing class, the state-run TV channels, the police and large companies. They were guilty of manipulation to suit their own ends. This was one of his favourite words and he repeated it often.

The next morning I set off across the plateau with mist still rolling around the Rhône Valley. There had been a storm the night before and the vegetation in the verges smelt rank with moisture. Pinned to a post I found this manifesto for the free spirits who live in the mountains:

A private non-commercial welcome for anyone who wants to accept it
A space for unconventional encounters
A place to experiment with living in a different way based on Love of the Spirit of Truth
Refuge with a dormitory in the hay
Exchange of ideas
Think, Speak and Live differently in the mountains
This farm is self-sufficient in heating, electricity, water and almost in food
At Planvanel a visit is not minted out of what comes from a purse, but with what comes from the heart. It is not free, but comes at the price of your friendship.
Signed Gérard the shepherd of Planvanel
Entrance and Exit Free

The farm house enjoyed a clear view of Bellegarde-sur-Valserine in the valley and the Jura mountains beyond. The tip of Lake Geneva was just visible in the distance. Outside the house I bumped into two French couples coming from the opposite direction and we decided to put this manifesto to the test.

Gérard appeared, but he was not wearing a smock. Tall, serious and ascetic looking with a beard, bare feet and bronzed legs under his shorts, he was reluctant to engage in conversation. I could tell that the French were as puzzled as I was about the basis on which he expected to receive visitors. They asked if they could buy some red wine, but this was not the thing to do and he refused politely. It seemed he did not sell anything and obviously our commercial approach made him clam up. He just received people. We noticed some young men throwing a Frisbee around and a few motorbikes outside. Maybe some people did stay here. He offered us his own cheese and said we were welcome to use his table with the beautiful view. The French knew a number of people pursuing an alternative lifestyle in the mountains. We discussed whether Gérard was an ordinary or an intellectual shepherd and decided on the latter. He looked about the right age for a 1968 drop out.

Gérard was typical of several people I met who had rejected contemporary society to find a simpler way of life. They are part of a movement which started after the Second World War and which gathered pace after 1968, as some revolutionaries left Paris. Communes of what the French call neo-rurals appeared in the most sparsely populated areas of southern France. This was the beginning of a return to the land of France after nearly a century when the rural population fled the countryside.

Shortly after meeting Gérard I found a farm at the beginning of a long open meadow with woods on either side. Several herds of cattle grazed across the path. This was the Plateau de Retord and looking north to the plain was a massive farmhouse belonging to Jean. An engaging character who ran the hostel with his son and daughter, he was much busier than Marc. "I hope Marc makes a go of his business, but it's going to be tough. The pig-headed *commune* has left it with few facilities," he said.

I also suspected that Jean was more commercially aware than Marc, for example charging me €7 for a packed lunch rather than €3. Jean had certainly been around: "I bought the farm twelve years ago, but I have only worked here full-time since 2002. I learnt English working as a waiter in an Indian Restaurant in Tooting Bec. I have also lived in California for a year."

Like a lot of free spirits in the mountains he had been to Nepal and also spent three months in Tibet, climbing over a high pass near Everest. He talked very enthusiastically about the beauty of the Pays de Bugey, the name for this southern tongue of the Jura Mountains. Wedged between the Rhône and the Pays de Gex, the flatter land near Geneva, it is the shape of a triangle. A little south of Culoz the Rhône hooks back to the north, enclosing the mountains, before flowing south again to Lyon.

With eighteen miles and a steep climb ahead I left early. A massive viaduct over the Rhône totally overshadowed the approach to the depressing town of Bellegarde-sur-Valserine. It carried the motorway between Lyon, Geneva, and the Mont Blanc tunnel. Disused factories and a railway line stood underneath the arches. Bellegarde is only three-quarters of an hour's drive from Geneva where many people work, while others also cross the frontier from other parts of the Jura to work in Switzerland. An hotelier further north told me that in his area 15,000 *frontaliers* crossed into Switzerland every day. He added that the Swiss came to France to buy properties, just like the British in the south-west.

A forest track turned left up a precipitous side valley where I was immersed in the beech forest. Under an overcast sky the deep chasm felt claustrophobic with the sound of an invisible ghostly stream somewhere at the bottom. At the top of a meadow above the Valserine stood the Borne au Lion, the site of two important episodes in France's history. In 1944 the Germans attacked the *maquisards* in the south of the Ain. They retreated to the Borne au Lion and 3,000 of them set up camp with a radio link to London. *Borne* means frontier stone and a short distance down the hill I found such a stone with two crests. Much earlier, in the sixteenth and seventeenth centuries, France and Spain were locked in a titanic struggle. The Spanish Emperor at one time controlled the Low Countries, stretches of eastern France, the Franche-Comté, as well as lands in Italy. Savoy owned a small corridor along the Valserine which linked the lands of Spain, Savoy's ally, with Italy. The emperor's troops used to march down this so-called Spanish road, which thus took on great strategic significance. The frontier stone, the Borne au Lion, was one of several erected to mark its boundary. Savoy eventually ceded this strip of land to France in 1760. Mercenaries, brigands and smugglers also used it. Later the Valserine was the border of the Vichy zone during the German occupation from 1940 to 1944.

At Les Rousses lorries and cars rumbled past my hotel room all night and hail clattered on the roof and windows. I tossed and turned on an uncomfortable bunk in a cramped room, the landing light streaming through a glass panel in the bedroom door. At 1.30 a.m. I put an end to this torture by descending the stairs and disconnecting the offending light bulb. Next morning *monsieur*, who was both chef and handyman, looked harassed and complained that customers stole everything. After breakfast I made haste to replace the offending light bulb in its proper place.

*

Just as the waitress was clearing my table the mobile rang again.

"Terence, I've been talking to my physio. He says I can't cope with the stairs and that I ought to move to a flat on the ground floor. So I am going to. I have found somewhere suitable in a block with a warden. It's cheaper than this one. I thought you would be pleased with me."

Changes in my mother's life usually happened like this. If I had suggested such a move, I would probably have been told not to be bossy. Now she wanted to do it immediately because someone else she liked had made the same suggestion. She was too old to organise a move and no doubt realised I would have to come home.

"Well, I'll have to interrupt my walk and come home for a bit."

"I am sorry but I think it's the right thing for me."

I walked over the frontier by the Swiss railway station showing my passport to the policemen standing at the side of the road. "No need to do that. Have a good trip," they shouted cheerily.

My mother was full of excitement at the prospect of another move. She insisted on going to a kitchen and bathroom showroom to order new fittings. "I must have a decent kitchen where I can cook. It will cheer me up. I shall have plenty of money left over."

I did wonder how much cooking she would be doing when she was having difficulty working a microwave. I met the salesman at the showroom, a cheeky young man who knew exactly how to handle older women. This explained the euphoria. "Well OK, perhaps some improvements are needed but you can't spend all your money. You must keep most of it in case you need care."

The result was a frown and a concession that she would make do with the existing carpet.

There was a lot to organise and I could see I would not be going back to France for some time. The next task was to squash a lifetime's possessions into a pint pot. My mother has been an avid collector of china and glass all her life; not antiques, just things she likes. Waterford cut glass acquired during trips to Ireland for American Express; Royal Worcester; Lladro figurines. She had at least four tea services with matching tea knives. Then there were boxes and boxes of mementoes, old programmes, cuttings of King George VI's coronation and soft toys. I grumbled to myself about sorting through all this stuff but I have a similar weakness. My study and attic are just as cluttered—the habit must be in my genes. One of the pleasures of walking is that all this debris is left behind. Everything I need is in the rucksack.

We threw out unwanted furniture and a huge amount of other rubbish. Nonetheless, when the removal van arrived at her new flat, it was obvious there was no room to unpack the boxes. I turned the spare room into a warehouse and stacked the boxes so tight that only those nearest the door were accessible. There they remained for some months. If I had tried to leave the flat in perfect order, I might as well have given up on France altogether.

All this upheaval was a strain for an eighty-five-year-old woman who walked with difficulty and whose memory was failing. There was one last trauma to go through. My mother no longer felt confident driving and so we sold her car. She was tearful. Ever since her divorce it had been her lifeline, her escape. Whenever she was lonely she could drive off somewhere. Now she was trapped in three small rooms, reliant on taxis to get around town. She said she could manage on her own. I booked my flight back to Geneva.

*

SWITZERLAND'S NEIGHBOUR

Soft green beech leaves sparkled with water drops while dark green pines looked down like elderly relations. Cuckoos called from the tree tops. Outcrops of limestone covered the forest floor. Woodland accounts for forty per cent of the *département* of the Jura, and wood is widely used for house building and making furniture. From the top of a cliff near the Swiss frontier I enjoyed a panorama of Alpine meadows and lakes. This is dairy country. The local breed of cows known

as Montbéliard, piebald red-brown and white, stared as if to say "what are you dong here?" The breed is over three hundred years old. I rested for a moment by a typical Franche-Comté farmhouse, with its low walls and high pitched roof. Spacious and cosy, it was large enough to shelter cows as well as humans.

The scattered village of Chapelle-des-Bois contained a dairy for making cheese and a church. The dome on the tower resembled many others in the Franche-Comté and the spike on top would have suited an Imperial German soldier's helmet. The building looked like a local farmhouse. Started in 1633 when the Franche-Comté still belonged to Spain, it was completed after Louis XIV destroyed this last vestige of the Duchy of Burgundy in 1678.

At the hostel at Combe Simon a group of walkers from Boulogne provided an evening's entertainment. I arrived in the bar and only gathered that something was afoot when the manager started to pour 28 *kirs*, a mixture of sparkling wine from the Jura and Crème de Mûre (blackberry liqueur), rather than the more usual Cassis (blackcurrant). Mûre has a softer taste than Cassis and mixes well with the light sparkling white wine of the region. I was reluctant to take a glass, but they all said *allez-y* so I accepted and that broke the ice. The manager then mentioned I was an English walker and questions were soon flying at me from every quarter. A plump red-faced man in a royal blue shirt seemed to be in charge of the group. He let me know pretty soon that he was a Sarko supporter, as were most of his friends, except for one lady who said all politicians were rogues. They told me the French were never happy with the government's policies: "They are always complaining."

We all sat down to dinner together round a large table and, with the effect of wine, volleys of jokes were soon flying back and forth across the room. The red-faced man pushed me into a seat between two ladies. "They are women with secret vices," he said. "You might have some fun!"

Several of the group had stopped work at sixty, but some were teachers who had taken a full pension at fifty-five. What a life! One woman from the other side of the table was desperate to talk English to me, but struggled to make herself understood. My blue-shirted friend told her she was a chatterbox. Turning to his audience he remarked that he had run out of money to make the machine work, pointing to her mouth. At this there were more gales of raucous laughter. At the end I brought the house down by breaking a glass full of white wine on the floor. Don't worry, they said, a broken glass of white means good luck…

Lizzie joined me again at Mouthe, the coldest place in France. Together we climbed the Mont d'Or, which rises gently and then disappears into nowhere. On the summit ridge at 4,793 feet we looked down a six hundred-foot wall of rock a mile long where the limestone had cracked open, like a massive ice flow breaking in the Arctic. There are few signs to warn the unwary of approaching doom. What about Health and Safety? The view reached far into Switzerland only a mile away. To the north the rounded *ballons* of the Vosges Mountains were clearly visible.

Standing on the edge of the drop we met a crew of cameramen and actors. They were making a promotional film about Vieux Comté cheese. Lizzie looked quizzically at the group and one of the young men said to an actor, "You have an admirer!" "No," he said "she is a gourmet." He promptly offered her a slice of cheese and a sip of Vin Jaune in a plastic cup. Vin Jaune tastes like a dry fino from Jerez and is the only wine in Europe outside Spain to develop the sherry yeast called *flor*. It will keep for up to fifty years and complements the tangy two-year-old Vieux Comté very well. The camera continued to film as we made appreciative noises.

Our mountain path skirted the plain of Pontarlier. After a trek through dark

Mont d'Or, 4,793 ft

pine woods we suddenly came to an open field. At the far side was a sign saying "welcome to Switzerland" and stone boundary marker number 162. Waving our passports at the wind and rain we soon reached the hamlet of Les Petits Cernets and a welcoming Swiss inn. There we found our Scottish friends Hugh and Sheina who had already trekked with us in the Cévennes and the Rhône Valley.

On the following day I lost count of the number of times we crossed the frontier in both directions. It also rained hard most of the time. Eventually a building appeared out of the mist, looking like a barn, but without a light on anywhere. What was it? Then a man with a gold earring stuck his head out of a small porch and welcomed us in. The inn at Vieux-Chateleu occupied a massive old Franche-Comté farmhouse built of overlapping wooden panels and a corrugated iron roof. The restaurant was all wood with a roaring fire in the grate. Antique farm instruments cluttered the landing above. Monsieur Geff had the face of a savvy countryman, with blue eyes and an unshaven beard below a head of curly hair. He did not look particularly French and might well have been Swiss. He explained that the house was built in the eighteenth century using wooden rafters. Movement was essential for its survival. "You need to feel the roof give if you bounce on it. My house is like a tree that bends under the weight of snow, but does not break."

The wood creaked at night as if ghosts were moving around.

A plaque on the front door explained that a Resistance network had operated from the building during the Second World War. They smuggled a number of people over the border: agents, British servicemen, Jews. One of the network's members got into Switzerland to warn the British about the development of the V1 rockets, some months before they became operational. No doubt crossing into Switzerland was a lot more difficult than going for a stroll in the woods. The Jura was part of the Reserved or Forbidden Zone during the Occupation and directly controlled by the German Army.

BOUND TO THE SOIL

The owners of the Auberge at Villers-le-Lac were entranced when they learnt that Sheina came from the western isles of Scotland. "If you live near the island of Jura you must come and see our film," they said. In 1978 the Swiss Jura became a canton separate from Berne after a long campaign. At a festival to celebrate local culture the Swiss Jurassians invited not only their French cousins, but also a small group from the Scottish island of Jura. They only found out about the island by accident and could not believe it had the same name, which is in fact pure coincidence. (The name for the Jura Mountains comes from a Celtic root, *jor*, meaning forest. The Isle of Jura, in Gaelic Diura, comes from an Old Norse word for deer. The geological term Jurassic originated from the Jura Mountains in Europe.)

A film showed this small Scottish group setting off for their first visit to Switzerland and ended with one of their number playing his bagpipes with a Jurassian rock band. The participants talked about the importance of preserving the identity of people who are bound to their own soil. This concept, which is readily understood in France, explains why so many French people seem hostile to globalisation. Products and culture are an expression of the land from which they spring and they want to avoid being swallowed up by what they see as a homogenised Anglo-Saxon lifestyle which dominates the world: the same factory-produced food, the same global brands, the same free-market approach to business. It is hard not to sympathise with this point of view. In England, if not in the rest of the United Kingdom, we have lost much of the distinctive character of each region which gives a country its flavour. We may all end up living in a version of Milton Keynes, towns without roots.

I learnt that the Franche-Comté, and the Jura in particular, does have its own identity. It is a long way from Paris and many of its citizens feel closer to Switzerland. Some of them work there and they speak the same language. Physically the Swiss and French Juras are very similar and they have their own distinctive products: cheese, wines based on their own grape varieties, wood and clocks. They also have economic links, not least in the watch industry which operates on both sides of the border. The architecture of churches and farms is quite distinctive. France did not conquer the Franche-Comté until relatively late in the seventeenth century.

Arnaud was a plump fellow, with a yellow tee-shirt hanging over his ample belly. He moaned about the struggle he had to make a go of his business but I suspected a touch of laziness. Arnaud jumped up and down during the film to prepare supper. It was obviously going to be something quick and easy. My heart sank when I saw lots of cheese being weighed into a bowl. Packet cheese fondue did not seem very appetising after a long walk, and I had eaten so much cheese in recent days that I was sick of it. A young couple from Alsace joined our table and it was then that the fireworks started. He was placid enough and talked about how he worked in Switzerland while living in France, and was saving for a Swiss pension. She was Italian in origin and hated all German speakers. They were *moches*, a French word with different shades of meaning but indicating something or someone to be criticised and despised. Above all she did not like cheese and, when booking, had specifically asked not to be given fondue. Arnaud protested that he always gave people fondue, but presented her with some dried-up recycled pork and soggy pasta instead. That was the end. She stormed out followed by her partner. Our patient British party ploughed on politely through cheese and cold meats and managed to insist on a salad before the desert of profiteroles and hot chocolate sauce. No one here, it seemed, was worried about cholesterol. The next morning the young couple said that they had enjoyed a wonderful meal in a restaurant in the town, the young man in raptures about the vegetables which were so conspicuously absent at the Auberge.

Arnaud now embarked on a tirade about the country going to the dogs and how it was always someone else's fault. "I am delighted by Sarkozy's victory but will it change anything? Firms are moving over the border to Switzerland and many people are working over there. The Swiss economy is doing very well. The Swiss seem to protect themselves from the worst ravages of capitalism. For example, they won't allow foreigners to buy their companies. I hate private equity groups, who are using bank debt to buy up French companies and then sack the workers. The Germans make high quality products. All the French companies can do in this region is act as sub-contractors to German concerns. The trouble with France is that taxes are too high. If you want to leave something to your children a lot of it goes in tax, so it is a waste of time. The Swiss are buying up old properties here because we cannot afford to restore them as a result of the high inheritance tax."

"Agriculture in the valleys of the Jura is completely dependent on subsidies," he continued, "particularly with the guaranteed price for milk. Money is being pumped into farming to keep communities afloat, including the infrastructure for tourism. There would be no leisure facilities in the countryside, not even footpaths, without this high level of support. The environment in the villages is very artificial."

Next morning we stood on a belvedere overlooking the Doubs before it flows through a narrow gorge for thirty miles. Fishermen had moored their skiffs on the placid water of Lac Moron ahead of the first dam, one of several used to generate electricity. No doubt they were hoping to catch pike and *sandre*, a delicate freshwater fish much appreciated in France. Despite the gorge's apparent isolation the Swiss industrial town of La Chaux-de-Fonds is not far away. Thick beech woods dripped with moisture, swags of moss festooned rocks and branches and huge fungi clung to trees like giant plates. Large brown snails devoured juicy leaves and black slugs fed on the faeces of wild animals. Little light filtered into these depths from the grey sky above. The water flowed pure and clear over the rocks, while a wagtail bobbed up and down on a stone.

The personality of the river changed as the cliffs parted. Poplars lined small meadows. Banks of gravel appeared on the Swiss side where trout fishermen could venture out into mid-stream. The inn at La Rasse looked like a smuggler's haunt, tucked in the gorge alongside a waterfall. The owner was a German-speaking Swiss from the Bodensee, which explained the simple comforts and calm efficiency of the place. He was something of a buccaneer, having worked in unusual jobs all over the world. We relaxed with three Irishmen on a jaunt together, one taking it in turns to drive the Mercedes while the other two walked. They did most of the talking.

Although the Ladders of Death sounded formidable the reality was much less startling. In the nineteenth century smugglers carried cargoes of flour, sugar, coffee and tobacco up ladders made of tree trunks and without handrails.

Accidents were frequent. Now steel staircases have replaced the wooden horrors of old. The second ladder rises over the rocks at a forty-five degree angle and it was alarming enough bouncing over the void, even if the dramatic name provides an opportunity to brag at home.

The hills folded around the gorge like a stage curtain and our forty-eight hours of isolation were over. Half the village of Goumois lies in France and half in Switzerland. There is one cemetery for the two settlements and one church. French cars streamed back from Switzerland after a public holiday. The Swiss customs post was open but the French was not. As the bars were shut in France we crossed the bridge to Switzerland to find a beer.

The French are probably more in love with their dogs than the English and certainly more fastidious about their appearance. A young woman dragged her clipped lapdog with button eyes along the pavement at St.-Hippolyte. When he saw us he yapped ferociously and she shortened the lead, dangling him in the air like a clockwork toy. "Stop! Stop!" she cried, while continuing to jerk the recalcitrant animal after her. He resisted valiantly and danced in the air like a circus animal. Hugh and Sheina departed for England at St.-Hippolyte and Lizzie a couple of days later, leaving me to cross the industrial basin ahead on my own.

8 ALSACE AND THE VOSGES MOUNTAINS
FACING THE RHINE

ON THE CANAL du Rhône au Rhin east of Montbéliard a wire fence blocked the towpath behind a "road closed" sign. I could see workmen repairing a lock. Now I faced a diversion of at least three miles. There was nothing for it but to beg. "I'm hiking and I've had a tiring day. I face a long detour. It might be nothing for a cyclist, but it's more serious for me. You've closed one of the major long distance paths in Europe without adequate warning."

The foreman looked at my map but said there was nothing he could do. I pleaded one last time. Slowly he retreated to his shed and emerged with an enormous pair of wire cutters. Clunk! Clunk! They cut through the barrier in two minutes. "*Allez-y. Bon courage*," they said, and promptly wired it up again.

I had been lucky. Further along the towpath an official notice threatened anyone who tried to climb through with prosecution.

A valley about twenty miles wide, known as the Belfort Gap, lies between the Vosges and the Jura. The geology of this whole area is very varied as the calcareous Jurassic rocks change to schist and alluvial soil in the middle of the Gap. The Vosges, however, are basically granitic. Together with the Black Forest they took shape in a great upheaval in the Tertiary era. Later the centre of this upland area collapsed to create the valley of the Rhine.

The Belfort Gap was strategically important in the aftermath of Prussia's victory over France in 1870. The peace treaty ceded Alsace and Lorraine to Germany, but a sliver of territory around Belfort was detached from the *département* of the Haut-Rhin and remained French. The area in question was predominantly French-speaking. Moreover, the fort at Belfort had put up a heroic resistance during the struggle. This Territoire de Belfort became a separate *département*, which it remains to this day.

The French built several forts to prevent a future German invasion through the Gap. I arrived at one after a steep climb through woods north-west of Belfort. Small railways were constructed up the hill to feed the Fort du Salbert and its guns with the necessary supplies. Today the tracks have gone and the railways have become a network of paths. I found a group of stone bunkers next to the trail. Further on a section ran on an embankment above the forest floor. From the south side of the summit there is a magnificent view of Belfort in the middle of the Gap, and it is clear that the big guns would have been able to destroy an approaching army. The remains on top of Mont Salbert show that the fort

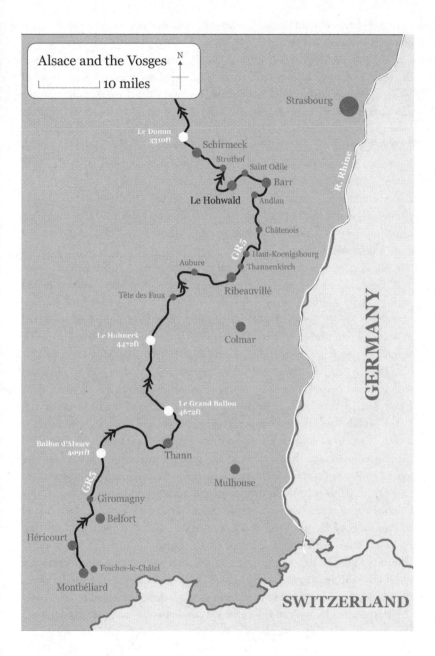

Alsace and the Vosges
10 miles
N

Strasbourg

Le Donon
3310ft
Schirmeck
Struthof
Saint Odile
Barr
Le Hohwald
Andlau

Châtenois
GR5
Haut-Koenigsbourg
Aubure
Thannenkirch
Tête des Faux
Ribeauvillé

Le Hohneck
4472ft
Colmar

Le Grand Ballon
4672ft

Ballon d'Alsace
4091ft
Thann

Mulhouse

GR5
Giromagny
Belfort

Héricourt

Fesches-le-Châtel
Montbéliard

R. Rhine

GERMANY

SWITZERLAND

must have been massive. A bridge crosses a large ditch in front of iron doors and concrete walls marked Fort Lefebvre 1874-1877.

The Pays de Montbéliard also has an unusual history. When France annexed the Franche-Comté Montbéliard remained independent, ruled by the Duke of Württemberg as part of the Holy Roman Empire. During the Reformation the duke decided to become a Lutheran, and as a result his territory was mainly loyal to the Protestant faith. During the French Revolution the French party in Montbéliard got the upper hand and the territory became part of the First French Republic. Apart from Savoy and Nice it is the youngest part of France, still retaining its distinctive heritage. In a wood north of the city I found boundary stones marking the limits of three *départements*: the Doubs to the south, the Haute-Saône and the Territoire de Belfort. They also mark the older boundary of the territory of Montbéliard, and on one of them I could just make out the ducal shield and the date 1764.

The duke's castle still stands in the old town centre of Montbéliard. Some buildings look more southern German than French, with heavy wooden beams on the façades and high gables, while the Lutheran church is severe and classical like others in the region. The Protestant church at Fesches-Le-Châtel glowed in rose red sandstone. It was built in 1869 to accommodate the increasing manufacturing population of the area, no doubt all hard-working Lutherans.

The Pays de Montbéliard also had its own folklore. Deep in an old hazel wood I came across a small limestone cliff and the grotto of La Tante Airie (Aunt Airie). A teacher accompanying some children told me the local legend. In the Middle Ages, around Christmas time, everyone in the villages awaited the arrival of an old woman on her donkey. Something of a sorceress, she inspected the houses to see that they were clean and gave presents to youngsters who had left a carrot and an apple for the donkey at the front door. She also punished naughty children by making them wear a donkey's bonnet but gave deserving families a gold coin. People came to her for advice on how to find a husband or keep in good health. One school of thought has it that the legend of Aunt Airie was based on Henriette, a fourteenth-century Countess of Montbéliard who defended the rights of people and was much loved as a result (Airie is a diminutive of Henriette). Others believe that her origins go back to the era of the Gauls. Her story is still re-enacted in the Pays de Montbéliard to this day.

Beyond St.-Hippolyte I approached an industrial zone stretching from the dormitory villages south of Montbéliard, through the city itself and on to small towns like Héricourt and the conurbation of Belfort. The latter developed very quickly after 1871, in part because former French industrialists from Mulhouse, then in Germany, invested heavily in the area. The famous French engineering company Alsthom, which makes the TGV engines, started in this way. Montbéliard is also the home of Peugeot, which is still French-owned and operates a large plant here, close to the factories of its numerous suppliers. Yet life in this industrial town sounded difficult. I was warned about gangs of unemployed youths mugging passers-by. I stopped for the night in one of Montbéliard's suburbs, and my host told me about the impact of today's economic climate on his life.

"I used to own my own building business," he said in a quiet voice, "but under the Socialists the market got more difficult and my bank refused credit. Now I'm on the production line at one of Peugeot's suppliers. I've worked shifts, including nights, for eighteen years. Tonight I only got home at nine o'clock. The work is soulless and the bosses tough. I'll have to work on the Ascension Day public holiday without extra pay. They give us very little notice of these demands. The new boss at Peugeot insists on ever lower prices from suppliers. My company doesn't value my contribution. I hope my son will do better in the computer industry."

Rapid industrial change has created a precarious existence for many workers in France, and *précaire* is the adjective commonly used to describe this aspect of modern life. The area is highly dependent on Peugeot, with alternative employment limited if the company cuts back. After Montbéliard I walked through Héricourt, which showed signs of industrial decay. Near the station a lone factory chimney stood in the middle of flattened rubble, probably one of the last textile plants to be cleared for redevelopment. Héricourt, like many towns in the plain near Mulhouse, used to be a major centre of the French textile industry before production moved offshore to Asia. The hotel by a dirty canal was not inspiring, but the waitress brightened up when she told me about her dream to visit her friend in Tahiti. She only needed to win the lottery to afford the air fare.

Giromagny at the foot of the Vosges also looked as if it had seen better days. On arrival I started to look for a restaurant for the evening because the hostel did not provide food. A search of the three main roads into town proved fruitless. The only choice seemed to be doner kebab and chips, not an appetising prospect. I wandered into a bar to see people smoking and staring silently into space. Two barmaids with lank greasy hair seemed crushed by the cares of life. The bar at least provided three forms of solace for those who have little hope: alcohol, tobacco and gambling.

Giromagny used to be a textile town, but now there are just a few suppliers to the big firms near Belfort and Montbéliard. I went to collect the keys for the hostel from the guardian of the campsite, who told me: "The cost of a night's accommodation is €8.50 to be paid in advance with the exact money."

I offered him a €10 note and told him to keep the change.

"I can't accept this," he said. "I would have to divide the note with the *mairie* and I can't do that. You must find the right change somewhere and come back by 5p.m."

I went off to buy some food and to bring the right money. Once I had paid up the guardian grunted that I would find the hostel in an industrial estate to the left. That was all the help I got. A series of shed-like barrack blocks stretched up one side of the road, housing various small businesses. My abode for the evening looked like one of the sheds, but was comfortable inside once the gas heating was working. Despite the sound of motorbikes at night, I got some sleep.

It is not surprising if some people find it difficult to thrive in an uncertain economic environment. Nadine, my hostess in Montbéliard, was also an artist. Slim, pale and slightly vulnerable, she moved her hands nervously as she talked. Although she had limited means, like many artists she cared passionately about her physical environment. She had chosen every item in the house carefully to bring out the characteristics of the property built around 1900: the stripped woodwork, the old oak cupboards and tables, the conservatory, the artist's studio. The next morning every detail of her breakfast table was coloured blue. She talked at some length about her artistic vocation and about a Czech who taught her for nothing. I sensed that this vocation was very important to her, even if she had difficulty selling her paintings. She taught calligraphy part-time in a local school and enjoyed encouraging children. "One of my colleagues ripped up a child's work in front of him and told him it was rubbish," she said. "That upset me a lot."

Nadine went on to talk about stress. "So many people feel stressed, whether it's managers working long hours or Algerians being made to feel like outsiders."

ALSACE

At times Alsace hardly seems French at all. Looking down the eastern slopes of the Vosges towards the Rhine, I often felt as if I was in Germany. Recent history has left deeper marks in Alsace than anywhere else in France.

Several hundred thousand people speak Alsatian today, a dialect of German. I heard it spoken several times during my visit, the first time in a café twelve miles north of Colmar. Characteristically, grandfather spoke Alsatian, his granddaughter French and his son both languages. Quite a few people speak German with the many visitors who come across the Rhine. In one inn my companions at dinner were a young German couple from Heilbronn in Baden-Württemberg. I noticed that the young woman serving us spoke to them in German. "I can understand her perfectly," said the husband. "The Alsatian and southern German accents are similar. Few young people in Alsace speak German. The Alsatian language will die out eventually."

In the Vosges the weary walker can find hospitality in a number of inns run on farms, where the atmosphere often feels Bavarian or Austrian. It is not just the wooden beams and satisfying rustic cuisine which give this impression. The hearty hospitality is in itself different from the more reserved welcome in French boulevard cafés. Climbing the Hohneck I was delighted to find one of these inns, where a raucous party of Alsatians had taken up residence. Two older men played guitars with colourful tassels hanging from the top of the fingerboards. Why weren't they wearing *Lederhosen*, I wondered? But they did sing a verse of a drinking song and everyone chimed in with a chorus of "da-da-da!" The steamy, hugger-mugger atmosphere reminded me of a bar after a day's skiing. We ate a tasty meat pie with salad, followed by a stew and more salad. The *fromage blanc* with kirsch and crystallised sugar built up my energy, but two glasses of red wine probably had the opposite effect. What did I care? It was warm inside and pouring with rain on the mountain.

Alsatian cuisine is similar to German. I remember filling dishes which kept out the cold, like boiled beef stew, boiled ham, quiche made of cabbage, cream and cheese, *tarte aux myrtilles*, local quetsch fruit, like a plum, with *fromage frais* on a sponge base. Unlike the rest of France, Alsatians have always marketed their white wines by grape variety—the scented Gewürztraminer, Riesling, and Pinot Gris. They also make their own spirits from local fruits such as quetsch and mirabelles, which are quite similar to the schnapps found in Germany and Austria.

The domestic buildings look Germanic too. Ribeauvillé among its vineyards is a picture postcard example. It boasts a ruined castle on a hill, two old squares, a market cross, a tower with a gateway below and two churches. Elaborate carvings decorate the wooden beams of the old houses. Window boxes of geraniums hang next to balconies and dormer windows, while wooden signs festoon the shop fronts. Chocolate brown is the dominant colour, along with pink and ochre. The pointed roofs huddle together for comfort within the town walls. At Châtenois brightly coloured tiles blaze down from a many-pointed steeple, while the gables in Andlau twist upwards in opulent scrolls.

The castles dotted along the crests of the Vosges would not look out of

Ribeauvillé

place on the Rhine. The round-arched windows of the magnificent Knight's Hall of St.-Ulrich, suitable for use as scenery for a Wagner opera, look down on Ribeauvillé and the plain of Alsace. Haut-Koenigsbourg is the most visited monument in the region, its heavily restored castle a magnificent recreation of the medieval past, even if somewhat controversial in execution as Ebhardt, the architect, copied features from other castles in Germany. The church architecture also has a distinctive style. The first town I stopped in was Thann, where the roof of the collegiate church brightened up a dark rain-soaked evening with its brightly coloured tiles. It is an outstanding example of the south German late

Gothic style, but the rich colour of the local sandstone is characteristic of Alsace.

Catholic belief has always been stronger in Alsace than in any other part of France, except perhaps Brittany. Along the path I saw numerous shrines, often dedicated to the Sacred Heart. At Thannenkirch a particularly charming Virgin had been carved in a niche in a tree. A stag and a rabbit join in adoration of the Christ child. Such roadside shrines are often placed near springs said to cure diseases. Unlike in the rest of France, religious instruction and religious symbols are not banned in state schools and priests are still paid by the state. There is also a Protestant presence, Calvinistic as well as Lutheran.

The monastery and tomb of Ste. Odile stand at the very tip of a rocky promontory overlooking the Rhine Valley near Strasbourg. If there is one place which is the spiritual heart of Alsace, this is it. Throughout the upheavals the province has experienced, the monastery has become a symbol of continuity. The legend of Ste. Odile is a touching story. Etichon, Duke of Alsace, was by all accounts a bully. He looked forward to his first child and wanted a boy, so when his wife gave birth to a blind girl he flew into a rage and ordered the weakling to be killed. His wife sent the baby secretly to a convent, where miraculously she recovered her sight during baptism. Etichon's next tactic was to try and marry her off to a young prince, but she told her father she had other plans. She wanted to be a nun and fled to the Black Forest Mountains. Etichon lost his temper again and rushed after her. It was time for another miracle, and a rock duly opened up to give her refuge. Despite everything Odile was a good girl and prayed for her father to be released from purgatory. She died in 720, a byword for piety, charity and miracles. The number of pilgrimages to her tomb soared, people with eye illnesses praying to her for a cure. She still has feast days on 7 July and 13 December.

A long time ago Alsace was part of the German Holy Roman Empire; the one that Voltaire famously said was neither holy, Roman nor an empire. After endless fighting the French grabbed Alsace in 1648, but the Alsatians did not automatically become Frenchmen, remaining just German subjects of the King of France. Later, the leaders of the French Revolution dreamed up the idea that the Rhine was a natural frontier and they tried to persuade Alsatians to think of themselves as French citizens. Imperial Germany recovered Alsace and part of the neighbouring province of Lorraine (the modern French *départements* of Haut-Rhin, Bas-Rhin and Moselle) after defeating France in 1870. I saw the old frontier on a plateau south of the Ballon d'Alsace above Giromagny; granite blocks with the D for Deutschland still clearly visible. A French walker stopped by one of them and pointed to a D gouged out after the First World War. "Despite their efforts, you can still see it," he said.

The mark left by Imperial Germany is still quite obvious, even in the most surprising places. Le Hohwald had the air of a mountain resort from another age, when Europe's leisured classes sought fresh air away from the unhealthy cities. In the pine trees I found a memorial to Fürst Chlodwig von Hohenlohe-Schillingsfürst—a mouthful even for a German aristocrat. The stone did not look very imposing but Chlodwig was in fact a political big shot in his day; German Ambassador in Paris and then Governor of the new German province of Alsace-Lorraine. In 1894 he was called to the top job of Chancellor of Germany. No doubt he used to stroll here, wondering how to keep the Alsatians in order.

The most obvious physical evidence of Kaiser Wilhelm II's rule is the castle of Haut-Koenigsbourg. He took a personal interest in its expensive restoration and his motives were mainly political, wanting to demonstrate German power with a prestige project on the Reich's new western border. In the Kaisersaal a massive eagle has been painted on the ceiling, its wings pointing to the crown of the Hohenzollerns over the chimney. What a pompous man he was, and sentimental. There is a small picture of his dog and an inscription reflecting his supposed distress at the death of a young German soldier in 1918.

Between 1871 and 1918 inscriptions on all public monuments, like the church at Andlau, had to be in German because French was banned. In 1871 inhabitants were given the choice of becoming German citizens or departing for France. On the northern edge of the Ballon d'Alsace, within sight of the old German frontier, I found a statue of Joan of Arc. This was erected before 1914 as an act of defiance. Many French nationalists could not accept that soil, which they regarded as an inalienable part of France, was now German. One such was Maurice Barrès, whose name caught my eye on a plaque in the monastery of Ste.-Odile. Barrès, a writer and politician, visited the site in the autumn of 1903 while working on his novel *Au service de l'Allemagne* (*In the Service of Germany*), which deals with the defeat of 1871 and the desire for revenge. Barrès was very attached to the land of France and the cult of its fallen heroes through the ages. The plaque records his impressions in ornate language which seems dated now: "Sainte Odile is a spot where I feel at home; where I can tread unwearied the paths of my sacred mountain and sing an exultant psalm."

Some of those who stayed on in Alsace tried to keep the flame of French culture alive. Yet it is a mistake to assume that German rule was universally unpopular. The German government introduced social insurance for workers long before the French or the British and, as a result, some social benefits are still more generous in Alsace-Lorraine than in the rest of France. Some fellow guests in a hostel said that these included more time off to look after sick children and better health care.

Alsace was the not the most active sector of the Western Front in the First World War, but the conflict left scars here as elsewhere in northern France. In August 1914 the French Army in the south could see the Rhine Valley below and rushed downhill to claim their prize. They were soon pushed back, but not all the way to the frontier, leaving a bulge in the French line which ran through the Grand Ballon. As I struggled up its southern flank, a sudden gap in the cloud revealed a tantalising view of the great river. I understood why the French were so determined to reach the plain and the Germans to stop them. Further north I came to the Tête des Faux, the scene of some of the fiercest fighting in this sector. Today 418 French soldiers lie buried in a dark glade in a pine forest. The German and French positions lie very close together on steep rocky slopes, and heaps of broken masonry and metal rails clutter the summit. A tall cross erected after the war stands on a base made of rails. Several German dug-outs lie along the path with twisted metal stakes used to support barbed wire defences.

Alsace-Lorraine was transferred back to France after the Treaty of Versailles before Hitler re-incorporated it into Germany in 1940. This had a serious impact on the whole population, not least on young men who were conscripted into the Wehrmacht. In Héricourt I met an old man of eighty-seven as I talked to the hotel owner about the war. Now he passed his time smoking his pipe and fishing, but traumatic experiences had scarred his life when the Germans had forced him to fight on the Russian front. In 1945 Alsace-Lorraine returned to France.

The Nazi concentration camp at Natzweiler-Struthof was right on my path. I did not know what to expect, never having visited the site of a camp before. This one stood in beautiful mountain scenery. Of course, the camp was well concealed from prying eyes and it was on German soil. In the giant granite quarry working conditions were barbaric, and many prisoners suffered appalling maltreatment and a cruel death. Beyond it the trail passed through another dark pine forest. I thought of lines of prisoners being marched uphill to work, some never to return.

The camp buildings were located on a series of terraces in a clearing, so wherever a prisoner stood he would have had a view of the mountains. Would they have given hope or been a cruel reminder of lost freedom? The camp has been tastefully preserved as a memorial to those who died. Visitors are asked to walk around in silence as a mark of respect. I tried to remain detached but then some small detail dragged me back to the horror: the hangman's noose silhouetted against the sky, the drain down which blood flowed, the table on which prisoners were beaten.

The camp is surrounded by a double barbed-wire fence, which would have been electrified. Some of the watch towers are still there. Most of the huts have been removed, but at the bottom of the hill two still remain. One was the crematorium, where victims were shot in a small room and their bodies recorded and incinerated. Another room was used for medical experiments, and yet another contains a slab used for autopsies. Next door is the solitary confinement block. Some of the cells were so small prisoners could only crouch.

The small camp museum recalls the facts of daily life: the roll calls for hours standing in the freezing snow, the beatings and hunger. The SS documented everything meticulously; the prisoners included Jews, Resistance workers, gypsies, homosexuals and political prisoners. Some members of the Special Operations Executive were killed here, including Vera Leigh and Diana Rowden. The SS killed many resisters just a few days before the Liberation as the Allies closed in. Some were given lethal injections and suffered atrociously.

Perhaps the most disturbing feature of the camp is the suburban villa, where the camp Commandant Kramer lived with his wife and children. It is locked now, but I imagined family life around the swimming pool only a few hundred yards from the camp gates. The Allies eventually captured Kramer and sentenced him to death. He personally supervised the execution of 86 Jews in the gas chamber. This was installed in an ordinary looking dance hall, which still stands by the path further down the hill.

A WALK IN THE VOSGES

From Giromagny I set off to climb the Ballon d'Alsace (4,091 feet). In Alsace all the great peaks are called Ballons, which means balloons in French. I thought this word was used because the tops are rounded, no doubt the result of past erosion. They are also naked; no trees, just hummocks of coarse grass and rocks. Walking across the Ballons I felt I was taking a sort of balloon trip, floating over the Rhine Valley where the mountains rise abruptly out of the plain. Then I checked in my large French dictionary. Although balloon in French only has one "o", *Ballon* in Alsace derives from Belchen in German—there is a mountain called Belchen in the Black Forest which also has a bare dome-like top. I should have known.

The ascent of the Grand Ballon was more strenuous. From Thann I had to climb 2,600 feet, and then descend before struggling up a further 2,000 feet to the summit. Below the top two lines of beech trees ran straight down the mountain and dead centre between them was Mulhouse, its office blocks sprawling across the plain. From the crest of the Vosges you can often see the valley of the Rhine spread out like a carpet, with the Black Forest in the background. I was the only guest in the Chalet Hôtel des Vosges. Owned by the Club Vosgien Strasbourg, it is delightfully old fashioned like a traditional London club, with dark wood panelling and a library full of battered armchairs.

My day on the Hohneck (4,472 feet) was one of the wettest I have spent walking in my life. As I approached the summit the cloud came down and the wind reached gale force, threatening to knock me over. I staggered on into the teeth of the tempest and reached the Refuge de Tinfronce at the Col du Calvaire after four hours hard effort. I wondered how long my waterproofs would keep out the blasting rain and soon felt pretty damp underneath. I hoisted my umbrella into the wind, like Don Quixote jousting with windmills, but it buckled under the impact. My hood was plastered against my face and eyes. Shit! Where is the way among these rocks? I stumbled around a peat bog, hopping from rock to rock like a drunken ballet dancer.

At the refuge there was a fire to dry my things, a filling meal, plenty to drink and cheerful company. I wallowed in the luxury of it all. After several beers a carafe of Alsace white slipped down easily, followed by Mirabelle schnapps. The heat of the fire and the alcohol soon worked their magic on my aching limbs. I lurched upstairs to my bunk, slipping on the rungs of a wooden ladder.

Ten hours later sun poured in through the window, waking me up with a start. I forced myself out of bed, head throbbing, but could not focus on what to do next. I thought of going back to bed, but that was not allowed, and even the kind girls downstairs would want to kick me out after 9 a.m. Packing a rucksack is normally fine if your mind is clear, but strangely difficult if recovering from a hangover. Normally I have a system. I lay a number of waterproof bags in different colours on the bunk and assign my possessions to the correct one; blue for shirts and trousers, black for underwear and so on. My rucksack has seven compartments of varying sizes and a plan dictates which bag fits into which compartment. I line the main one with a plastic rubbish sack to keep out the rain. Then I have to master ten different straps and buckles, two draw strings and two zips, to secure everything. In a befuddled state, I thumped the sack in frustration as I got everything muddled up. I had to repack the main compartment twice, once because I got the wrong items at the bottom and once because I left something out. I tore the bin liner, before accidentally pulling a toggle off one of the drawstrings and damaging a buckle.

You might think packing the sack is the end of preparations before departure. Not quite. First of all I have to adjust the walking poles to the correct height. Why do the spring mechanisms never lock shut when you want them to? Then the boots have to be laced up correctly and the socks straightened to prevent rubbing and more blisters. The map needs inserting in the map holder—right way up. Then I clip my camera to my belt, so I don't have to take my sack off to get at it. The list is endless.

Eventually I stood in the middle of the room with an uneasy feeling that

I had forgotten something. Then I remembered that I meant to ask the girls downstairs to make me a sandwich. Thankfully they were very obliging and rustled up something delicious in next to no time. I stood in the entrance and heaved the sack onto my aching shoulders. It weighed thirty pounds but felt like a ton. I'll never drag this thing any distance, I thought. Fortunately the track through the forest was dead easy, and I felt pleasantly cool walking in shirt sleeves after two days encased in a rubberised jacket and leggings, which made me perspire profusely. After the storm it was unbelievable.

Nearing Aubure I heard the tap-tap of the poles of a faster walker behind me. It was as much as I could do to amble. The village was a homely spot with several simple guest houses. A Belgian ex-banker called Jean-Pierre had run the hostel for twenty-five years. "I'm retired now. I find living in Aubure on my own resources much less stressful. Some people can't stand the quiet."

I asked Jean-Pierre why his hostel was such a big building and why there seemed to be so many hotels and large houses in Aubure. "When I arrived here it was still an active health resort. People came to take a cure in a sanatorium. This building was a hotel with several long-term guests. That tower in the corner of my vegetable garden conceals the hotel's ice house. There are huge cellars underneath the lawn."

Towards the end of our meal a large party of long-haired German motorbikers drifted in. Bottles of Jack Daniels and Johnny Walker appeared, followed by loaves of bread, pieces of chocolate and sausages. There was a lot of nibbling and then they took over the kitchen. Jean-Pierre gave up and let them get on with their meal. He said they came to drive their bikes faster than allowed at home.

The walk along the wooded ridge above Ribeauvillé is known as the path of the three châteaux. St.-Ulrich is perched on a rocky outcrop next to Girsberg, which is much smaller. Haut-Ribeaupierre makes up the trio, poking out of a sea of trees, a tower right on the edge of the void. Haut-Koenigsbourg made the fourth castle in my collection. Beyond Châtenois I was able to visit three fortresses next to each other: Ramstein, Ortenbourg and Bernstein. My score in castles rose to seven. Next day I found Landsberg, castle number eight.

The trail now ran west into France. The landscape looked much wilder; a vast ocean of conifers frozen in time. Schirmeck is a small industrial town spread over several valleys. There is not a great deal of work here and many people commute to Strasbourg. I finally arrived in the square by the church at 7p.m. in desperate need of food and drink after ten hours on the road. The

Restaurant de la Bruche was very much the local workers' bar. A group of men were puffing away at their cigarettes and drinking heavily among much noise and laughter. They asked me what I was doing in Schirmeck. When I explained I had been walking all day, and still had to get to Wackenbach two miles away, they cheerfully said I was mad. In the dark I headed up a wide road across the railway tracks. The headlights of oncoming cars blinded me and it started to rain steadily. It was difficult to see where I was going and I might have blundered into a nearby stream by accident. It was 10p.m. before I reached Wackenbach. Pierre looked at me very seriously. "I am sorry but I am full. You are late and I cannot put you up."

I looked at him open-mouthed, the very picture of dejection. "You cannot be serious," I said. "What am I going to do?"

I stood in the rain for what seemed an eternity with Pierre staring at me intently. Then he laughed out loud and slapped me on the back. It was only then that I realised that Pierre was very fond of jokes. I was dying to flop into bed but he insisted on talking. In the space of a few minutes we covered Sarko, George Bush, Tony Blair and Iraq. It turned out that Pierre had been brought up in French Tunisia before coming to France. He was also desperate to tell me more jokes, mainly rather unsubtle puns.

"This hotel is the Lion d'Or, *lit en dehors*, bed outside, Ho! Ho! Ho!"

I struggled to sleep because of some agricultural snoring from the bedroom next door and was convinced that a large beast was about to burst into the corridor. The next morning the beast revealed himself as a huge Frenchman with a pot belly and a beard. Taciturn and scowling he grunted in my direction, unaware I had taken some of his breakfast. I set off up the valley in a drizzle. After 1,300 feet of climbing it was time for elevenses. A hotel at the Plateforme du Donon offered coffee and apple strudel that was too much to resist.

*

The mobile phone jingle went off in my pocket. I wondered whether it would be another unwanted salesman. There was a voice the other end which I did not recognise.

"I am a District Nurse speaking from your mother's flat in Stratford-upon-Avon. She is suffering from a urinary tract infection which has caused temporary dementia. She was found on the floor last night after a friend called the police. She did not know where she was. We have organised some carers to come and live in her flat until she is better."

I felt as if I had been thrown into a waterfall and was struggling to reach the surface. I stood silently for a second looking at the mountain of Le Donon ahead. Lizzie raised her eyebrows.

"Is it your mother?"

The District Nurse's voice cut across our silent exchange. "Are you there Mr. Cudbird?"

"Yes."

"We can cope for a few days but there is one problem. There is no money in the flat and your mother needs a few things."

I could feel the ties of responsibility drawing tighter. I was the only child and there was no one else sufficiently close to her. I wanted to help, but some other time; not today.

"Can I speak to my mother please?"

"Yes, of course, but she may be rather confused."

I heard the plaintive tones of my mother's voice. Like me she had acted in many plays. She knew the effect her words would have. "I'm all right, Terence. When are you coming home?"

I knew I would have no peace if I did not leave for England now.

"I'm coming home straight away. I hope to be with you tomorrow."

I ended the call. Lizzie's eyebrows climbed a bit higher.

"I'm sorry. You've only had a few days in Alsace but if I don't go today, I'm only putting it off. I won't be able to walk all the way to Nancy, let alone the Channel."

"I know," she said wearily. "You have to go, but she has stopped you living your own life so many times. Now she can't help it. She should be in a care home."

One of the advantages of walking is that in an emergency you can move very quickly in any direction. In a quarter of an hour a taxi arrived and an hour after that we were at Strasbourg station. The TGV whisked us to Paris in just over two hours where we jumped on the Eurostar to London. As we whistled over the plains of Lorraine I hoped I would be back before long.

The live-in carers became a permanent feature of my mother's life for a few weeks. She resented their interference and complained constantly, sometimes with justification. When she felt better we dispensed with their services and relied on regular cleaners. I stocked up her fridge with food. She assured me she could get a taxi to Marks & Spencer for her weekly shopping. With some trepidation I broke free again two months later, telling her I was always on the end of my mobile.

*

The beech trees were resplendent in their autumn coat of yellow and brown and a dense mist shrouded the mountain of Le Donon. Apart from drops of water pattering onto the leaves, all was silence. At 3,310 feet the summit is the most northerly peak of any importance in the Vosges. I knew it would be the last big hill before the Pyrenees and I had hoped for a fine view. Instead ghosts kept looming out of the cloud and the atmosphere was decidedly eerie. I was completely alone.

The path came to the foot of a monumental stairway built of rock. This was the most recent vestige of the past, constructed by German soldiers in the First World War to enable the Kaiser to walk up to the summit. The top of Le Donon is an elongated plateau which has been completely deforested in recent years. It is now covered with sandstone rocks and heathers. The remains of successive occupation by Neolithic peoples, Celts and Romans lie scattered across the hillside. Carved stones show that the Roman god Mercury was worshipped here, but also Vosegus, a Celtic deity who gave his name to the Vosges. A platform of rock, crisscrossed by huge cracks, covers the highest point of the plateau. Here the Forestry Commission built a crude temple of rough-hewn blocks in 1869, just as they imagined it would have looked two thousand years before. It was probably an advantage to see it with the mist softening the harsh outline of square columns and a triangular roof.

Below Le Donon the great forest of the Vosges seemed to stretch for miles in all directions. Trees covered every peak and valley with not a building in sight. And then in a small gap between two ridges I suddenly saw a flash of yellow, which might have been a field of stubble in the far distance. This was the first intimation of the way ahead to the rolling plains of Lorraine. The only sound was a bird of prey calling out across the hills. I strode along the crest and then dropped down a deep comb to the Sarre Blanche river. It was difficult to think that this stream, in a remote mountain valley, flowed into the industrial heartland of Lorraine.

9

FROM LORRAINE TO THE NORTHERN PLAINS
WOODS AND WATER

MOST BRITISH VISITORS speed through northern France on their way south, unless they want to visit the battlefields of the First World War. They imagine it to be full of factories and mines interspersed with featureless countryside. Walking across the region I saw much more variety than I had expected: constantly changing landscapes and architectural styles in the different *pays*, from Lorraine to the Ardennes, the Thiérache and then Flanders and the Nord. For a hiker bent on discovery it was an ideal environment.

The plains of northern France stretch all the way from Lorraine to the English Channel, rising and falling in a gentle rhythm. Three rivers pass through the north-eastern corner of the hexagon and I crossed them all: the Meurthe, the Moselle and lastly the Meuse. They drain into the Rhine and the North Sea. Later the Oise flows south to the Seine and the Canche due west to the Channel. Canals link many of the rivers and dotted among all these waterways are clusters of lakes, man-made and natural, large and small. The walker is never very far from water and the mirror it holds up to a vast sky and its changing moods. The landscape constantly alternates between plateaux of open fields, mainly devoted to arable farming, and depressions where meadows full of cattle surround a meandering stream. Massive forests cover much of the region: circling Nancy, on the slopes above the Meuse, on the battlefield of Verdun, in the French Ardennes near Charleville-Mézières, and at Mormal east of Valenciennes.

These northern plains were largely empty of people, which seemed incredible given how close they are to the most densely populated area of Europe: the Low Countries to the north and the Paris basin to the south. The north may contain much of France's industry, but there are huge open spaces in between. The large towns come in clusters: Nancy and Metz in Lorraine, Sedan and Charleville-Mézières in the Ardennes, Lille and Valenciennes in Le Nord alongside Arras in the Pas-de-Calais and lastly Boulogne and Calais on the coast. Otherwise it is a region of small towns and scattered villages, which have suffered rural depopulation as the cultivation of the great plains has been mechanized. Only around the major conurbations are workers in the towns starting to re-populate these villages. Otherwise many seem asleep, only coming to life at five o'clock, when cars return from a long journey to work. In the open fields I saw the occasional tractor silhouetted against the sky. Unlike in the nineteenth century when many hands made light work, agriculture is now a lonely business. Many

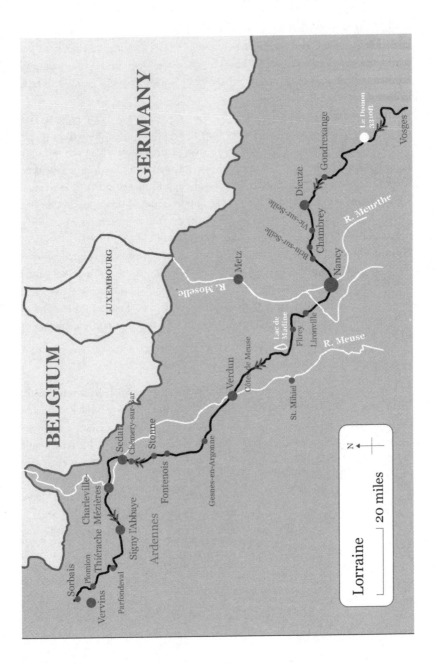

of the villages might have a part-time *mairie*, if they are the centre of a *commune*, and also a church. Occasionally there is a hall for local activities, but rarely a shop or a café. I had to take all my provisions for the day with me and accommodation was scarce. Even a bench on the village green to rest my legs seemed to be a luxury.

The memory of past conflicts is ever present in northern France. War plagued these open plains long before the nineteenth century. Then the struggle with Germany between 1870 and 1945 scarred the north. There are not only many graveyards, French, German, British and American, and monuments to mark the sites of different battles, but also thousands of reminders of individual acts of sacrifice. Memory is kept alive by the activities of voluntary bodies like Le Souvenir Français, in the naming of Places du Souvenir Français, both in big towns like Nancy (Place Carnot) and also in small villages. In 1976 President Giscard d'Estaing made an official visit to Nancy and the city council ordered the following inscription on the Arc Désilles: "On the Twenty Fifth of November 1976 Valéry Giscard d'Estaing, President of the Republic, solemnly consecrated this monument in memory of all those who have died for France in the course of its history." No doubt the attempt to include everyone in a non-partisan spirit was quite deliberate.

LORRAINE

Nancy has a population of around 500,000 but its growth is relatively recent. In 1870 it was a sleepy provincial capital. Then came the war with Prussia and the annexation of "German" Lorraine only twenty miles away. Many Lorrainers poured into Nancy, which before the First World War enjoyed a remarkable period of prosperity. Metz is now the capital of the modern French region of Lorraine, but Nancy is the cultural centre.

But what exactly do we mean by Lorraine? Is it a geographical region? Does it have a cultural identity? Within the new Europe of the EU in what sense is it French? I decided to play the tourist in Nancy and see if I could find some answers.

I headed straight for the Musée Lorrain as the best place to discover Lorraine's identity. The museum is situated in the former ducal palace, part of which is an exuberant late Gothic building dating from 1501. The artefacts include glassware and porcelain for which the region is famous, art nouveau furniture and the contents of farmhouses. The visit included the Église des Cordeliers and the mausoleum of the ducal family, a classical rotunda complete with dome and coffered ceiling.

Lorraine knew its golden age in the aftermath of Duke René II's defeat of the Burgundians in 1477. He built the church, started the ducal palace and today sits on his prancing war horse above the main gateway on the Grande Rue. Unfortunately this single military victory did not rid the duchy of its major strategic weakness, as geographically it is a border region where the Paris basin meets the Vosges. In the sixteenth century it sat at a crossroads in northern Europe, sandwiched between two powerful monarchies, the Holy Roman Empire and France, who were determined on a fight to the death. The disaster of the Thirty Years' War followed, so movingly portrayed by Jacques Callot whose engravings hang upstairs in the Musée Lorrain. In 1633 he started a series called *Les Grandes Misères de la guerre* (The Great Miseries of War) which are every bit as horrific as Picasso's *Guernica*. It was the France of Louis XIV which emerged triumphant from all this destruction, so that by the eighteenth century Lorraine was firmly in the French sphere of influence.

Francis, Duke of Lorraine, had to step down because he married Maria Theresa, the Empress of Austria. The French could not tolerate the Austrians controlling Lorraine, so Francis graciously agreed to accept Tuscany in compensation. No doubt he felt that Florence was a better bet than Nancy, which can be miserably cold in the winter. As I chewed a baguette in a churchyard above the city, an interesting gravestone had caught my eye: "Here lies the body of Marie Chelkepfin, the widow of Mr. Balthasard Schreber, a pensioner of the King of Poland. She died on 25th February 1809 aged 90 years... General Jacopin her son-in-law and his wife, her daughter, put up this monument."

The King of Poland was Stanislas Leszczynski, who was thrown out of his native country and succeeded Francis as Duke of Lorraine, an event engineered by Louis XV's ministers. His daughter Marie was the wife of the French king and it was agreed that, once Stanislas died, the duchy would revert to France. They did not bargain for the fact that Stanislas would last for thirty years, albeit as a French puppet. He spent his time building grand houses, including an immense château at Lunéville, but kept away from Nancy because his foreign origins did not make him popular with the locals.

In the streets of Nancy it is possible to trace the evolution from proud independent duchy to client state of France and finally to French region. The medieval streets of the very oldest part of the city contain the soul of the former:

the Rue du Maure qui Trompe which used to house the brothels; the walls and towers at the Porte de la Craffe; the huge wolves on the gateposts of the duke's chief huntsman. No doubt my memories are gilded by the scent of a good chicken tajine in a Moroccan café, the succulent hare served at *Le Cul de Poule* in the Place de l'Arsenal and the second-hand bookshops.

At the end of the seventeenth century the ostentatious grandeur of the Sun King's baroque began to make itself felt: from the classical cherubs on the house of the duke's silversmith to the overpowering columns and façade of the cathedral and other churches such as St.-Sébastien near the market. In this commercial quarter the streets are so wide that even on a busy weekday the place looks empty. When you reach the Place de la Carrière you see the full expression of the power of the French state: a long vista of pillared buildings leading the eye to the Palais du Gouvernment. Next to this square are the obligatory triumphal arch and the huge open space of the Place Stanislas, which lies between the medieval and modern cities. It is one of the finest public squares in France, with elaborate wrought-iron grilles resplendent in black and gold and imposing eighteenth-century buildings.

I sometimes wonder what has happened to town planning in modern France. There are prestigious projects, some of great originality, alongside ugly excrescences of concrete and plaster detracting from their surroundings. Crude apartment blocks dominate the skyline on the hills to the west of Nancy, yet the city has a native tradition in modern architecture which emphasized the organic growth of buildings out of the surrounding environment, the École de Nancy. The Maison Huot is the most entertaining example of this style, fun and quirky, a real *jeu d'esprit*. A Moorish window takes the shape of a leaf surrounded by vitreous turquoise tiles. The front door looks like a tree; mouldings of plants surround the other windows and chimney stacks. In the commercial district art nouveau principles have been applied to the Graineterie Genin-Louis, which is unusual in that the basic structure is entirely of metal. The ground floor façade and the bay windows of the tower have an abundance of fine wrought-iron work. A profusion of vegetation and poppies appear in the decoration.

So Lorraine certainly had a sense of identity but how can this be summarized? It was a political and legal unit of sorts, as a duchy within the Holy Roman Empire. However this duchy never covered the whole of what was known as Lorraine in early modern times. It was also a distinct geographical area, but with boundaries which were not altogether clear. Lorraine has its own languages: the

Maison Huot

French patois of the west, now virtually extinct, and Francique, a Low German language distinct from Alsatian, still used in the extreme north-east.

"My grandparents and parents spoke patois," said Josette in Dieuze. "The nearer you get to the north-east frontier, the more German words it contains." Other cultural differences have persisted too. Josette continued, "In the *département* of the Moselle, as well as in Alsace, the priest can visit the local school once a week to teach the catechism, and his salary is paid by the state."

Lorraine has its own cuisine. Josette produced a satisfying home-cooked meal, which perhaps inevitably included Quiche Lorraine and the local fruit called mirabelles. These have the consistency of a greengage or plum, but are smaller. In Lorraine they have yellow skins with a touch of red, the *mirabelles de Nancy*, or are just plain yellow, the *mirabelles de Metz*. A good accompaniment to ice cream, they are also used for making liqueur. Later in my walk I enjoyed a *menu Mirabelle*: a hefty Lorraine pie filled with veal and bacon, quails with mirabelles and *soufflé glacé* of mirabelles to finish.

The characteristic features of Lorraine villages became familiar as I walked towards Nancy. The long village streets had wide verges, used in former times to keep carts and equipment, stack wood and pile manure. Niches above decorated door frames contained statues of the Virgin and high arched gateways led to yards behind. Some of the houses dated from the eighteenth century. At one time they would have contained the items displayed in the Musée Lorrain: box beds and solid country furniture; fireplaces full of iron cooking implements; old pumps for drawing water; stills for making schnapps; farm carts.

Unfortunately for Lorraine it came into contact with France, which during the Revolution and the nineteenth century imposed a cultural and political uniformity throughout its territory. It was not the only area of Europe with a somewhat uncertain sense of difference to suffer this fate. It is perhaps because the French sense of identity resulted from the crucible of conflict over territory that it has seemed so strident to Anglo-Saxons. After 1871 the French educational system of the Third Republic ensured that peasants, as well as bourgeois, spoke French. Regional political expression was strictly taboo. After Germany returned the *département* of the Moselle, the French wanted to reinforce Lorraine's destiny as an integral part of France. It was only after 1945 that the French state felt confident enough to relax its grip, and the region of Lorraine emerged with others to take some responsibility for its own destiny, particularly in the economic field. It is ironic that the French state now supports publicity for France's various local cultures in order to promote tourism. They are all regarded as part of France's heritage.

Lorraine is struggling to come to terms with the globalised economy of the twenty-first century. The towers of an ancient cement works belching steam appeared on the horizon as I strode towards Gondrexange in eastern Lorraine. The industrial town of Sarrebourg was only fifteen miles away. The wealth of modern Lorraine was founded on steel and coal, and Germany grabbed the heart of the industrial region around Metz between 1871 and 1914 precisely because of this wealth. But steel making is now in decline and the coal mines have all closed. I visited the small town of Dieuze, which has a population of only 3,600. It lost 800 jobs some years ago when a sulphuric acid plant closed down. An interview given on TV by the Vice-President of the Regional Economic Council highlighted the lack of new jobs, plants moving to countries where production costs are lower and the numbers of local people working over the border in Luxembourg, Germany and Belgium. There are 54,000 of these so-called *frontaliers*, according to one newspaper report. "Economically we are closer to Germany and Luxembourg than to the rest of France," said Jean-Pierre in Dieuze. "We draw strength from our neighbours."

Further west unemployment is well above the national average in Verdun. The army has reduced its presence in recent years and the town is dependent on visitors touring the battlefields. The situation is even worse in Sedan where one in four is out of a job. The traditional textile industry has disappeared and more recent enterprises have suffered from foreign competition.

A WALK THROUGH LORRAINE

Friesians populated meadows dotted with copses and red berries rotted in hedgerows reminiscent of the English countryside. The mewing of a buzzard added to the mournful atmosphere. Gondrexange is a functional village not far from the cement works and a railway line. Yet here the landscape changes suddenly, as the trail enters a network of canals and meres (*étangs*). The Canal de la Marne au Rhin flows past the village in an elegant curve to enter the Étang de Gondrexange, protected on both sides by large dykes. Above and around me was a huge expanse of pale blue water, with the lines of the canal stretching into infinity. A heron skimmed across the surface of the mere looking for food. I moved quickly on a frosty morning, as the slanting light of a crisp autumn sun threw my shadow across the dyke ahead. Patches of mist started to disperse and I saw a group of fishermen warming themselves over a glass of red wine.

The trail crosses the canal at a junction; left to Nancy, right to Sarreguimines. I followed the Canal des Houillères de la Sarre (the Sarre Coalfield Canal). It is some time since barges laden with coal ran along this waterway, and now the only noise was the plop of a float dropping into water as a fisherman greeted me from the opposite bank. The canal entered an azure-roofed tunnel of trees, the reflection of their dying shades perfect in the motionless water.

I had crossed into the Moselle just after Le Donon. The southern boundary of this *département* was the frontier between France and Germany from 1871 to 1918 and also from 1940 to 1944. I followed its direction westwards and promptly thought I was in Germany. A local village tip had notices in French and German and I passed holiday chalets with German family names on the letter boxes and German security fencing. I met German hunters in the woods.

There was no accommodation in Vic-sur-Seille.To find a bed for the night I had to battle along a main road in the rain, constantly and hazardously jumping out of the way of the traffic. Many French country roads are built on embankments, the verge is narrow and the drop to the surrounding fields steep. Some kind souls swerved to give me room, but others did not see me as it got dark. After two miles I saw a great barracks of a farmhouse three storeys high. At one time it must have housed an army of farm workers. An Alsatian eyed me suspiciously as the farmer unlocked a large wooden door to let me into a draughty hall. He was a man on his own with a young child and explained that there would be no supper. He could only offer bed and breakfast. My bedroom might have been airy in summer, but with its high ceilings it was freezing during a cold snap in late autumn. I sat and shivered under a blanket and then went downstairs to beg a cup of hot coffee.

Hoping to reach Nancy the next evening I walked on the *route départementale* 77 through anonymous villages. The buildings of Chambrey were completely destroyed during the 1914-18 war. At Brin-sur-Seille I crossed an unremarkable bridge over the river, about forty feet wide at this point and flowing quite fast. An old man was chopping wood and chatting to his friend. Seeing I was obviously a visitor he said suddenly, "That used to be Germany over there in 1914, and in 1940 when I was a boy. The Seille was the frontier. The Germans closed it in the Second World War. You couldn't cross here then. Too many soldiers about; far too dangerous."

The steep slopes leading up to the Forêt de la Haye contain the western suburbs of Nancy. A bitter northerly air flow whistled through the pines and I needed all the warm clothes I could muster. A series of long straight *allées* brought me to an escarpment overlooking the Moselle. This winding stretch is at the top of the massive arc which the river cuts around Nancy before joining the Meurthe on its way to Metz. I crossed the river and huddled on a bench to bolt down my baguette. After twenty minutes my fingers were frozen, so I pressed on fast only to find an exposed plateau of open fields. There was not a shaft of light in the grey clouds above. Facing north-east towards the wooded hills of the Moselle valley I met the full force of the Arctic air stream. At Rosières-en-Haye my legs felt they had had enough, so I devoured some dark chocolate to get a kick of energy. Fortunately a country road led quickly to an inn.

The inn-keeper looked like Astérix the Gaul with unruly hair. His sparrow-like wife bounced around attentively. She took me to my room, where I promptly fell on the bed and went to sleep. *Monsieur* gathered his flowing locks into a ponytail for the evening, but did not bother to change his track suit bottoms. I was the only guest and fortunately he had lit a fire in my honour. He liked to grumble but Yvette was constantly cheerful. When I came down for breakfast she was doing a crossword. "I did not have much education. I have run a small business all my life," she said, "so I am trying to improve my mind. I enjoy a chat with my customers and I can't just discuss the weather! Saying it's cold or windy doesn't make for very exciting conversation. I love my language and learning new words. So I do crosswords and play Scrabble."

I walked along the River Esch with the warmth of the sun on my back. This was an intimate valley, with little enclosures and old woods dissected by twisting paths. I crossed the river at Martincourt, as it bubbled exuberantly between sluice gates, and came to a parting of the ways with the GR5. It turned right to run north towards Luxembourg, but my route led straight on to Verdun. Although the spot was unremarkable, I felt as if I was leaving an old friend who had accompanied my struggle all the way through the Alps, the Jura and the Vosges.

THE MARKS OF WAR

The track passed through a small gorge in the woods ahead, where a notice told me all about the Battle of Lironville in the St.-Mihiel salient. This was one of the most active sectors of the Western Front for the French Army of the Great War, especially when the Germans advanced a long way south-east of Verdun during the early fighting in 1914. This bulge was called the St.-Mihiel salient after the small town of that name a few miles away. On 21 September 1914 the southern extremity of the salient passed through Martincourt. The French wanted to roll it back by taking the village of Lironville on the other side of the wood. The order to attack was given at 3 p.m. on 22 September. When the French reached the crest above the village German machine gunners in the church tower decimated their ranks. It was only after two more days' fierce fighting, and the use of heavy artillery, that the French took the village and pushed the German line back two miles.

In woods north of Flirey I stumbled across the remains of several German trenches established after the battle. The French front line was only about 550 yards away in the fields. A large wooden cross stood in front of the trees marking the spot where Sergeant Rochas was killed on 11 April 1915 as he led an attack against the German lines. He ran fifty yards ahead of his company brandishing his rifle and shouting "forward!" before being shot down. He was a law student from Grenoble and only 19 years old. In a similar action nearby 700 French went over the top and only 200 came back. A large memorial by the road recalled the sacrifices of the French soldiers, who during four years knew how to "*lutter, tenir, souffrer, mourir.*" The word *tenir* is particularly significant. After the failed offensives of 1914-1915 French soldiers simply wanted to hold their ground and stay alive.

French troops were ordered over the top in more useless attacks in 1917 after the carnage of Verdun. Some of them mutinied. They thought it was time for peace but tragically this was only available on Germany's terms. I understood their dilemma when I read some words spoken by my pacifist grandfather in front of a military court at Blackdown Camp on 18 July 1918:

"I resist conscription because I am opposed to war and every form of militarism, and after two sentences involving over 18 months' imprisonment with hard labour, I am still resolutely opposed to any compromise whatever with compulsory military service, whatever the consequences, and I feel that in maintaining my resistance I am doing a work not only of national but also of international importance.

This Tribunal administers certain laws, but what is the justification for these laws? They enact conscription, they have militarised British rule and they have destroyed in a few years the whole fabric of religious and political liberty which the genius of England had built up by centuries of struggle. They have combined with the military licence of other countries to devastate Europe, to destroy countless lives and break numberless hearts; is it not time they were disobeyed? The war has immeasurably increased every danger it was intended to avert. The peoples in Russia, in Ireland, and in Austria, cry aloud that the laws must be broken if humanity is to be saved from the projects of selfish imperialism, the rivalry of ambitious powers and the intrigues of diplomats, and the cry finds an echo in every part of Europe."

The Lac de Madine was created in 1965 to provide water for Metz, a reserve for wild life and opportunities for leisure activities. It lies in the wet clay soil of the Woevre plain which has been drained over the centuries for agriculture. The brown lakeside reeds rustled as I watched flocks of ducks and pairs of swans searching for food. Mist covered the distant hillsides of the Côtes de Meuse. To the south the isolated hill of the Butte de Montsec rose out of the plain crowned by a monument. I could just make out the classical columns of what looked like a Greek temple. This was the American memorial to the Battle of the St.-Mihiel salient of September 1918, which marked America's arrival on the world stage as a great power. The Butte was the jumping-off point for an attack to clear the area of German forces. A total of 216,000 US troops took part alongside 48,000 French. A further 200,000 Americans stood in reserve. It was the first independent US operation of the war under an American Commander-in-Chief.

The wooded slopes of the Côtes de Meuse run north all the way to Verdun. Vineyards used to cover the Côtes, but the phylloxera beetle devastated most of them. Orchards of mirabelle, cherry and apple trees replaced the vines, but some of the Côtes were also planted with conifers or left to grow wild. The silence of the forest swallowed me up. It was a damp and airless day. The only sound I could hear was the noise of my feet shuffling through the carpet of dead leaves. The remains of a German memorial from the First World War stood near a crossroads with its top hacked off.

At St.-Rémy-la-Calonne the trees retreat to the surrounding hillsides, leaving the flat-bottomed valley as a giant cradle for fallen French soldiers. There is a simple graveyard next to the church, with several rows of plain white crosses running across immaculately mown grass. I had come to find the last resting place of one of France's most famous writers, Alain-Fournier, author of *Le Grand Meaulnes*. The cemetery did not contain a map to tell me where the grave was and I had to walk along the rows until I found it: "FOURNIER Henri dit Alain-Fournier Lieutenant 288e R.I. Mort pour la France le 22.09.1914."

Alain-Fournier fought with the 288th infantry regiment and the Germans buried his remains in an unmarked trench, along with many others. There they lay unnoticed for seventy-eight years until identified and transferred to their present location in 1992. Alain-Fournier published his famous novel the year before the war, when it narrowly failed to win the prestigious literary Prix Goncourt. A tale of the lost world of youth in *la France profonde*, it makes his early death particularly poignant. Despite his neat uniform and trimmed moustache, the photograph in the cemetery does not portray a military man. The deep dark eyes and slight refined features are too sensitive.

I very much wanted to visit the site of the ferocious battles which took place in April 1915 around the hill on the Côtes known as Les Éparges. The French tried to drive the Germans off this high ground because they saw it as the key to the St.-Mihiel salient. They only succeeded in capturing it at enormous cost and had to withdraw when the Germans attacked Verdun. Huge bomb craters litter the battlefield, the result of each side's efforts to undermine the other's trenches by blowing them up. One of these massive holes must have been seventy feet across and fifty feet deep. Such events mark a man for life. Another writer, Maurice Genevoix, repaid his debt to his fallen comrades by describing what they went through together in a series of moving memoirs (*Les Éparges*, 1923), as devastating as a series of crisp black and white photos. Here is an extract from his diary for 21 February 1915: "Why? Why is my trench full of dead bodies? All these dead bodies torn to pieces, their stomachs ripped open, pulverised, fallen next to each other without having fired a shot. Why is the bomb crater full of dead bodies? Why has a point of cold steel been driven into Raynaud's head?... The commander bleats like a lamb; Petitbru starts shouting again; Biloray runs, falls, gets up and runs again; Laviolette finds a place to hide and die, his hand trembling on his head in a woollen glove..."

Near Verdun my route ran into the Autoroute de l'Est. I turned off and took refuge in a restaurant crowded with families enjoying Sunday lunch. The prospect of a large coffee and a calvados was very tempting, so I hoisted myself on a stool and placed an order. The *patron* behind the bar had a painful hip, which caused him to limp badly, but still found time for some banter. Inevitably his curiosity got the better of him. "What are you doing in Verdun with a rucksack on a chilly autumn day?" he asked

"I've just come through the forest on foot avoiding the hunters," I said.

"They're a nuisance. The season is far too long."

I had to agree with his opinions on hunting. I had a stand-off with some German hunters near Dieuze and was challenged several times to keep out of the way on the Côtes de Meuse. Hunters are a powerful lobby group in France and their rights seem to prevail over everyone else's. If you get in the way, *tant pis*. Any local resident with a licence can hunt in the woods. It was hardly surprising therefore that I had encountered men with their guns all the way from the Pyrenees. I remembered a jovial hunter in the hill country above Montaillou. He had winked at Lizzie and said he would not shoot me so she could take the insurance money.

I started feeling in my pocket for change.

"The bill is €6.50 but give me five; that'll be enough."

I must have looked like a real down and out who could not afford very much.

The Meuse meandered though the meadows on my left. Ahead lay an estate of concrete bungalows, uniform in appearance with neat privet hedges. It was a very suburban introduction to Verdun where the duty to remember is felt more strongly than anywhere else. The French writer Ernest Renan once said that a nation is kept alive by the shared experience of strife and adversity. In that case Verdun, more than anywhere, should symbolize the spirit of the French nation. What would it be like?

Walking down the hill to the centre I passed the embankments of the old Verdun fortress dating from the time of Vauban. The suburbs of the old town looked the worse for wear. Weeds grew out of a bridge crossing the Meuse Canal which was lined by decaying houses. More care had been lavished on the quays by the river itself and the shopping street behind. Pleasure launches lined the river banks.

The hills on the right bank of the Meuse may be only 1,100 feet high, but they seemed very close. To retain Verdun it was essential for the French defenders of 1916 to hold onto these heights at all costs. But why fight to the death to defend this small town, whose forts were regarded, even in early 1916, as of limited military importance? After all the French had virtually evacuated the famous fort of Doaumont and the Germans walked right into it. Verdun's importance was symbolic as much as anything else. Because the Germans launched such a massive attack the French felt they had no option but to hold on. I retired to bed with two questions on my mind. What is Verdun's raison d'être today and would I be able to recapture the atmosphere of the desperate struggle which raged here in 1916?

I decided to take a day off walking to join millions of others who have toured the main sites of the battlefield on the right bank of the Meuse. The terrain is not at all as it was in 1916. The war scoured the hills of vegetation. In place of woods and fields the struggle left mounds of blasted earth, the skeletons of destroyed villages, remnants of fortifications, twisted scraps of metal and broken equipment, unexploded ordinance and human body parts, all buried in mud. It was totally impossible to return the land to its original state, so trees were planted to hide the main area of conflict. Today the site of the battle is covered in a rolling forest, which conceals the soft undulations of the tortured earth. It was no doubt the only thing to do, but it has taken us several steps from the original horror. Standing in the large open graveyard on the ridge at Thiepval on the Somme, you get a much better sense of what it must have been like for the Tommies to walk across the fields on a July morning. In Verdun I could not grasp the scale of the battle close up because the trees obscured the big picture like a curtain.

The best introduction is to climb the hill of the Fort de Bois Bourrus. From this vantage point on the left bank I had a panoramic view of the arc of hills which dominate Verdun. The eye can sweep from Côte 304 and the Mort-Homme in the west, across the Meuse to the Bois des Caures where it all started on 21 February 1916, and south on the right bank to the cluster of invisible forts overlooking the town itself. While the Mort-Homme is some seven miles from Verdun, the furthest point of the German advance on the right bank, on 23 June 1916, was less than half that distance. The French resistance was desperate, the Germans ran out of impetus and the Somme offensive came in the nick of time.

The ruined fort of Doaumont has been left more or less as it was during the battle: the long dimly lit corridors of arched stone constantly dripping water, metal bedsteads, washing-troughs and an old gun turret. When the Germans captured it there were no latrines and the resulting stench during their occupation made the soldiers sick. Then an explosion killed several hundred of their men inside. There is now a small chapel to commemorate their loss. The ossuary at Doaumont, with the massive cemetery in front, is unfortunately one of the ugliest buildings you can see; a long curved vault with an enormous tower. Strangely the ossuary itself was the result of a private initiative and is not maintained by the French government. After the battle the local bishop formed a committee to give a decent burial to the many remains which could not be identified, both French and German. There are 130,000 men commemorated in this way.

Verdun seems like a small town overburdened with its history, which stretches not just back to 1916 but a thousand years earlier. The massive Romanesque cathedral was started in 990 AD, the century after the Treaty of Verdun which divided Charlemagne's empire. That treaty created a Middle Kingdom which the French and the Germans fought to control for the next eleven centuries. In the former bishop's palace a museum dedicated to peace was staging an exhibition of old slides from the First World War, processed to look three-dimensional when viewed through special glasses. Here at last I glimpsed the real life of soldiers during the height of the battle. The slides showed horrific pictures of troops in the front line, dead and mutilated bodies in a devastated landscape. But there were also many shots of unguarded moments during breaks in the rear: enjoying a wash, queuing for the latrines, drinking wine and marching up and down the Voie Sacrée (the Sacred Way) from Bar-le-Duc, the only route that supplied the beleaguered fortress of Verdun in 1916. Today there is a plaque marking the Voie Sacrée by the railway station.

My path on leaving Verdun ran over undulating downs to Chattancourt. Several villages destroyed during the fighting of 1916 never rose again, but the inhabitants of Chattancourt rebuilt their homes. One combatant described in graphic terms the dangers of crossing the village to reach the French front line at Mort-Homme: "Shells rained down on the village and several houses were burnt out. There was only one road through, which was constantly under fire. To make matters worse drainage pipes had been destroyed by the bombardment and the whole area flooded. The writer had to wade through water up to his waist."

Mort-Homme is about three hundred feet above the valley floor, an insignificant hill among many. Having attacked first on the right bank in February, the Germans opened a second front here in March. Terrible hand to hand fighting took place. The intensity of the artillery fire from both sides meant that the central part of the ridge could not be held by either army. The struggle continued all summer until the French counter-attacks of August gave them the upper hand. All that is left is a peaceful clearing in the woods, a number of monuments and a military cemetery. Now there are joint Franco-German visits to remember the dead. A cross erected in 1984 records the old enemies' reconciliation.

THE ARDENNES: THE EMPTY QUARTER

I walked on departmental roads all day in the Argonne and very few vehicles crossed my path. Just outside Gesnes-en-Argonne the road left the Meuse to enter the *département* of the Ardennes and soon became more like an English country lane with high banks on either side. The next settlement looked like a place cut off from the world as I sat on the church steps looking at lush meadows, ditches, orchards and cottages. Three bored boys sped up and down the road on their small motorbikes. I left them to find a repetitive landscape of arable plateaux and intervening valleys populated by more small villages. This was the Empty Quarter of northern France. The population density in the rural Ardennes and the neighbouring *département* of the Meuse is as low as in many areas of the Massif Central. The soles of my feet were sore after seven and a half hours' road walking for twenty miles. I ate often to keep up my energy levels and rapidly became addicted to chocolate and bananas—one great plus of French supermarkets is that you can buy high-quality black chocolate with delicious nut fillings.

At 8.30 a.m. on 1 November I started off under a brilliant blue sky, as the sun melted a crisp frost and dispersed the mist filling shallow folds in the landscape. I was walking on a trail which followed the path of retreat of the French armies in August 1914, as well as the victorious advance of the Americans four years later. Near the hamlet of Fontenois a monument commemorated the death of members of the 128th infantry regiment, harried by German columns on 31 August 1914. A week later these apparently demoralized formations turned round to defeat the Germans on the Marne. A ruddy-faced man, with grey wispy hair squashed under a woolly hat, was tending his vegetable plot.

"Where are you walking to today?"

"Chémery-sur-Bar."

"That's a long way."

"Yes, twelve miles further at least."

"Well, before I retired I used to cycle fifteen miles to work each day and fifteen back in the evening. *Bon courage!*"

*

He looked at me quizzically as my mobile rang in my anorak pocket. It was Lizzie.

"Your mother has been on the phone. It's unusual. She doesn't often call me." Lizzie laughed.

"What's the problem?"

"She says she can't find anything to eat. I did some shopping for her not long ago. I think she can't make the effort to look in the freezer. Perhaps we should find someone to cook for her, like she had after she suffered that infection."

In the middle of such a remote French hamlet it was difficult to focus on my mother's needs.

"The problem is finding someone she will accept," I replied. "Perhaps we can soldier on until I reach the Channel and come home. Let's talk about something else. Northern France is surprisingly interesting. Apart from the battlefields lots of hidden corners no one knows about. Last night I stayed with two Dutch who own a small hotel in the middle of nowhere. They said they loved the peace and quiet compared with Holland, but I wondered. A large statue of a Second Empire general in the square; just my period."

*

Eventually I entered the village of Stonne built on a prominent ridge. Just before the houses an inscription on a stone warned me that this was the site of an important tank battle in May 1940. "Here the tank Chinon was destroyed with all its crew, in the course of fierce fighting which took place at Stonne on 15-18 May 1940."

The crossroads at Stonne was full of memorials. General Guderian's 19th Corps had crossed the Meuse near Sedan on 13 May. The French had three armoured divisions in the region, but they were too slow to counter-attack. The Third Division was ordered to deploy around Stonne, supported by motorized infantry. It was equipped with the B1 bis tank, an example of which stands by the road today. It performed well but unfortunately, as a plaque records, only 377 were manufactured. In the fighting which followed the village changed hands many times and the French lost between 4,000 and 5,000 men. All this effort was in vain. By 15 May Guderian had broken out to the west, driving for the Channel to cut the Allied armies in two.

I dived into a forest until I reached the soggy meadows of the Bar valley and the village of Chémery-sur-Bar. As the Germans crossed the Meuse, there were extraordinary scenes of panic at Chémery and the next village called Bulson. A French general at Bulson wrote, "A wave of terrified fugitives, gunners and infantry, in cars, on foot, many without arms but dragging kitbags, was hurtling down the Bulson road screaming 'the tanks are at Bulson'."

This rumour turned out to be totally false, but 20,000 troops fled in panic. These troops were ill-trained and ill-equipped, and had not originally been intended for battle duty. The Germans had subjected them to heavy aerial bombardment using Stuka bombers. Today Bulson is a quiet and attractive village in hilly country three miles south of Sedan. Terraces of cottages in honey-coloured stone surround a large green, at the centre of which stands a twelfth-century fortified church built of the same material.

Once on the heights of Marfée the memories of past conflicts came thick and fast. A terrace overlooked the valley of the Meuse, the town of Sedan and the wooded hills of the Ardennes on the far bank. From here I surveyed the site of three battles in the extended Franco-German conflict between 1870 and 1945. On 1 September 1870 William I of Prussia watched from further along this escarpment as his armies encircled the French trapped in Sedan. In September 1914 the retreating French counter-attacked against the advancing Germans on this spot. In 1940 waves of Stukas bombed French positions on the Marfée as Guderian's troops crossed the Meuse below.

The Meuse is a lazy river which wanders into Sedan past rows of factories and a railway station. The town suffered extensive damage in the last war, and older houses clustered under the castle are interspersed with ugly modern flats and commercial buildings. Sedan is down at heel. Many of the shops sold factory seconds and young men hung around listlessly outside the few cafés. Despite all this the winding streets built in the eighteenth century have a lot of charm, particularly the area known as la Petite Italie. The castle, a massive pile of masonry surrounded by ramparts and bastions, is said to be the largest fort in Europe. It is refreshing to find an old town which has not been restored as a tourist honey pot.

A large statue of a French soldier protected by an angel dominates a square in the town centre. A national subscription provided the funds to pay homage to those who gave their lives in September 1870 to save French honour. The defeat at Sedan, when a whole French army had to surrender, was long felt to be a national disgrace, the responsibility of incompetent generals and the Emperor Napoleon III. The latter departed from Sedan to captivity and exile, never to be seen on French soil again. Standing on the castle terrace it was not difficult to imagine the scene on 1 September, as the fire of the Prussian cannon rained down on a demoralised French army crushed into the narrow streets and surrounding fields. Moreover, France's humiliation happened in full view of a glittering assembly on the heights near the Marfée, comprising the German princes and representatives of the British, Russian and United States Armies, accompanied by William Howard Russell of *The Times*, one of the first war reporters. Russell had already made his name exposing the weaknesses of the British military in the Crimea. No one has described the atmosphere better than Émile Zola in his novel *La Débâcle*: "It was a bombardment from hell, the ground trembled and the air was set alight. Around Sedan eight hundred German cannon in a ring of bronze all fired at once and struck the surrounding fields with continual thunder. The effect of this fire converging on the town from the surrounding heights would have pulverised and burnt it within two hours."

At Charleville-Mézières the Meuse makes two massive meanders before disappearing into Belgium. Intersecting canals, railway lines, roads and low-cost apartment blocks dominate the townscape. The town's favourite son seems to be the revolutionary poet Arthur Rimbaud (1854-91). A sign board announced that Charleville-Mézières, apart from being twinned with three German towns, is the puppet capital of Europe and the birthplace of Rimbaud. The inhabitants have made him into a successful cultural commodity. There is a museum and his family's house, while numerous clothing and media shops have borrowed his name. This is ironic as Rimbaud, like many other favourite sons, detested the bourgeois society of his native town. He rebelled by escaping to Paris at the age of sixteen, a few days before the Battle of Sedan. He came back but his rebellion continued. He grew his hair long, drank too much alcohol, behaved boorishly and stole books. Later he lived with the poet Paul Verlaine in Paris and travelled to three continents. He only returned to Charleville at the very end of his short life.

The must see site is the Place Ducale, a splendid square built in 1610. The *place* is more or less contemporaneous with the Place des Vosges in Paris, a harmonious structure in the classical style with lots of red brick, rusticated stone work around the windows, classical pediments, square-topped pavilions and graceful arcades at ground-floor level. This perfectly preserved architecture stands in stark contrast to the dilapidated stonework and graffiti elsewhere. Charleville-Mézières is suffering from economic depression. On Saturday evening there was no life in the cavernous streets and most people seemed to be scuttling home. Some drunks had propped themselves up on the fountain in the middle of this huge open space. I found shelter in a Savoyard café and ate one of the worst meals I have had in France. The *tartine* consisted of a large piece of toast covered in potatoes, cheese and tomato with a fried egg, smoked meat and salad. It was cold and only just edible. A mound of Chantilly smothered the *crêpe gourmande* filled with banana and chocolate sauce.

THE THIÉRACHE

The Forêt Domaniale de Signy-l'Abbaye is a magnificent stretch of oaks, ash, wild cherries, maple and beech, at one end of a range of hills and narrow valleys which stretch from the Ardennes to Artois. Streams, springs and ponds cover these slopes, draining into the river systems of northern France. Hedges and ditches interrupt the sweeping plains of the north. The cackling of geese outside a farm suddenly interrupted the sound of silence. This stretch of countryside, from the Ardennes to the towns of the north-west, also deserved the title of the Empty Quarter.

At Rocquigny the material used for building changed from the honey-coloured stone of the Ardennes to red brick. Here I saw the first of the fortified churches of the Thiérache region, built entirely of small red bricks in the seventeenth century. It is a massive construction, with a square keep and two tall round towers at the west end. Arrow slits allowed defenders to fire across the path to the west door.

Next to the rows of undistinguished cottages was something very unusual in these villages, a café which was open. I dumped my rucksack and ordered a large *café au lait* from the burly owner behind the bar. His hair was slicked back and a ginger moustache curled across his upper lip. There were three customers in the café. A man sat next to his wife, a sack of slack flesh hanging in folds over his trousers. Another man in his sixties blew rings of cigarette smoke towards the ceiling. Perfect silence reigned. When I entered the three faces turned and stared blankly at my walking clothes, but said nothing. After a quarter of an hour sipping coffee I plucked up courage and remarked that it was not cold outside.

"Where are you going dressed like that," they asked.

"Parfondeval."

"Uh! It's six miles by the road."

That was all they had to say, so I left.

I joined trail 122 and followed it for around a week across northern France. I was now in the *bocage* of the Thiérache, with more hedges and ditches than elsewhere in the north. The next village, Parfondeval, turned out to be a little gem.

Neat red brick houses surround the village green and the pond. Parfondeval boasts a fortified church also built of small bricks, with two monumental towers either side of the keep. White Renaissance stone work dating from 1547 surrounds the double doorway. A gatehouse and a ditch guard the entrance to the churchyard. In the domed lobby I could see the remains of two staircases leading to the upper storey of the keep.

My host talked about the restoration of his old house. He explained that it was originally built of mud and wood, with some areas filled in with brick. The previous owners had covered the wooden beams with concrete, causing the wood to rot because it could not breathe. He replaced many of the old beams.

Monsieur was a slim old man, who was still vigorous and active. He had been the mayor for eighteen years and on the *conseil municipal* for another ten. When he was not helping his son on the farm he had found time to write a short history of Parfondeval during the Revolution. "My family have worked this land continuously since the time of my great grandfather. Now I have passed the business on to my son. I have seen enormous changes in agriculture. My father's farm was 100 acres. My father and mother worked full-time on it with a dairy maid and a ploughman; four of them in the 1930s. I farmed 150 acres and now my son manages 170 and works entirely alone. We have improved our labour productivity by a factor of seven."

This enormous change had happened since 1945 and particularly since the 1970s. What really shook me was that he was using horses to pull his plough until the mid-seventies. "I introduced automatic milking machines in the 1970s. Before this I milked by hand. You needed supple fists to do that. You also needed a lot of strength to plough with a horse. When farm work was done mainly by hand life was hard. Now we have more leisure time to occupy ourselves with nothing!" he said.

At the back of his house *monsieur* had an astonishing collection of old farm implements and machinery stored in his barns. The biggest had a broad high roof supported by beams. There he kept a four-wheeled cart, some old-fashioned threshing machines and an old harvester. He was proud of these reminders of his life from forty or more years ago.

Our dialogue continued while we sipped his homemade laurel wine. "In my father's day there used to be a lot of smallholdings of 12-15 acres. Now they're being consolidated. Financial incentives are encouraging many farmers to give up. A lot of young people have left for the large towns because there's little alternative employment. It's very quiet in Parfondeval with about 150 people living here. Some Parisians visit their second homes in July and August. A few Dutch and Flemish Belgians own houses. There are lots of retired people. Many used to be farmers, but some arrive from outside. Rural life with few services is difficult. Parfondeval is very remote. There's only one small town in the vicinity. The school bus takes children attending the primary school and *collège* to the next village. If you're good enough to attend a *lycée* you have to go to Laon thirty miles away."

From here the fortified churches came thick and fast. At Jeantes there was an added bonus. Over 4,000 square feet of expressive modern frescoes cover the church walls: contorted limbs and elongated necks. The Virgin floats in a haze of lapis lazuli; the cockerel which accompanied Peter's betrayal of Jesus is full of character. Plomion boasts the largest castle-church of all. The whole village could have taken refuge in the keep. Turrets still project from the north and south transepts.

Plomion Church

Vervins is a draughty town of narrow streets on a hill overlooking the Route Nationale 2. Lorries rumbled underneath the battlements on their way to Belgium. Dust covered the furniture in my hotel and the incongruous cyber café was empty. My room was from a bygone age. Pale blue paper decorated with pink roses covered the walls, while several large mahogany pieces surrounded a marble fireplace. Terraces of red brick cottages, more typical of Flanders, lined the streets. Vervins seemed like a frontier post bypassed by the rush of modern life, despite being the home of the *sous-préfecture* of the Aisne *département*. The Minister of Justice had just decided to close the local court, an indication of Vervins' diminishing status. The young waiter in the hotel looked forlornly out of the window after serving me, his only customer. He came from Guise, fifteen miles away. This was the only job he could find after leaving school. Not a lot of fun, I thought, for a young man living on his own in a quiet provincial town.

The trail led to the valley of the Oise east of Autreppes, where Robert Louis Stevenson finished a canoe journey in 1876, two years before his trek in the Cévennes. I crossed the river to enter Sorbais. Carole and her husband thrust a glass of local cider in my hand as soon as I arrived at their comfortable *chambre d'hôte*. "We moved down from Lille seventeen years ago," she said. "We took early retirement here because our families originated from the Thiérache."

She had a dark tan from a recent holiday in Tunisia. I enquired about the number of visitors she received in this beautiful spot. She told me that business in the main season had been down fifty per cent and promptly launched into a long attack on the policies of Nicolas Sarkozy. "President Bling-Bling does not understand how ordinary people have to struggle," she said.

At dinner they plied me with a sweet sparkling wine followed by red. For the first course we ate a tart covered with the local Maroilles cheese. It had a strong salty taste, was certainly full fat, and made, Carole claimed, out of unpasteurized milk. It also filled the room with a very distinctive odour. While we ate the television was on in the background and I feared for Carole's blood pressure as she exploded at each item of news. We watched fishermen in Brittany demanding a special reduction in the price of petrol to save them from extinction, barristers demonstrating against court reform, students protesting against more independence for universities and public service workers complaining about having to pay more for their pensions. Once the TV was turned off we talked a little about the locality. I remarked that I had seen a lot of sugar beet being harvested in the fields. They said this work was usually done in early November. Although small sugar factories dotted the area, once the EU had removed preference for French beet sugar these would have to close. A sugar plant at Laon was due to shut down shortly.

I left Sorbais on a misty autumn morning with a slight hangover and spent one more day in the forests and small fields of the Thiérache. And then I reached the northern plains; the flat country.

10

FROM LE NORD TO THE CHANNEL
THE FLAT COUNTRY

LE NORD HAS NOT always enjoyed a good image in the rest of France. It is associated with cold weather, grimy industrial cities and beer drinking inside dark cafés. Henri Matisse, who was born in the Nord town of Le Cateau-Cambrésis and is remembered in a museum there, is known for his bright colours, but he fled to the sun to work. Walking around France I met several people from the north who had escaped further south. Northern cuisine, for one thing, is not really French, a favourite dish being the *flamiche*, a little like a pizza and often covered with cheese. Some of the region's inhabitants even speak a distinctive dialect called Ch'ti. The film *Bienvenue chez les Ch'tis* (2008) tells the amusing story of a postmaster from Provence who is sent to a small northern town as a punishment for misconduct. Judging from the reaction of his wife and friends, he could just as well have been sent to Devil's Island, the notorious French penal colony. A gendarme stops him on a motorway for speeding, yet when he discovers that the poor man has been sent to work in Le Nord, he lets him off. In due course the postmaster discovers that life there is not so bad and is eventually reluctant to leave his new friends. A northerner told me that local people are warm-hearted because it is so cold outside.

Le Nord is suffering similar economic problems to Lorraine. At Le Cateau-Cambrésis a local hotelier told me, "Since we came here a textile factory has closed down and four hundred workers have lost their jobs. Another two hundred and forty jobs went when a German-owned company making car interiors reduced their work force." He contrasted the fate of Le Cateau with nearby Valenciennes, which is larger and has the advantage of being on the motorway network. "A member of the government is Mayor of Valenciennes and he is putting a lot of drive into modernising the town."

I discovered later that the government is studying a project to build a test railway track twenty miles long through attractive villages south of the city. It wants to build up Valenciennes as a centre of expertise in locomotive manufacture. Naturally the nimbies (there is no French translation) are protesting. A poster on a gate said, "No to the circular rail track! Not in my garden!" There are signs of economic upheaval in the north-west too. A businessman who lived near Arras told me, "The regional economy has seen enormous changes since the last war. The mines have closed and now textiles have almost gone, undercut by competition from China. Steel making struggles on near Dunkerque. New

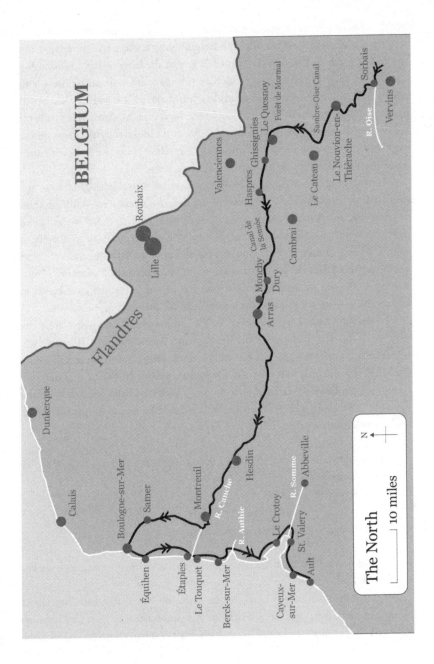

wealth is coming from computer software, tourism and car manufacturing."

The Cambrésis is an industrialised region which takes its name from the city of Cambrai. At Catillon-sur-Sambre I joined the bank of the Sambre-Oise Canal, a 44-mile stretch of water which Stevenson paddled down on his way to Sorbais. The enormous square in Catillon was deserted. I huddled on a bench to eat my baguette and then saw a light in the local café. Madame was sitting on her own by the bar, smoking and trying to finish a Sudoku puzzle. "Most people work in Le Cateau or Cambrai," she said. "Very few boats use the canal these days. There are plenty of fishermen but not much else."

Approaching Ors the water level in the canal was a lot higher than the surrounding fields. A deep ditch beyond the dyke formed a second line of flood defence. The meadows beyond were full of cattle and surrounded by pollarded trees. Every year long thin branches, like spiky hair, are cut back to a bulbous stump. I tried to talk over the sound of a chainsaw to a young man pruning one of the rows. He said he had this job to do every autumn. Pollarding is now starting to die out. It used to be characteristic of wet lands and river banks in France and provided a valuable source of wood for fuel.

I reached Ors on 9 November 2007, almost exactly 89 years after the advance of the 32nd Division of the British Army across the canal. The date was 4 November and the Armistice was only a week away. In the battle to capture the bridge by the lock four Victoria Crosses were won. It was on that day too, about half a mile north of here, that the poet Wilfred Owen was killed on the towpath. The Western Front Association has erected a memorial plaque by the bridge, which contains these lines by Owen.

Let my death be memoried on this disc.
Wear it, sweet friend.
Inscribe no date nor deed.
But let thy heart-beat kiss it night and day,
Until the name grow vague and wear away.

I measured half a mile on my map and stopped at an appropriate spot on the canal bank for a minute's perfect silence.

Next morning I took a track in the Forêt de Mormal, which ran ahead in a never-ending straight line. Blocks of flats lined the way into Le Quesnoy, followed by the massive ramparts and ditch of Vauban's fortress, one of the most important on the northern frontier. Le Quesnoy looked like a threadbare suit which needed a clean. After peering up at the eighteenth-century belfry an unusual mural attracted my attention: a scene on the New Zealand coast with a Maori, a nun and a Kiwi bird. Underneath the biggest rampart on the other side of town I found a memorial garden. On 4 November 1918 the New Zealanders stormed Le Quesnoy by scaling the sheer face of the walls on ladders, an amazing exploit against hostile fire from above. Beyond this rampart is a network of ditches and two big lakes. Le Quesnoy looked like an island surrounded by a marsh.

The muck of agriculture covered Ghissignies, but it had plenty of smart houses. In a rural lane wide drives ran through well-groomed lawns to big picture windows. In Ghissignies incomes are one-third higher than the national average but in Le Quesnoy twenty per cent below. According to a local, city folk are repopulating some villages near Valenciennes, but this trend creates social divisions as villages are abandoned during the day to the old and a few young families.

Heavy skies covered the immense plain like a pall. The trail took me on a series of ancient cobbled tracks through sodden fields. It was Sunday and city workers were taking their weekend exercise jogging or cycling. Groups of men wandered the fields shooting at anything they fancied. Diamond patterns of red and black bricks decorated cottage walls. Farmhouses stood at right angles to the street.

I got caught in heavy rain twice during the morning, the second time as I approached Haspres across a bleak plateau of open farmland. I trudged into the village dripping wet, looking for a café which also served food. No such luck. In desperation I selected an establishment which only sold alcoholic drinks, not even coffee. As I came through the door the eyes of all inside swivelled through ninety degrees to stare at me in silence for what seemed like an eternity. I must have looked like an apparition, with water streaming off my waterproofs, rucksack and two walking sticks. At last, one of the men said, "It's not the season for doing the St. Jacques pilgrimage!"

I struggled to get my wet layer off while people and dogs pushed past. *Madame la patronne* behind the bar was very grumpy. No doubt I had lowered the tone for her regular customers. Very reluctantly she gave me a small plate of sliced sausage and nuts to nibble with a brown Leffe. Veterans were enjoying a few drinks after the Armistice Day procession. One old soldier wearing his medals struggled on crutches, while a man standing alone was dressed like a bandmaster in a blue uniform with red lanyards and a pill box cap. When he discovered I was British he suggested visiting one of the two British cemeteries where members of the York Regiment were buried after the battle in October 1918. He said that they had once entertained the descendants of the British soldiers who lost their lives.

The café culture in the north in winter is quite different from the south, mainly because customers have to sit inside. Many of the *estaminets*, as they are called here, are really drinking dens aimed at working-class men. My dictionary defines them as *petits cafés populaires*, which just about sums up the establishment at Haspres.

Along the Canal de la Sensée I encountered a landscape typical of Le Nord: the wharves, the curving lines of the banks, the chugging of long barges, the flat open fields on either side, the screens of trees, but above all the light of a wide open sky reflecting off the water. Large ponds enclosed by dense undergrowth line the canal. Here small huts on stilts provide an escape from urban living in a leisure landscape that is replacing the industrial past. As I left the canal, the sun set across the plain of Artois ahead.

There are no better words to describe this northern landscape than those of Jacques Brel, a Belgian but one of France's most popular singers. He bites on his words as fiercely as the north wind. Here is his song *Le plat pays*, the flat country.

> With a sky so low that a canal gets lost
> With a sky so low that it makes obeisance
> With a sky so low that a canal has hanged itself
> With a sky so low that it must be forgiven
> With the north wind which blasts in all directions
> Listen to it crack.
> The flat land which is mine.

ARTOIS

In total, 1,884 British soldiers and 173 Canadians are buried in Dury, casualties of the final British offensive in the autumn of 1918. In the gathering dusk it was poignant to see so many headstones with the simple inscription "a soldier of the Great War." I stayed the night in an old farmhouse called l'Abbaye des Quinze. In fact, it was rebuilt after the First World War because virtually all the houses were destroyed around here during the British advance. Next morning the open ground rose and fell like a swell on the ocean, until I reached the ridge where Monchy-Le-Preux stands overlooking Arras. For the British this town is famous because of the battle fought here in April 1917. The soil is chalky and it must have stuck to the Tommies' boots as they fought their way uphill under German fire. Monchy was as far as the Allies got that April. It was not until 1918 that they penetrated all the way to Dury. I had walked the distance in two and a half hours.

After crossing the motorway and TGV line to Paris, the next sight was a panorama of muddy fields stacked with sugar beets. Factories and warehouses ran along their southern edge and the high-rise apartment blocks of Arras marked the far horizon. I stopped at a small walled enclosure called Bunyans where fifty British soldiers were buried after the 1917 offensive. It was a mournful scene, grey and overcast. I imagined the desolation of the battlefield, with the chatter of machine gun fire and the whining of shells.

The majestic gables of the Grand' Place in Arras rippled away from me, like the tail of a kite in a strong wind. Scrolls and pillars spoke of solid Flemish prosperity: merchants, markets, and fine cloth. Squinting into the sun in the arcaded Place des Héros, I managed to stare up at the massive belfry above the Renaissance town hall. It looked like a tiered wedding cake. A watchman at the top would have warned the citizens of an approaching army. In the sixteenth century Arras had wealth worth protecting. It was not part of France, but belonged politically to the Low Countries, the richest corner of early modern Europe. The narrow streets are damp and dark, but secret courtyards hide elegant town houses of a past age, like the Hôtel de Guines painted in canary yellow. Near the white classical façade of the theatre is a sombre side street where Maximilien Robespierre lived before he went to Paris in 1789. In the eighteenth century Arras was a town where new ideas were discussed and grand building projects undertaken. I came across the huge classical Abbaye St.-Vaast from this period, now housing the Musée des Beaux-Arts. It was completely out of scale for a town of such modest proportions, as if the Louvre had come to Artois. From a distance the Musée looked imposing, but close up you could see its stonework was crumbling, as if pockmarked with bullet holes. Arras still has the air of a town which has not recovered from two wars: façades streaked with industrial grime, concrete and plaster encroaching on the elegant brick. The streets seemed to have gone to sleep in the eighteenth century and never fully

Place des Héros, Arras

reawakened in the twentieth.

In Artois I came across farmyards entered by an arched gateway off the street and churches of white stone, with stocky towers supported by stout buttresses. Small ponds appeared enclosed by dykes and soon the tell-tale sound of quacking echoed round the woods. Rearing ducks for shooting must be a major pastime in this region of France. The River Canche flows north-west for forty miles into the sea at Étaples, passing Hesdin and Montreuil. Ivy covered trees and tumbledown barns, clumps of hazel sprouted in boggy woods and broken water wheels languished by stagnant mill streams.

A desert of ploughed earth covered the plateau. Factory-fields stretched for several miles, without hedges or fences. Only the faint outlines of the next village broke the horizon, with a stark concrete water tower completing the picture. Most of these were built after the Second World War because in 1945 only thirty per cent of rural homes had piped water. In this area farms are grouped in villages and farmers go out to work in fields some distance away. I passed through a series of sad settlements where the prevailing impression was one of poverty and neglect.

Fabrice and Mireille had a number of permanent guests at their house, French people working in the area on a temporary basis. There was a company director, a teacher, a young jewellery maker and the manager of the fish counter at the local Intermarché supermarket in St.-Pol. For him everything was a catastrophe, including business in the hypermarkets. He wanted to work in Belgium, but not in England where life was too "precarious." French politics were also a catastrophe. He had a pot belly and munched his way through a bowl of pasta.

Next morning a skylark in full song kept me company. The war memorial on a village green included a statuette of the Virgin, a replica of a medieval carving which used to stand on the spot. Overt religious imagery is unusual on war memorials in France with its secular tradition in public life. The north, however, has a strong Catholic tradition and I passed many private shrines to the Virgin. One statue of her stood next to a praying figure giving thanks for twenty-two cures granted at Lourdes between 1936 and 1984. I could not help thinking that this Virgin looked like a china figurine in a souvenir shop. Holiness is in the eye of the beholder.

Vieil-Hesdin, some three miles short of the modern town of Hesdin, was on the front line of the struggle between the Habsburgs and the French kings. The

French managed to seize this Imperial fortress, but in 1553 Charles V's army fought back in a war which became merciless and brutal. After this episode the town of Hesdin was rebuilt on today's site, but still under the emperor's control. Pavement cafés are, of course, one of the great pleasures of life in France, and what better way to study the old buildings of Hesdin than while drinking a beer in the sunshine? Squinting across the Place d'Armes I made out another belfry towering above the town hall. The watchman must have frozen two hundred feet up on wintry nights, looking for a French army, so out of consideration the builders provided a small lodge to keep him warm. The church is a fine example of sixteenth-century Flemish architecture and a strange mixture of styles. Branches and foliage, characteristic of late Gothic, decorate the twenty-three windows with their rich stained glass. Yet the doorway is a magnificent Renaissance construction, with its coffered Roman arch and Corinthian pillars. There are four coats of arms on top including the Habsburg eagle of Imperial Spain.

Next morning I forgot about history and got on with the practical business of finding provisions for a twenty-mile walk. I bought a delicious slice of terrine, but squashing it into an overloaded rucksack did not add to its appeal. Placing a baguette on top of a sack is tricky. If you wedge it under the top flap it is liable to strike passers by on either side, so better to break it in half.

After the old beech woods above Hesdin the bleak plateaux started again, even today a forbidding environment in which to work in all weathers. The prevailing tones were brown and grey and I imagined armies of peasants tilling the earth in wind and rain long ago. The Canche and its tributaries dissect these chalk plateaux, creating valleys where most of the villages lie. Georges Bernanos evoked the atmosphere of this region in his novel *Sous le soleil de Satan* (1926), in which an anguished priest fights his lone spiritual struggle. The film version won the Grand Prix at Cannes in 1987. He refers several times to the immense plains. This empty countryside takes on an eerie supernatural quality in the darkness:

"He was standing alone, facing the darkness, as if on the prow of a ship. The great dark wave rolled around him making a superhuman sound. The invisible fields and woods came rushing towards him from the four corners of the horizon. And behind the fields and woods, other villages and little towns, all the same, bursting with plenty, hostile to the impoverished, full of hunched-up old skinflints, icy as winding sheets."

Bending double I squeezed through a tunnel in the massive walls which surround Montreuil. The main fortress has a commanding view over the valley below and the ramparts stretch right round the town, enclosing its squares and narrow streets in a tight grip. The millions of red bricks were first laid by Louis XI in the fifteenth century, but it was Vauban who established Montreuil as one of the twenty-six forts shielding the northern frontier. The Canche brushes its walls and then flows through a marshy landscape towards the sea. I was now only twelve miles from the Channel.

*

Christmas was approaching and I decided to go home for a rest. Speeding down the M40 to Oxford on the bus I thought about the 2,400 miles I had covered since leaving the Pyrenees. I was well over half way with roughly 1,600 miles left. Psychologically this was a boost.

Lizzie met me at the Park and Ride. "Well which one are you going to visit first, your father or your mother? What are we going to do about Christmas? I suppose we must have your father to stay as your mother came last year. Will you go and see her on Christmas Day?"

I replied in the affirmative. In over twenty years of marriage we have always tried to be fair; mother one year, father the next. Both my parents were living on their own, immobile and with no other friends or family to invite them. The negotiations became more complicated than usual. I acted like a peacemaker engaged in shuttle diplomacy. It was agreed that I would collect my father from Hornchurch. On Christmas Day I would drive over to my mother's and cook her lunch, returning to eat another Christmas meal with my father and Lizzie in the evening.

I was concerned about how much longer he would be able to live on his own. He never made an effort to meet other people, although perfectly happy to be agreeable if they came to him. In retirement his main passion was playing bridge—several times a week if possible. Like his father he always had a pile of books by his chair and read his way through the local library A-Z. When he ran out of new classical CDs he turned on the television and watched snooker, a bizarre contrast with his normal tastes.

Then he gave up bridge because his memory started to fail. Gradually he became a complete recluse, only talking to me and one or two neighbours. Every suggestion of more social contact met with a blank stare. His clothes were thirty years old and several sizes too big for him. The curtains were torn and encrusted with black dirt. Stuffing grew out of his armchair like a fungus. All the tiles on the kitchen floor were loose. Every surface was covered with papers and copies of the New Statesman, which the Cudbirds had read since the 1930s. Empty bottles and old suits filled the cupboards. He would not let me disturb anything. More serious were the large cracks appearing in the walls at the back of the house. Our exchange on this subject was typical of so many others.

"I think you may have subsidence. Look at those cracks in the walls."

"There have never been any problems like that around here."

When the neighbour told him about his own subsidence problems my father called a surveyor. "If only he had taken action earlier," I thought to myself. His reaction was the same to every other issue Lizzie and I mentioned. Later that year he had an attack of shingles which affected one of his eyes. In his usual stubborn fashion he refused treatment. "I don't believe in taking medicines."

"Well this time you are going to. Get in my car and come to the hospital. I am not going to let you lose your eye sight."

Years of playing competitive tennis and badminton in his youth had resulted in crippling arthritis in his hips and knees. I knew an operation was out of the question but suggested an extra hand rail on the stairs to lessen the risk of a fall.

"No."

It was like a mantra. Lizzie and I heard an advertising slogan on one of our trips to see him. "Stop saying no; start saying yes."

We both burst into hysterical laughter and tried to make this into a joke when we saw Peter. Inevitably it fell on deaf ears.

Before setting off to collect my father I phoned a traffic information service and held my breath. "Junction 19 to Junction 25 slow moving traffic; journey time 45 minutes longer than normal. Junction 27 to 29 slow moving traffic: journey time 11 minutes longer than normal."

On the return journey worse was to come. Snow started falling at Watford. By the time we reached the Chilterns it was a blizzard. Gradually the traffic ground to a halt. We sat for three hours with the engine off getting colder and colder. My father was desperate to go to the toilet. Eventually the snow eased and we moved forward slowly, reaching Oxford at 10 p.m. Lizzie looked at me and we both had the same thought. For how much longer would we have to make this journey?

When I saw my mother over Christmas she seemed more confused than before and struggled to cope with everyday life. She ate mainly cold food and found dressing and getting out of a chair difficult. She tried to walk to the communal lounge but did not make it very often. The other residents were kind but few of them were kindred spirits. Increasingly her life revolved around medical appointments. On the plus side she could make eyes at two handsome men, an eye surgeon and a physiotherapist. I took her in her wheelchair to the hairdressers where she came alive talking to the young stylists dressed in the latest fashions. She had few contacts locally. Old friends from far afield kept in touch but inevitably she spent long hours staring out of the window at the passing traffic. Every time an old man in a terraced cottage opposite came out of his front door she would say:

"What's he doing now?"

She started to make up stories about his life, but she never met him.

SAND AND SHINGLE: THE CHANNEL

The outskirts of Boulogne lie on hills reminiscent of the South Downs. When the sun appeared from behind the clouds it threw a garish light on the ugly jumble of concrete sprawling over the slopes ahead. I crossed the A16 motorway and marched past a large hospital into an industrial estate.

The atmosphere was thick with smoke in the bar opposite. There were three customers on this quiet Sunday afternoon, apart from the couple running the establishment. One man wearing an old cap was propped up on a bar stool. Every time he smiled you could see that half his teeth were missing. He was already very well oiled with *pastis* and slurred his words. I must have looked like a man from the moon with my rucksack, stick and walking clothes. Once I had finished a beer and sandwich they could not restrain their curiosity any longer.

"What are you doing here?"

"I am walking around France."

They raised their eyebrows as if they thought I was mad.

"Are you a soldier?"

"No," I replied, "retired!"

"Do you really do this for pleasure?"

"Is there anything going on in Boulogne?" I asked.

The answer was slow in coming. "Not much."

One person in four is out of work in Boulogne.

"The introduction of the euro has put up prices," they complained. "Our salaries aren't keeping pace."

Napoleon's column, Boulogne

This got us onto politics. They were obviously pretty discontented with all their leaders. I noticed that the TV was turned off when some election coverage appeared on the screen. "All politicians are useless," one of them said. "Why should we bother to vote at all?"

Then they turned on the English. "Why are you so sceptical about Europe and why haven't you adopted the euro?"

I tried to explain some economic arguments about setting our own interest rates and made a hash of it. They looked unconvinced. They thought the English were conservative Eurosceptics and were equally suspicious of the United States. "The USA has been making war on everyone ever since they dealt with the Indians in North America!" said the old man on the stool.

Among some Frenchmen there is a strong streak of anti-Anglo-Saxon sentiment. Their politicians play up to it by regularly criticising market reforms as Anglo-Saxon. Our little debate was all very amicable, however. I shook hands with everyone round the bar, before leaving on my mission to find a dead Frenchman who also had no great love for the English, the Emperor Napoleon.

He stands on top of a column, about as high as Nelson's, set on a hillside north of Boulogne. Below is a magnificent view of the coast towards the white cliffs of Cap Gris Nez south of Calais. The English coast traces a faint line across the horizon. King Louis-Philippe authorised the column's construction a year after transferring Napoleon's mortal remains to the Invalides. It commemorates the first awards of the Légion d'Honneur, not a planned invasion of England, yet you cannot help noticing that Napoleon, in his inimitable greatcoat and cocked hat, has his back to the Channel. Perhaps he is looking towards future conquests on the Continent and muttering about the tiresome English.

I was now at one corner of my journey around the hexagon. Turning south to walk downhill to the old city of Boulogne, I lost my way in a maze of empty streets with dirty houses and council flats painted pink, grey and blue, where the appearance of the passers-by suggested a hasty exit might be prudent. The old city, on the other hand, with its walls, narrow streets and old houses, had charm and character. The cathedral looked like a smaller version of St Paul's. Inevitably old Boulogne also had a belfry; another to add to my collection

A city banker once told me that any budding entrepreneur has to pass the wet Monday morning test. Are you sufficiently motivated to get up early on a miserable Monday morning and get stuck in? This was the challenge ahead. I decided to lighten my load for the long walk to Étaples by calling in at the post office and sending some things back home. The clerk asked me to fill in a form specifying what should be done if the parcel could not be delivered. I looked puzzled. "I am posting it to myself," I said.

"Presumably *monsieur* knows where he lives, so we will mark the parcel for destruction if it cannot be delivered, because such an eventuality is impossible!"

It was too early to follow this impeccable Gallic logic.

The coast path started off through the fishing port, which meant walking past a never-ending row of loading bays designed for refrigerated lorries. The old Hoverport lay abandoned, a monument to rapid changes in transport technology. What is the point of battling on top of the waves when you can fly to France for the price of a cappuccino? The character of the coastline now changed radically from cliffs to dunes dotted with pine woods, which continue to the Bay of the Somme. At Équihen my plans for the day went completely wrong. Surging waves at high tide covered the coast path along the beach. I must have been stupid not to have thought of this possibility. Clearly the seaside route to Étaples was a write-off, and there was nothing for it but to scramble over the dunes. Climbing in sand is hard work.

I was now near the beginning of the Atlantic Wall, a system of coastal fortifications which the Germans built all the way to the Spanish border. I came across the ruins of these bunkers and artillery emplacements almost every day I was on the coast. Much of it was built by slave labour from occupied countries. Just after Équihen the footpath was named the Jews' Way, in memory of thousands of Jewish workers who suffered and died in appalling conditions.

Étaples is a modest town of small cottages and closely knit streets which are dark and draughty at night. My host and his three brothers had owned a fishing smack for twenty-five years. He proudly showed me the picture. "I used to fish the Channel right over to the English coast and up as far as the Belgian border. We caught sole and cod but had to give up."

He explained that fish stocks had fallen and the European Union had imposed quotas. Also petrol had become very expensive. He realised that fishermen were having a difficult time everywhere in Europe, but the Spanish were better off than most because fishing had more electoral weight there. "France has a magnificent coastline and 11,000 fishermen, but the French government doesn't care about them. Their numbers are falling every day."

So now he runs a bed and breakfast and also works as a guide in a new museum dedicated to the history of fishing. The local fishing community has started other enterprises. A top quality fish restaurant on the quay called *Aux Pêcheurs d'Étaples* also has a branch in Boulogne.

As I walked along the dyke separating Le Touquet airport from the Canche estuary the sky turned black as night. Hail stones clattered on my umbrella, but as long as I faced the icy south-westerly it did not blow inside out. The storm had emptied the tidy streets of Le Touquet. A waterlogged golf course succeeded rows of neat villas with immaculate lawns. Passing four-by-fours sprayed me with dirty water. Their occupants looked askance as I huddled in a bus shelter for a cold picnic.

The River Authie is the border of the Somme *département* and here the character of the landscape changed yet again. The fields surrounded by drainage ditches contain alluvial soil providing rich grazing for cattle. I followed tracks on top of a succession of dykes. Isolated farmsteads replaced the clusters of farm buildings in the villages of Artois. A single-storey farmhouse dating from 1775 with a tall steep roof offered bed and breakfast. Enormous barns enclosed a farmyard the size of a football pitch. Apparently it used to contain a big pond for watering cattle.

The husband and wife were in their fifties and two of their sons also worked on the farm. Farmers can be reserved and this couple were no exception. The large fireplace, oak table and tiled floor in the dimly lit dining room suggested a Spartan existence. No doubt they worked hard and felt remote from the big cities. Small talk with an eccentric English visitor who insisted on walking everywhere was probably irksome.

"I have eighty milking cows," said *monsieur*, "and others for beef. I grow cereals somewhere else. Agriculture is our biggest exporter but the French government doesn't care."

My surprised expression did not stop his sudden flow. "Prices are too low. We only receive thirty cents a litre for milk. The hypermarkets pay us a pittance."

Monsieur and *madame* seemed reasonably well informed about English agriculture. They had once stayed on a farm in Sussex which was diversifying into non-agricultural activities. This persuaded them to start *chambres d'hôtes* and now they were busy all summer. The new A16 motorway down the coast meant that Paris was only two hours away. They welcomed many stressed Parisians who wanted to relax.

The shore of the Bay of the Somme is forty miles long and merges imperceptibly with the sea. On the far side the church towers of St.-Valery-sur-

Somme seemed to rise straight out of the water. This was a vision of infinity, the sun bouncing off a huge area of sea, dazzling my eyes. When mudflats appeared in the early evening I was disappointed to hear that the guide across the bay had cancelled his trip for the next day. I was not foolhardy enough to try it on my own, particularly when a lady told me at breakfast that she had sunk up to her thighs, even with a guide.

A massive dyke runs around a reservoir, which stores up water draining off the fields before releasing it periodically into the sea. Although St.-Valery is only two and a half miles from Le Crotoy as the crow flies, I had to walk eight miles round the bay. The salt marshes provide excellent grazing for sheep, their flesh supposedly given a unique flavour by salt resistant plants. These marshes also serve as killing fields for duck and migrating sea birds. Specially constructed grassy knolls have slit openings for wild fowlers' guns and shooting hides stand on pontoons anchored on the sea bed. The River Somme becomes a canal at Abbeville before flowing into the sea at St.-Valery. Now only fishing boats and pleasure craft use the port. The tide raced in across the mudflats and swept up the canal mouth within ten minutes.

The countryside between St.-Valery and Cayeux-sur-Mer is a characterless void in which few landmarks break the monotony of level fields and drainage ditches. Navigation is difficult without signposts. I followed the map very carefully, counting the number of turnings to left or right before changing direction.

The meal at the only restaurant open in Cayeux started with *ficelle picarde,* a pancake filled with mushrooms and ham and swimming in cream. The *choucroute* with fish was healthier, but followed by banana ice cream in another pancake covered in hot chocolate sauce. All this followed omelette and chips for lunch and mussels and chips the night before. In the dairy country of the north-west everything seemed to be floating in cream or fat.

The view of Cayeux from the back had not been inspiring; a crane, a tall radio mast, industrial sheds, a church tower and scattered modern villas. In the murk to the south the outline of higher land appeared. A long east-west ridge several hundred feet high came to an abrupt end where white cliffs dropped into the sea. This was the beginning of the chalk plateau of Upper Normandy.

11

NORMANDY
CHALK, CHEESE AND CIDER

I HAD BEEN TRAMPING down the coast for five days. Ahead lay what the French sometimes call Le Grand Ouest, an arc of *départements* stretching from Normandy down to Bordeaux. This was the first time I had walked along the French coastline, having avoided the beaches of the Languedoc and the Côte d'Azur. Inevitably the coast was much more developed than the mountains and empty plains I had already crossed. The populations of all these *départements* have grown substantially in recent years, mostly at the expense of the older industrial areas to the north and east. Retired people have moved in, as well as young families seeking work in new industries and a more pleasant environment to bring up their children. I discovered a less exotic aspect of modern France: hotels, holiday villas, tourist attractions, new roads and bridges, nuclear power stations, oil terminals, industrial estates. A visitor among so many other visitors, I found it more difficult to form a rapport with the local inhabitants. In Le Grand Ouest I had to create a different journey of discovery.

WALKING IN NORMANDY

I do not remember my trek in Normandy as particularly beautiful or challenging. There was too much road walking and often my knees begged for mercy. If every day was not packed with adventure or interest, I was at least always busy as I wrote copious notes and took hundreds of photographs. Here is an example of my undigested observations on a day in Normandy. "Path along flat fields by cliff often indistinct. Rough grass, ploughed earth, poor waymarking. Turn left over fence down track to Penly. School: posters in window: *non à la fermeture, école occupée*. Back on road again; go around huge electricity generating plant. Massive pylons and compound of offices. 5.30p.m. tired. Sit on park bench in St.-Martin-en-Campagne. Amazing change from previous villages. Well laid out public garden. Large monument with a quote from Gandhi about need for tolerance. Bed and breakfast with retired couple in old house. My room has green flowered wallpaper and orange bed spread. Brown floral curtains. *Monsieur* and *madame* invite me into living room for beer and slices of tart. They watch TV quiz show. He has given up farming. Glad not to have to get up to milk cows any more."

Normandy did have its attractions and sometimes I was given a very hospitable reception. Pierre and Séverine had moved from Alsace to renovate

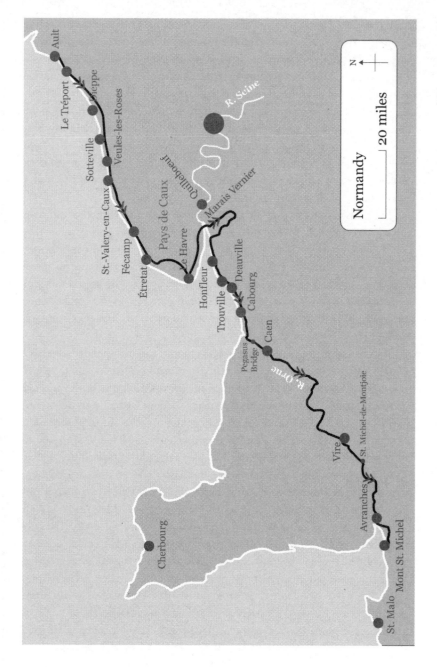

Normandy

20 miles

Ault
Le Tréport
Dieppe
Sotteville
Veules-les-Roses
St.-Valery-en-Caux
Fécamp
Étretat
Pays de Caux
Quillebœuf
R. Seine
Marais Vernier
Le Havre
Honfleur
Trouville
Deauville
Cabourg
Pegasus Bridge
Caen
R. Orne
Vire
St. Michel-de-Montjoie
Avranches
Cherbourg
Mont St. Michel
St. Malo

185

an old Norman farmhouse and start a *chambres d'hôte* which offered stabling for horses. They wanted to escape the extremes of the continental climate as Normandy is mild in comparison. Both spoke some Alsatian. Pierre was a professional chef and we certainly enjoyed a hearty Alsatian meal around the kitchen table: onion and bacon tart, a huge stew with everything in it, cheese and clafoutis made with pears and apples. It might have been a little heavy on the stomach but no doubt contained enough calories to keep me marching onwards. It also soaked up the liberal supply of alcohol. After two aperitifs Séverine kept opening bottles of red wine. I lost count of how many as the conversation became more and more animated. We also tasted a twelve-year-old Calvados liqueur made on a local farm. It seemed to be very strong.

The riding group staying the same night were surprised that an old man with a pack could walk twenty miles in a day, when they were only covering that distance on horseback. Conversation was treated as an opportunity for repartee and jokes at each other's expense. The only intellectual flashpoint was when one of the women, a *lycée* teacher of history from Blois, attacked the role of the USA in the Second World War, claiming that in reality the Americans had not done so much to liberate France—after all they had only joined in halfway through the conflict.

The chief comic was a man whose close-cropped hair incorporated a number of totally bald strips around the back of his neck and semicircular patterns above his temples. Two diamond studs adorned his left ear. He came from Paris and Séverine thought a Parisian hairdresser could have done a better job. He did not take offence, but said he had his hair cut like this purely because it pleased him. Elaborate tattoos covered his arms. Séverine asked why he did not have a stud in his tongue: had he thought of having it divided surgically to make him look like a Gothic vampire? The suggestion was followed by gales of drunken laughter. There were three other women in the party, all young. One was a plump and jolly Toulousaine who giggled and rolled her eyes at everything that was said. As the evening wore on there was more and more sexual innuendo. The *lycée* teacher asked whether English women talked like this too and I assured her they were no different when they had finished a bottle of Chardonnay. Next morning I had a hangover, but discovered that our hard-drinking cavaliers had stayed up until 4.30a.m. No wonder they departed quietly. The Toulousaine winked from beneath a broad-brimmed felt hat and wished me *bon courage*.

The accommodation at the next village provided a stark contrast. I passed the night on my own in a hostel owned by the *commune*, which was situated on a housing estate. The bare tiles of the cavernous rooms echoed to my footsteps and the temperature was freezing. But at least the electric stove worked so I switched on the oven and opened the door to create a pool of warmth in the kitchen. A small local restaurant and bar had offered to provide me with a meal, but the reception was frosty. It seemed that the owners also managed the hostel for the *mairie*. When I asked if they had any visitors, *monsieur* said "only walkers" with a sneer. A handful of local farmers propped up the bar, flushed with wind and alcohol. I was thrown a piece of dry pizza, a slab of ham steak, some cheese and an ice cream from the fridge.

Most British buying properties in France want a holiday home, but some decide to settle with their families. It was not a complete surprise therefore to find an English pub at Le Petit-Celland near Avranches run by Miles and Jackie from Newbury. When I went in to enquire about an evening meal, Miles was behind the bar pulling pints in an England rugby shirt and watching a match on the television. "We came out two years ago and won't go back now. Lots of English settlers give up after a few years. I like the space for my children and don't worry so much whether they are safe or not. I don't get as many aggressive drunks in the pub as in England. Bureaucracy and the level of taxes in France are a pain if you are running a business, but the pub is breaking even, which surprises me in a village with so many old people. I stay open late and have lots of video games, so the young come here. Most of my customers are French."

I wondered how well he and Jackie integrated into the community, as they spoke very little French and had not so far made the effort to learn. The local French vet dropped in for a drink with his girlfriend, but he spoke good English. It was different for the children. Miles' eldest daughter worked in Paris, while his youngest went to the *collège* in Avranches and was much more confident in the language.

NORMAN LANDSCAPES

Normandy certainly has enough unusual geographical features to maintain the walker's interest, starting with the chalk cliffs which run one hundred miles from Ault to Le Havre. In his novel *Pierre et Jean* Guy de Maupassant talks about "a tall cliff running straight, jagged, cut out like a printer's die, proud, a huge white defensive wall, in which every indentation hides a village or a port." The open downland often drops straight over the edge which is subject to constant landslips. The novelist captures exactly the appearance of the small valleys which run down to the coast: "a small sloping valley, which ran down from the village towards the cliff. The latter rose eighty metres above the sea. The grassy slopes framed a triangle of sea in the distance, silver-blue in the sunshine, and a sailing boat on its surface looked like an insect." Unfortunately, however, the trail did not hug the cliffs for long distances.

The best place to see the coastline is Étretat, where Maupassant had a villa and which Monet made famous all over the world. His imagination turned the cliff into a kaleidoscope of colour and shifting light, but the weather on my visit was more prosaic and the predominant tones white and grey. The sea has created two great arches through the cliff, the first of these slender and Gothic, almost French in appearance, the second rounded and rugged, more English in character.

Étretat

Inland lies a chalk plateau known as the Pays de Caux. Serge, a retired teacher, explained to me the origins of the word Caux. "In the patois, which my grandmother used to speak, the 'ch' as in 'achat', purchase, was a hard 'k' not a soft sound. Therefore the word for chalk, chaux, was pronounced as caux, hence the Pays de Caux, country of chalk."

A thin layer of clay topsoil in the open fields covers solid chalk below and it is greasy to walk on when wet. The plough turns up flints with every furrow. Serge explained some aspects of the local geology. "Water drains through the soil and creates large natural holes in the porous chalk, known as *bétoires*. They are dotted all over this part of Normandy. There are also pits dug by farmers to extract lime. There might be one large hole with a number of galleries running off it. These are known as *marnières*. Some of the older *bétoires* and *marnières* are marked on maps, but many are not. The plateau of the Pays de Caux is like a gruyère cheese, full of holes. They can create a problem when you buy a house. Before we moved to Gonneville we tried to buy a house near Fécamp. We had to withdraw at the last minute because a ground survey revealed a large hole underground, within thirty metres of the property."

On the south bank of the Seine rain lashed my face driven by a gale. The river is over five hundred yards wide as it approaches its estuary. The path descends into boggy land right at the water's edge. I realised with alarm that the river could easily burst its banks and sweep me away in an avalanche of water. The Vernier marsh stretched for five miles on my left, so there was not much security in that direction. Beyond the marsh a crescent of limestone hills reaches almost to the river at the Point de la Roque. I rushed along in the mud as fast as I could and breathed a sigh of relief when I reached higher ground.

The Marais Vernier is the largest peat bog in France. The Seine used to meander under the encompassing hills, but has long since changed course. Henry IV engaged Dutch engineers to drain the marsh in the early seventeenth century and subsequently their polders were extended to the river bank. Agriculture has never prospered here and now the marsh is part of a regional park within which is an important nature reserve. This unique habitat faces a number of threats, however. The withdrawal of EU and government funding has caused a financial crisis and, in addition, lakes and water channels are silting up, partly because of greater use of phosphates and nitrates to enrich the poor soil.

Lower Normandy south of the Seine is quite different. Approaching Honfleur I passed through a landscape of beech and horse chestnut woods, apple orchards, scattered farms and small fields. South of Honfleur the Bois de Breuil is thick and lush in the almost frost-free climate by the coast. Once beyond Trouville the cliffs disappear and sand takes over, stretching all the way to the D-Day beaches. Behind the dunes west of Cabourg is a reclaimed marsh, a featureless expanse of meadows intersected by drainage channels.

The way out of Caen was to follow the River Orne along the quays near the station. Two pretty young girls saw me striding along with my rucksack and umbrella sticking up behind. They shouted, "How many kilometres?"

"About twenty-five," I replied.

"Not bad," came back with much giggling.

Clearly I was old enough to be their grandfather.

*

Just then my mobile emitted a short bleep. It was a text from Lizzie.

"Mother fell out of bed last night. Ambulance came. She's OK for the moment."

*

The *bocage* of lower Normandy south of Caen is the famous region of hedges and small fields which frustrated the Allies after D-Day. Beyond Vire lies countryside typical of this landscape: bracken, oak and beech, hedgerows, pastures, streams and narrow dells. I noticed granite everywhere as I walked along: wall slabs, gateposts, wayside crosses and even a medieval jousting post. The Granite Way led to the village of St.-Michel-de-Montjoie, passing by huge blocks of the stone known locally as *boeufs* or *baleines*. Granite blocks, with earth piled on top to form an embankment, enclose the fields. Now there is insufficient labour to repair these banks every year.

The path around the Baie du Mont-St.-Michel is marked on the French maps as the Sentier du Littoral but is actually a long way from open water. Vast salt marshes surround the river estuaries and the bay, which silted up over the centuries, allowing the mudflats to dry out and salt resistant grasses to grow. It is a featureless landscape so that under heavy cloud I lost all sense of time and scale. At low tide the salt marshes run out in a sea of oozing sand. Walking across the bay is dangerous without a guide who knows the tides and the location of quicksands.

As I walked along I studied the local architecture as well as the landscape. The style of buildings in Normandy is distinctive and heavily influenced by available materials. On my first day in the province I passed a barn with walls of plaster between a framework of exposed wooden beams. Houses built in this way line the old streets of many towns, while thatched cottages in a similar style surround the Marais Vernier. Plants grow along the ridges helping to bind the roof together. These buildings must look fairly authentic because French TV decided to film a Guy de Maupassant nineteenth-century serial in one of them. One long narrow cottage had a roof like an outsize hat, sprouting from the brim. This style is so popular that builders of new homes have used a pastiche version in their developments, sometimes economising on construction costs by fixing wooden beams and plaster onto breeze blocks.

Town house, Pont-Audemer

In Normandy some churches were built of wood and plaster. Perhaps the best-known example is Ste.-Catherine in the port of Honfleur. The English destroyed Honfleur's church at the time of Agincourt and then occupied the city for half a century. After they had been ejected the local sailors and shipwrights started building a temporary church out of ships' timbers. Below the Gothic clerestory are two naves, side by side and separated by a single row of pillars. The first nave was finished in 1468 and the second added in 1496, as it was impossible to find beams big enough to span the whole space. The roofs look like upturned boats.

Flint is also a traditional building material in Normandy. I found an example at Ault, the first town I entered, where at the top of the village street a herringbone pattern of flints, like fine English cloth, covered the church. Other local stone is also used. There are granite quarries near Vire, and it is thus hardly surprising that Notre-Dame de Vire was constructed using this material. Almost totally destroyed in the fighting following the Normandy landings, it was rebuilt in the same stone, which changes in colour from grey to pink and brown as it oxidises.

Traditionally Normandy is dairy country. I saw plenty of cows in the fields, but fewer people work on the land than previously as farms are consolidated into larger units. Smallholders can only survive if they also work in industry, like one old man I met whose complexion had been well weathered in the sun. "Smallholdings like mine aren't viable any more," he said. "Land is being concentrated into larger farms. My nephew has 250 hectares growing nothing but potatoes; it's a real factory. He has difficulty getting labour for his farm because people prefer easier jobs."

Lower Normandy also grows apples in abundance and produces cider, but sadly orchards are closing. Gonneville on the outskirts of Honfleur used to be an area celebrated for its cider, but now farms and cider-pressing barns have become houses or *gîtes*.

In the nineteenth century artists such as Monet and Boudin started to visit the coast, including ports like Honfleur. At the same time seaside holidays became fashionable. Now tourism provides much more revenue than shipping or fishing, and much of the Normandy coast has been developed for the Parisian bourgeoisie. South of Dieppe the coast path ran through the outskirts of Varengeville, which contains some expensive properties owned by media personalities. I watched as gardeners lopped trees and manicured the shrubbery. South of Honfleur smart houses occupy the wooded outskirts with large gates, entry phones and barking dogs.

Unlike Deauville on the other side of the River Touques, the older resort of Trouville is packed between the cliffs and the sea. It has two faces, the large sandy beach and the quays along the river, and between the two the tawdry carbuncle of the casino, which looks as if it has seen better days. Not far from this temple of chance is a small statue of Gustave Flaubert, who spent family holidays here. He returned in 1853 to recover his creative powers during the composition of his most famous novel, *Madame Bovary*. The statue has an inscription which claims that Flaubert's strongest emotions originated from Trouville and that he was excited by the sensations of the natural world here: "All the memories of my youth reverberated under my steps, like the shells of the seashore. Each wave of the sea, which I see breaking, awakens in me distant echoes." I think he would find it difficult to feel the same way about the place today. Tennis courts and concrete cafés on the beach obscure the view of the sea. Behind the promenade are many ostentatious bourgeois palaces built around 1900 in Renaissance or Norman style with huge chimneys, windows surrounded by pilasters and decorated brickwork. The town's appearance gave the distinct impression that it had dropped in the social pecking order.

Across the bridge I entered a different world, the much smarter avenues and shops of Deauville. This was the last of three major resorts which were created from scratch by property speculators in the mid-nineteenth century: Cabourg 1853, Houlgate 1854 and Deauville 1859. The 1850s were the glory years of the Second Empire. Baron Haussmann was driving his great boulevards through the centre of Paris, railways were spreading out across the country and bankers were falling over themselves to lend money for property development. The nouveaux riches came here to flaunt their wealth during the season, and

Prosperous Deauville

it was not surprising therefore to find a statue of the Duc de Morny next to a pile of vegetables in the market at Deauville. The Round Table objected to my photographing their stand and were even more puzzled when I explained that it was the statue behind which interested me. Morny was the illegitimate half-brother of the Emperor Napoleon III. A co-conspirator in the coup d'état which brought Louis Napoleon to absolute power, Morny personified the raffish world of business and pleasure of the mid-century. He made a fortune and spent some of it on racing. After creating the race course at Longchamp he turned his attention to Deauville, which he founded as a resort with another famous race course.

The streets of Cabourg radiate in straight lines from the Casino and Grand Hotel, while a number of lanes join up these arteries by following a semicircular path. On the map the whole town looks like one half of a bicycle wheel. Marcel Proust used to stay at the Grand Hotel and Cabourg is recreated as Balbec in *À la recherche du temps perdu*. He refers to the clients of the hotel as "commonplace rich and cosmopolitan people, with a number of eminent people from the surrounding area, top lawyers, officials and doctors." He satirised the snobbish pretensions of the place, the director "who thought that people who only had an income of five hundred francs a month were pariahs who did not belong in the Grand Hotel, forgetting that he did not earn such a sum." He also poked fun at new gadgets such as the lift: "The director came to push the button himself: and a person unknown to me called 'lift' (who was installed, like a photograph behind a glass screen or an organist in his room, at the top of the hotel building where you would find the lantern of a Norman church), started to descend towards me with the agility of a domesticated squirrel, hard-working but a captive."

Many of the villas in Cabourg still put on a painted face to the world, with mosaics, high gables, arched patios and pyramids of dormer windows pointing to the sky. I stayed in a modest villa built for Berthier de Wagram, the son of Napoleon's Chief of Staff and himself a member of Napoleon III's court. However, the Grand Hotel and its surroundings do not have the cachet they once enjoyed.

I also walked through the industrial landscape produced by the modern economy: the warehouses and cranes at Fécamp, the docks at Dieppe, the car showrooms and factories around Vire, the storage tanks and chimneys on the Seine estuary. I marvelled at the Pont de Normandie, a powerful symbol of modern France, and at the skill of its engineers. It was svelte and chic like a

French model on a catwalk. How could all that weight be supported by a spider's web of wires? It is the biggest bridge in the world that uses such cables, one and a quarter miles long and with pylons over six hundred feet high.

Post-war buildings, drab and utilitarian, lined the wide boulevards of Le Havre which looked empty day and night. Admittedly it was the weekend but there was no life in the streets, only the rustle of leaves and litter. The scale of the buildings dwarfed the few passers-by. Jean-Paul Sartre spent five years teaching in Le Havre in the 1930s and used it as the model for Bouville in his novel La Nausée (1938). The town retains some of the empty soulless character of the fictional Bouville despite extensive post-war reconstruction. "Vegetation only encompasses Bouville on three sides. On the fourth side there is a large hole, full of black water which flows of its own accord. The wind whistles between the houses. The smells hang around for a shorter time than elsewhere: pushed out to sea by the wind, they skim over the black water like little will-o'-the-wisp fogs. It is raining... I am going to come back to Bouville. *Quelle horreur!*" says the novel's anti-hero.

Everywhere the large towns are spreading out into the countryside, gentrifying many villages and creating dormitory communities. On the edge of the Marais Vernier a small paddock surrounded each house, providing space for ducks, chickens, sheep, goats and apple orchards. I did wonder whether the occupants were city workers playing at farming. Some of the plots looked far too manicured, with geraniums in hanging baskets and even gravel drives. Many local people work in Le Havre and Rouen and also at the oil refinery opposite Quilleboeuf.

On the other bank of the river the owners of villas had little aesthetic sense. No one had tried to soften the harsh edges of their houses with shrubs and trees, but green wire fences anchored to concrete posts surrounded most properties, their sole function to keep the guard dogs inside. These gardens may have lacked plants but were well furnished with gnomes, wheelbarrows, pumps, fountains, wells, statues, lions, manicured ponds, islands and bridges. Some had ceramic plates or even little clogs fixed to the walls of the houses.

Normandy, like everywhere else in France, has seen enormous economic changes in recent years. A conversation in Fécamp illustrated for me how hard it is for people with limited education to survive. Near the promenade I found a tea shop in a small hotel and a young man served me tea and a madeleine while apologising that his mother did not make cakes because a pâtisserie had opened next door. Tall, slim and slightly anxious, he told me a lot about the hopes and fears of some young Frenchmen. His mother owned the hotel and, although quite young, he was already married with a baby of thirteen months who was crawling around the floor. His wife was a Spanish teacher at a local *collège*. He and his friends felt there was no work. "Factories are closing down and manufacturing is being moved out of France. Every day you hear people talk about factory closures. Unemployment in Fécamp is high. We have achieved a seventy per cent occupancy rate in the hotel, but struggle to make a margin because of rising costs. My mother pays me the minimum wage of €1000 a month but it costs her €1500 to employ me because of the high level of social security contributions which employers have to pay. She needs my help because running a hotel is hard physical work, but she can't afford to pay more. It's impossible to raise prices because of competition. I have a small terraced house over the street, but it needs a lot of repairs. We have just enough money to live on but nothing to spare. It is all right for the big companies, but the smaller enterprises are being squeezed. In twenty years' time many of them will have disappeared."

Suddenly England seemed to be the Promised Land.

"I adore London because it is so cosmopolitan," he said wistfully.

I left feeling concerned for the young man. He had very little opportunity to improve the hotel, which offered rooms and breakfast only. Maybe he should leave Fécamp altogether, I thought, and continue the training course which he had already started. Unfortunately he was trapped with a child to support. I remembered his parting phrase, "one survives in France."

1940-44

Like other parts of northern France, Normandy was embroiled in the Second World War and will always be remembered by the British as the site of the D-Day landings. Yet my first reminders of the conflict concerned the end of the Battle for France in May and June 1940. Some units of the British and French armies made their last stand not at Dunkerque but on the cliffs north of Le Havre: at Sotteville-sur-Mer, Veules-les-Roses and St.-Valery-en-Caux, where a lot of the town was destroyed. There was a memorial to men of the 51st Highland Division who, with the French Ninth Army Corps, tried in vain to stop the German Army. A total of 424 soldiers fell, half French and half British, and they are buried in the military cemetery.

Serge, the retired school teacher, recalled his early childhood in Le Havre during the Second World War. "My father was a railway worker and we lived near the main station. In 1944 the RAF started to bomb the docks. I admired the bravery of individual pilots coming in low to target installations with their bombs. Later the Americans instituted high-level bombing with waves of planes, which destroyed the old centre of Le Havre. My family's house was hit, but not completely destroyed. It was made of wood and ended up leaning at an angle. After the war we managed to push it straight again. We were so pleased when the Germans left Le Havre and the Americans arrived, throwing oranges and chocolate to us kids."

I did not walk along the famous D-Day beaches, but one memorial to 6 June 1944 sticks in my mind. The bridges over the River Orne and the canal at Ranville, the only ones between Caen and the sea, were the link between the main bulk of the Allied army and its left flank. Therefore it was vital that they were captured intact at the start of D-Day. The story of how Major John Howard and men from the Oxfordshire and Buckinghamshire Light Infantry landed in their Horsa gliders and captured Pegasus Bridge in ten minutes has become the stuff of legend. The café next to the bridge was used as a dressing station to help British troops and it is still there. The four-year-old girl who lived through that experience on D-Day still owns the establishment.

Madame Arlette Gondrée-Pritchett was immaculately dressed in a neat suit and black court shoes, with a scarf carefully draped around her neck. Formal and correct in her manners, she clearly did not believe in easy familiarity with her customers. While she was friendly she also seemed conscious of her place in history. The small café is overwhelmed by souvenirs and photographs of royal and military visitors over the years: General Gale, the commander of the Airborne Division, Major Howard and the Prince of Wales among others. Red check tablecloths and the simple menu are a conscious attempt to maintain the café as it would have been in 1945. Madame Gondrée would not allow photographs to be taken inside her café and was protective of her mementoes. She must resent the new museum, re-housed from a building attached to her café to a site near where the gliders crash-landed. Larger eating places now line the opposite side of the road.

Despite the destruction caused at Avranches in 1944 the visitor can still enjoy the old streets and squares. A roundabout near my hotel celebrated Patton's breakout with a huge granite memorial to the US Army. On 25 July the

Americans ruptured the German lines near St.-Lô and surrounded a German army corps. On 31 July Patton liberated Avranches and advanced from here to Brittany and the Loire. Next to the memorial is an American tank named Thunderbolt and, surrounding it, a six-pointed granite star containing the names of all the French divisions which took part in the Liberation. There is a small bust of Patton in a tank driver's helmet. The acknowledgement of what the Americans achieved here seems rather grudging.

The old stone bridge which I crossed at Pontaubault on my way to Mont-St.-Michel was the main access point into Brittany in 1944. In July Allied bombers tried to destroy the bridge to disrupt German communications. They succeeded in reducing most of the village to rubble, but failed to hit their target, only knocking a few stones off the parapet. It was ironic that Patton used this bridge to move his attacking columns into the Breton peninsula. What would he have done if the bombers had finished the job?

MONT ST.-MICHEL

Marching out of Avranches I felt morose under an overcast sky. A butcher, who sold me some excellent pâté, tried to cheer me up. "It would be fun to get out with a picnic and a bottle of red wine."

I protested that I had too much to carry to allow myself such a luxury.

"Perhaps you've got your priorities wrong," he suggested helpfully.

Later a rustic character in blue denim overalls and a cap was tidying up his vegetable plot, digging over the fertile soil and disposing of dead plants. A small bonfire smoked in a corner. "You only have nine miles to go now," he said.

This heartened me, as it was two miles less than I thought. I had reckoned on twenty miles that day. "You cannot miss the Mount," he said with heavy irony. "It's straight ahead!"

On the horizon the massive rock rose sheer out of the bay, keeping watch over the flocks of sheep. It could almost have been a desert mirage and it was easy to imagine why pilgrims thought of it as a vision of heaven. For them the journey would have been an epic adventure, with none of the comforts which we take for granted. As I strode alongside the cars and coaches on the causeway I felt infinitely superior. I had walked all the way from the Seine like a medieval pilgrim.

The Mont-St.-Michel is the most popular tourist site in France, with twelve million visitors annually, and some would consider it the country's finest Gothic building too. In my imagination I had not appreciated that the rock was so high and nor had I expected the soaring lines of buttresses, pinnacles and spires. The heavy fortifications were also a surprise. The Kings of France patronised this international centre of learning, worship and pilgrimage, which attracted visitors and money from all over Europe. It had to be protected and the walls were built during the One Hundred Years' War. The English tried to starve the fortress into submission, but were not successful.

The rock may have been remote when the only way of getting there was to cross the sands at low tide or go by boat, but once the causeway was built in the 1870s the era of tourism began. Now the rock welcomes swarms of visitors. On a quiet day there were still around twenty coaches parked below, yet often there is shuffling room only. The commercially operated museum looks as if it needs a makeover; there is one main street full of restaurants and tacky souvenir shops, and no such thing as normal life. A religious bookshop reminded me that there is still a small monastic community at Mont-St.-Michel and some people come here to seek God, but it must be difficult. The traditional place to celebrate the end of a pilgrimage is the parish church of St.-Pierre. I went inside to shut out the visual clutter in the street. Two nuns shrouded in black were praying in front of an icon of St. Michael whose statue in full armour stands in a side chapel.

I was the first to enter the abbey at 9.30 next morning, but at 9.35 the first busload of chattering Japanese visitors hit the grand staircase. I raced to stay ahead but eventually decided to let them pass. They swooped like a flock of sparrows wherever their leader took them. In the guest chamber he showed them a huge medieval fireplace and suddenly all twenty rushed forward and peered into the dark chimney. Then the flash guns started blazing away—they must have collected a lot of blank pictures.

Of course the Abbaye du Mont-St.-Michel was not conceived and built in one period by one man. It evolved over several centuries and must have been a continuous building site. Although its Gothic architecture is world famous, it was for many centuries a Romanesque building. Much of the earlier church survives, including the massive columns and barrel vaults in the nave and the crypts underneath the church. Notre-Dame-sous-Terre is the chapel constructed in the tenth century, when Duke Richard I of Normandy first brought the Benedictines to the Mount to reform the eighth-century monastery of St. Aubert, Bishop of Avranches. Many changes resulted from collapses caused by faulty construction; for example, the north wall of the nave of the abbey church fell down in 1103 because the mortar between the stones shrank. The wall had to be shored up underneath. In 1421 the Romanesque choir collapsed and was replaced by a Perpendicular Gothic construction. The medieval abbots had the self-confidence to rebuild in the latest style, rather than preserving the old as we do. They were not given to understatement, but showed audacity and conviction. They travelled in search of ideas and found inspiration in the abbeys and cathedrals which were rising all over northern France in the twelfth and thirteenth centuries.

The skill of the builders who constructed the huge abbey on a platform on the rock is legendary, and the building is full of innovative solutions to particular design problems. How do you make sure that everyone in a long dining hall can hear a monk reading the Bible? The side walls of the long lancet windows are angled towards the lectern to provide an excellent acoustic. How do you ensure there is no interruption to the rhythm of the arches of the cloister at each corner? The builders constructed a double row of columns, with the second offset from the first. How do you ensure that the crush of pilgrims does not create a traffic jam? The abbots planned the route past important chapels with great care. Today visitors focus on the structure of the abbey and its meaning because all the ornaments have gone. It now looks like an austere Cistercian foundation, whereas it would have been full of images and colour. Only a very few remnants of magnificent stained-glass windows, wall paintings, carvings and wooden panelling remain.

The simple ideals of St. Benedict became a distant memory as the abbey accumulated the wealth it needed to support its activities. A new order of Benedictines came to the Mount in the seventeenth century. While they gave a fresh impetus to devotion and learning, they could not afford to keep all the buildings in repair, which in any case became old-fashioned and dilapidated. Contemporary taste in architecture looked to the classical models of Greece and Rome, and when four bays of the Romanesque nave collapsed in the eighteenth century the occupants erected an austere classical west front on the shorter church. As a result there is now a large open terrace where the west end once stood.

It was during this period that the state started to use Mont-St.-Michel as a prison. This became its sole function after the dissolution of religious orders in the French Revolution. In the nineteenth century various well-known troublemakers were imprisoned here, including Auguste Blanqui, a revolutionary known as l'Enfermé because he spent half his life behind bars. In 1874 the Mount was classified as a historic monument and the great work of restoration began. After defeat by Prussia a cult grew up around St. Michael as protector of the French nation. His golden statue, placed on top of the new Gothic spire, became one of France's icons, visible for miles as I walked towards the Breton coast.

12

BRITTANY
STONES, SHRINES AND THE SEA

THE POLDERS OF THE Baie du Mont-St.-Michel lay ahead. But I could only think about groups of pilgrims approaching the Mount, the menacing ripples of the incoming tide sliding towards them across the sands as dusk fell. Suddenly a fierce sun blinded me and dust from the track filled my throat. All I could see was a drainage ditch, neat rows of lettuces, a brick farmhouse and a line of poplars. A long wooded escarpment marked the southern boundary of the land reclaimed by the monks in the Middle Ages. The map showed me I had now crossed the eastern boundary of the *département* of Ille-et-Vilaine and was very definitely in Brittany. Superficially nothing much seemed to have changed. But for five weeks I was to tramp west along the north coast to Morlaix, and then south through Rennes, Brittany's capital, to the mouth of the Loire, and during this time I discovered how much of Brittany's unique identity still remains.

The landscape of the Baie du Mont-St.-Michel is unusual in northern Brittany: rich alluvial fields as far as the eye can see; the land merging seamlessly with the ocean; Mont-Dol rising up like an island in a sea of earth. I encountered small patches like it further along the coast: east of Trebeurden an old sand bar holding back the run-off of several streams and creating a marsh; the Bay of St.-Brieuc, an infinite space of mud flats and sky. The sandy bays between Cancale and St.-Malo are full of dunes and fragile flora, while St.-Malo itself is built on an island joined to the mainland by a narrow sand bar.

These polders, marshes and dunes were the exception to the rule, however. For three hundred miles, from Cancale on the edge of the Baie du Mont-St.-Michel to Morlaix, I walked along the crumbling edge of the granite plateau which is the Breton peninsula. While the underlying geological structure is the same, it takes different forms from place to place. Sometimes the plateau's sea bastions are firm and strong, high cliffs with inspiring views of the ocean. The headland at Cap Fréhel, between Dinard and St.-Brieuc, comes at the end of a walk of exceptional beauty. The cliffs swoop high and low in an unending switchback, through woods of oak and pine and across streams cascading over the rocks. Beyond the pepper pot towers of the Fort de la Latte the grey cliffs thrust in a giant curve towards the two lighthouses at the cape, where the fissured rocks look like the gnarled skin of a hippopotamus wallowing in the sea. The plateau above is a blasted heath, swept by wind so fierce that only gorse and heather can survive. Past the headland deep chasms divide the rock. In the distance a vortex

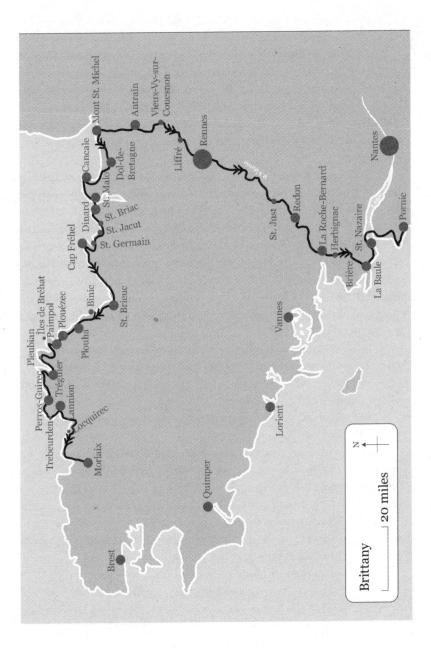

Brittany

20 miles

N

Mont St. Michel
Antrain
Vieux-Vy-sur-Couesnon
Cancale
Dol-de-Bretagne
St. Malo
Dinard
St. Briac
St. Jacut
Cap Fréhel
St. Germain
Liffré
Rennes
Nantes
Pornic
St. Nazaire
St. Just
Redon
La Roche-Bernard
Herbignac
Brière
La Baule
Binic
St. Brieuc
Plouézec
Paimpol
Îles de Bréhat
Pleubian
Plouha
Perros-Guirec
Trégnier
Trebeurden
Lannion
Locquirec
Morlaix
Vannes
Lorient
Quimper
Brest

of dark cloud swirled in a corkscrew down to the ocean's surface. It was a scene from one of Turner's paintings.

Generally the Breton cliffs are low, the limit of a massif which has collapsed into the sea, like the remains of a giant quarry. I saw this most clearly among the chaos of pink granite rocks on the way to Ploumanac'h near Perros-Guirec. These have been eroded into separate boulders like the tors of Dartmoor, only the stones are more rounded. Some of them looked like a giant brioche, that rich French bread which fluffs up into delicious knobs. A noiseless armada of islands lay at anchor.

The difference between high and low tide on the north coast of Brittany is greater than average, particularly near St.-Malo where the sea bounces off the Cotentin Peninsula opposite like water in a bathtub. Often the tide retreats beyond the horizon to create a new landscape for a few hours. I landed on the Île de Bréhat north of Paimpol after breakfast. By lunchtime I had to walk at least half a mile extra to find the ferry. Once the tide is out the sea bed resembles the floor of a crumbling quarry. Further along a sea of mud stretched for at least two miles, allowing visitors to gather shellfish. Submersible causeways crossed the sea bed to accommodate vehicles. Houses on isolated islets rejoined the mainland for a few hours.

Walking along the coast is not a simple matter because there are so many tidal estuaries and headlands to circumnavigate. I met a keen hiker in his sixties who knew the coast backwards. "Don't take short cuts across the headlands," he said, "you'll miss some of the best views!"

He had completed the Santiago pilgrimage twice; once from Narbonne and once from Le-Puy-en-Velay.

Pierre Loti gives an evocative description of this seaside landscape in his famous novel *Pêcheur d'Islande*. He wrote about the bay of Paimpol as it was in 1886 but his words still ring true, although there are many more houses today: "The rocky land rose up and down and you could always see the immense circle of the sea, which enveloped everything. There were no trees left; only the naked heath, the green gorse and the crucifixes with their great arms outlined against the sky, transforming this landscape into a hall of judgement."

When I turned south at Mont-St.-Michel I could have been in the Devon countryside. A track ran between two hedgerows, looking out across fields and oak woods. This was the first of many such ancient ways which duplicate the departmental roads and which local peasants would have used in the days before the national roads were built. As I progressed the valleys became deeper and the crests higher. This was the *bocage* so characteristic of much of Normandy and Brittany. Ferns covered the banks, remnants of a moorland landscape long since cleared. The steep-sided valley of the upper Couesnon was full of trees struggling for the light. Purple orchids had found an ideal environment in the shady undergrowth.

Leaving the River Vilaine south of Rennes I reached a typical Breton heath around the menhirs of St.-Just. The naturally eroded granite contrasted with the yellow of gorse and broom, the varied greens of grass and pine, the pink of tiny succulents and the white of rock roses. Approaching the coast again the soil became sandier and the trees were mostly pine. Soon I reached the vast peat bog of La Grande Brière, one of a number of wet zones stretching from the Golfe du Morbihan to the mouth of the Loire. A thick carpet of reeds and coarse grasses thrives in the saturated jet black soil, the occasional yellow iris shining like a beacon against a backdrop of rich green. Canals divide the marsh, constantly threatening to burst their banks. At one point I set off on a path on the edge of this morass, only to find my boots disappearing into a sea of sludge. Clouds of ferocious insects settled all over my hands, eyes and face and had to be picked off one by one, their bites making me scratch for days. Beyond La Baule the sleepy Loire slid into the Atlantic through an enormous estuary. On the horizon the tip of the Île de Noirmoutier looked like the remains of an ancient civilisation about to disappear under the waves.

The granite which is the peninsula's bedrock lends an austere character to many of its buildings. It is a rock of simple faith in thousands of churches and wayside crosses, a rock capable of resisting the Atlantic storms which batter the coasts, a rock which symbolises endurance in a harsh world where the peasant had to wring a living from the land and the seafarer sustenance from the sea.

In Dol-de-Bretagne the granite lends a rugged solidity to the medieval buildings along the main street: stumpy pillars supporting rustic arches under upper storeys of wood and plaster. The same could be said of the cathedral whose towers and buttresses rest heavily on the ground, rather than rising up to heaven. Inside pink stones are mixed with grey. Outside Dol I came across pink granite in a huge quarry gouged out of the hillside.

Tréguier looks like a town weighed down by its clerical past. The central tower of the cathedral is squat, pinning the great building down to earth. The narrow streets reinforce the introverted Catholic world of the great church:

buildings made of wood and granite, an imposing Episcopal palace now the *mairie*, the old bishop's quarters with a round tower, the Augustinians' house and the massive seminary now a school. But the decorations on country churches have a naive simplicity, charming and unsophisticated: an ancient worthy on top of a turret at Locquirec, a tower topped with balustrades like a tiered wedding cake at St.-Briac-sur-Mer, a pink granite spire with finials like pepper mills around the brim at Perros-Guirec.

Many of the domestic buildings of northern Brittany are also built of grey granite, from small cottages with dormer windows to gaunt manors with defensive towers. Some of the modern houses are built in the same style, and estates of ersatz Breton houses have been faced with granite to make them look old. Yet not all old Breton buildings are built of granite. I found many thatched cottages in the Loire-Atlantique constructed using local schist, particularly on the edge of the Brière regional park. The reeds grown here have been used for centuries for thatched roofs and there are still around 3,000 thatched buildings in the region. In the past they may have been insalubrious hovels, but now many have been restored to make prestigious holiday residences.

In Lannion I first came across the widespread use of wood in older houses.

Houses with wooden beams, Morlaix

In the main square the crazy composition of gables, dormer windows and carved beams looks like something straight out of Balzac. There are many magnificent wooden houses of the fifteenth and sixteenth century in the centre of Rennes, their patterned beams and exuberant carvings testifying to merchant wealth.

FROM CELTIC BACKWATER TO PROSPEROUS REGION

Brittany has always had a strong Catholic tradition mixed with popular faith in saints and sacred places. Belief is not confined in great churches but spills out over the landscape. North of Paimpol the countryside described by Pierre Loti is still rich in Christian symbols. On the way to Ploubazlanec I found one of the crosses to which he refers; a very unusual one on a triangular base representing the Trinity. The chapel of La Ste.-Trinité north of Porz-Even also appears in Loti's novel because it was customary for young married couples to walk to this spot "at the end of the Breton world". Wayside crosses are, of course, common all over France but particularly in Brittany, where they crown several islets along the coast. It is hardly surprising that there are many chapels and grottos to thank the Virgin Mary for a particular act of grace. I climbed up some steps to reach Notre-Dame du Bonne Secours on a small gorge above the River Couesnon. From this spot in 1826 a certain Mlle. Baudry fell down the cliff to the river's edge. When she found herself unharmed she attributed her good fortune to the divine intervention of the Virgin Mary.

St.-Brieuc is named after one of the seven founding saints of Brittany, who like several of his colleagues came over from Wales to evangelise the peninsula in the fifth and sixth centuries. The village of Plougrescant north of Tréguier is the site of a chapel dedicated to St.-Gonéry, who came from Britain at the same time. The chapel's lopsided spire leans at least 15 degrees out of the vertical, as if the lead has been melted by the sun, while its other curious feature is an open-air pulpit underneath the three figures of the Crucifixion. I imagined a priest from an earlier age preaching fire and brimstone to his peasant congregation gathered under the trees.

Some early evangelists travelled in the opposite direction. St.-Germain is another austere granite hamlet where St. Germain d'Auxerre landed on his way back from Britain, having been sent there in 429 to combat a heresy known as Pelagianism. According to legend he walked up the bay and made a spring gush forth, which still exists to this day. Followers of Pelagius believed that sinners could earn salvation by good works without God's grace. The saint is said to have defeated the Pelagians with his superior rhetoric, as Hilaire Belloc recalls in his "Pelagian Drinking Song":

And with his stout Episcopal staff
So thoroughly whacked and banged
The heretics all, both short and tall –
They rather had been hanged.

A belief in miracles was characteristic of the Breton church. Bretons expected their saints to be effective in curing diseases, safeguarding crops or sending rain. A site called St.-Samson, not far from Ploumanac'h, lies in a woodland clearing. Here I found evidence that this belief in miracles was built upon earlier pagan practices. Next to the pilgrimage chapel is a slender menhir which was supposed to cure back pain and also help infertile women conceive. In the woods nearby a stone dated 1632 marks the site of a spring believed to have had miraculous powers since ancient times. The water was thought to cure blindness and also to help children walk.

Yaudet is a religious site in which the link to pre-Christian beliefs is more specific. Ancient earthen ramparts, overlooking the mouth of the River Léguer west of Lannion, were occupied by Celts whose druids also waited for a virgin to give birth. The Romans built a temple here, and to win favour with the locals they included a statue of Cybele, the Goddess of the Earth and Mother of the Gods, representing her in bed suckling a small child. The Christian peoples from Britain adopted this idea when they worshipped the Virgin. The old church was rebuilt in 1855 and contains a charming, if sentimental, representation of the Virgin Mary behind the altar. She lies in a bed under a lace coverlet, with all the bedclothes of a nineteenth-century lady. The site would not be complete without a holy fountain dating from the Middle Ages.

Walking around Brittany I passed plenty of evidence of the purely pagan past. The shapes of the menhirs at St.-Just are as varied as the forms of nature: tall thin sentinels, rough stumps, pointed pyramids and piles of rubble. They lie or stand in lines, circles, covered ways and circular chambers. Some mark the spot where men and women lived; others may have had a sacred purpose, perhaps as tombs for the remains of the ancestors. Archaeologists have given them evocative names, like the Cross of St. Peter, the Tribune and the Saracen.

The menhir of St.-Uzec is a tall Neolithic standing stone situated on moorland near Trebeurden. The instruments of Christ's passion have been carved on the front and a stone cross placed on top. It was probably built over

Menhir of St.-Uzec

4,000 years before Christ. In this case a Christian mission of the seventeenth century tried to erase the evidence of earlier beliefs, rather than build on them. Catholicism has proved a potent force in Brittany up to the present day. My host Rémi in Herbignac said, "The Catholic Church is still strong in much of Brittany, including around here. There are plenty of Catholic schools. Some of the old superstitions which predate Christianity still hold sway."

If the Church is one pillar of Brittany's identity, another is the Breton language. There was a time when the majority of Bretons, certainly west of St.-Brieuc, spoke Breton. A plaque by the road side near Tréguier recalls the life of Ian Ar Gwen, a blind travelling storyteller of the old Breton society who brought the events of the outside world to his listeners, many of whom were illiterate and could not speak French. He related local and national news, sang comic songs and introduced some elements of religious teaching into his performances. North-western Trégor, one of Brittany's nine provinces, was the country of such popular singers.

Since the advent of mass education in French and the modernisation of the economy, most young Bretons have stopped using this Celtic language, which is closely related to Cornish and Welsh. It is mainly spoken by the old in the west and I met a number of older people on the north coast who spoke it, but virtually no one is monolingual in Breton. Several retired people told me how their teachers had discouraged them from speaking the language at school. Two old men propped up the bar at Pleubian while I ate breakfast. One of them had been a skilled cabinet maker. He was at school during the last war and remembered the teacher saying that, if they spoke Breton, they would not get any time in the playground. One man at Plouézec remarked that when children learn Breton in school today they study an artificial literary form, not the popular speech he knew as a boy.

At Redon a Breton couple joined me for breakfast. They came from St.-Brieuc and spoke Breton. *Madame* proudly showed me her Breton cheque book. *Monsieur* said, "I don't support the French government's monolingual policy. They should do more to preserve the other languages of our country." "I find the Irish very *sympa*," he continued. "Their Celtic culture interests me. Besides they're Catholic and they drink a lot like the Bretons! The Welsh and the Scots have an interesting culture as well, but the English have nothing to give to the world."

Rémi Le Marrec was keen to stress his Breton origins, telling me that his name meant knight in Breton. He had long blond hair and blue eyes, so I was not surprised to discover that his mother was Dutch. His wife Magali was totally French and they had moved from Paris. "I used to work in the merchant marine," he said, "but had to leave because the prospects were so poor. I have restored our home. Now I plan to re-train as a naval shipwright. I want to build traditional Breton boats out of wood."

Although he lived in the Loire-Atlantique *département*, he regarded himself as a proper Breton. "A lot of Breton music is still played," he said," and there are Breton dances too." His son treated us to a dance tune on his miniature accordion. The small boy took it very seriously and his tune was haunting. Rémi played a traditional Breton instrument called the *bombarde*, rather like a recorder. He too was critical of France's monolingual policy. "Breton is the only proper language in France, apart from French itself," he said, "and now only about ten per cent of the population of Brittany speak it. Few schools teach Breton. It has no special status in the world outside."

I asked why more people did not speak the language. "People think of it as backward, provincial and old-fashioned, particularly the young. It just isn't cool!" was the reply.

It is a paradox that while Brittany has become more prosperous and use of the language has declined, interest in Breton culture is growing. Even in the hinterland of Rennes, where people have not spoken the language for hundreds of years, they still think of themselves as Breton. The magnificent new Musée de Bretagne in Rennes tells the history of a society with its own unique identity.

Brittany was a separate state until its merger with France in 1532. From then on its prosperity grew steadily until the French Revolution. I could see the effect of this transformation at Rennes where the parlement (law courts) arrived thirty years after the union. The members had noble status and started to build grand residences suitable for their position. A fine example is the Hôtel de Blossac in the grand classical manner which in many ways is France's signature style: an elegant curving wrought-iron staircase; a gatehouse topped by a massive pediment and surrounded by rusticated stone work; two rows of high windows.

The Revolution marked a turning point for Brittany, as the province was torn apart in a civil war between supporters of the Republic, the Blues, and the followers of the monarchy and the Catholic Church, the Whites or Chouans. In the middle of a bog in a forest I came across a broken column commemorating the shooting of two Chouan rebels in 1796. The long story of the erection of the column shows that old hatreds die hard. It was put up in 1826 during the royalist restoration after Bonaparte, but not finished by the time a less favourable regime took power in 1830. More than a century and a half later, the memorial was finally completed in 1993. Recording history is often contentious in France and this column is a good example. The picturesque town of La Roche-Bernard on the Vilaine was also the scene of violence and executions during the Revolution. The royalist party was strong in Brittany and in March 1793 they killed two Revolutionary leaders here. Later in the month the town was re-taken by the Republicans and those held responsible for the summary executions earlier were arrested. One of them was garrotted over a cannon and then had his head cut off with an axe, just to make sure. Others were dragged away in chains.

In the nineteenth century Brittany took something of a step back into the past. If you had asked the average well-educated Frenchman what he thought of Brittany in 1900, he would probably have said backward, poor, superstitious, royalist, Catholic. The region was clearly on a divergent path from the rest of France, where secular anti-clericalism was in the ascendant. And while the rest of France was industrialising, Brittany's traditional industries such as textiles were declining and shedding labour. Many Bretons were leaving the countryside and some quarters of Paris became Breton towns. Nostalgia, allied to sympathy for the sufferings of the Breton people, developed in the arts, exemplified by Loti's *Pêcheur d'Islande*. This feeling of backwardness and decline continued until 1940.

The classic description of life in a Breton village in the early twentieth century can be found in Pierre-Jakez Hélias' *Le Cheval d'orgueil* which is a moving personal memoir. Poverty was the lot of most villagers and ruin always seemed to be around the corner. If circumstances became really desperate men might hang themselves but women preferred death by drowning. Hélias says "this obsession with destitution was such, that people expected it to overtake them on a bend in the road in the form of a mangy dog, its hair standing on end, its pendulous lips turned up to reveal yellowing teeth." They called it "the Bitch of the World, silent, cunning and likely to appear without warning." The saying went, "Look out for the Bitch of the World, which jumps on top of you and never barks."

The Second World War left its mark on Brittany. The massive German submarine base still stands next to the old commercial docks in St.-Nazaire, a massive hulk of grey concrete with a flat roof the size of a football pitch and fourteen pens underneath to protect the U-Boats from aerial attack. The thickness of the fortifications has made it virtually indestructible. The Germans built it in about eighteen months and on 27 March 1942 the British launched a commando raid called Operation Chariot, an attempt to neutralise a base which was strategically important in the Battle of the Atlantic. They failed, and so British and later American bombers tried to knock it out from the air. The city was reduced to rubble and life became almost impossible, but the base still stands. Now St.-Nazaire seems rather a soulless city, the post-war architecture dull and monotonous, a collection of concrete utilitarian blocks which have no spirit. Even so, St-Nazaire today is thriving economically, as the young owner of my hotel told me. "The population has grown to 66,000 since the wartime devastation. The city is doing well. The shipyards are busy building cruise liners for Italian owners and naval vessels. Don't forget that it was the ship works at St.-Nazaire which built the Queen Mary II in 2003. There is also an Airbus factory in the city which is busy."

Since 1945 Brittany's fortunes have been transformed by a period of unparalleled economic development starting with agriculture. Frédéric at Vieux-Vy-sur-Couesnon told me his story. "My father was sent as a forced labourer to a German farm during the Second World War. He came back determined to improve his own farm and studied agriculture. I took it over in 1964. Three years later I dispensed with horses for ploughing and started to use a tractor. My farm is probably twice as productive now as when I started running it. We raise cattle for both milk and beef, like most of the farmers in the region. We also grow maize and cereals, but mainly for cattle feed."

I asked Frédéric if there had been a *remembrement* in the village. Partly because of French inheritance laws, farms have traditionally been divided into small parcels in much of the countryside. *Remembrements* carried out mainly between 1960 and 1980 were voluntary agreements between local farmers to swap plots, so that they could consolidate their holdings and avoid the considerable costs of working widely scattered fields. *Remembrements* often involved rooting out hedgerows to improve access and drainage and for this they have been criticised by ecologists. Frédéric explained that there had been no *remembrement* in Vieux-Vy, unlike other parts of Brittany. His farm comprised different parcels east and west of the village. "There's no doubt that it takes more time to manage as a result," he added.

I had the impression that Frédéric and Jeanne's lives had been entirely bound up with the farm and their family, which was hardly surprising. Their income from one hundred and fifty acres would not have been enormous and until recently life must have been hard. Now they occupy a granite cottage in the village and have passed the farm on to a son who occupies the old farm house with his family. Running a *chambre d'hôte* is a retirement occupation for a lot of farmers, enabling them to meet people and keep a bit of pocket money coming in. Frédéric is still busy helping on the farm. He arrived home at 5 p.m. on a hot afternoon, having sown maize all day. In the past they would not have had a lot of spare money for luxuries like travel, but now they were retired they were going on a coach tour to Spain. They were enormously proud of what they had achieved. Given where the Breton peasantry had started from in 1945, they had every right to be.

THE COST OF TOURISM

Now Brittany is one of the agricultural powerhouses of France. The Bretons not only raise cattle, pigs and sheep but grow everything from cereals to artichokes and cauliflowers, both of which I saw in sandy fields near the north coast. In the past many Bretons found employment in shipping and fishing as well, but these industries are now a shadow of their former selves. Just after leaving Plouha

Gwin Zegal

I came across the deserted cove of Gwin Zegal, with forty-seven poles in lines on the beach like ghostly sentinels. They were once used for tying up fishing boats. At Plouézec I discovered that my host had served for thirty-five years in the French merchant navy, sailing all over the world. The last fourteen years he had spent on tankers. "Now the merchant navy is much smaller. Third World countries have taken over. They pay their nationals much lower wages than Frenchmen would be prepared to live on."

Brittany has a holiday coast afflicted by ribbon development: hotels, campsites, bungalows, mobile homes, flats, cafés, car parks, golf courses, casinos, marinas; a real coastal suburbia. Green lungs are few and far between. Some of the buildings do not blend well with the landscape and materials have often been selected for cheapness alone. Nothing looks more dilapidated more quickly than heavily stained concrete. Yet some local people are fighting to hold back the tide. Le Palus near Plouha had a sleepy air: a beach, a couple of cafés and a jetty. This atmosphere was not likely to last long, as the mayor had given permission for a major holiday development which the locals were fighting tooth and nail.

Inevitably many of the houses and bungalows are second homes. Outside one bungalow by the sea a seventy-five-year-old Frenchman lent over the garden gate and talked to me in perfect English. It turned out he had worked in England in his youth, in King's Lynn and Hammersmith, and had also spent seven years in Canada. "Regrettably England has changed for the worse," he said in a near faultless accent.

Clearly it was a lonely life on his own and he wanted to chat. "I'm the only resident who stays throughout the winter." He wanted to tell me about his English and German neighbours who only came in the summer. He said that there are 20,000 British in Brittany. No doubt large parts of the coast have lost their purely French character and there is little sense of community.

Many resorts are eerily quiet out of season, as I discovered at St.-Briac-sur-Mer. My hostess there dismissed any suggestion that restaurants might be closed on a stormy night in March, but I wandered the darkened streets to find every eating place firmly shuttered, except for one pizza house. Despite my pleas the owner said firmly that he did not serve food mid-week. There was nothing for it but to dive into a bar next door where a few locals were sheltering from the weather. I ordered a beer and looked enviously at a group next door devouring a plate of nuts. Quietly I asked the bar man, "can I have some nuts too?" Reluctantly he put his fist in a large can and doled out a few into a round dish.

Several beers later the owner of the pizza house came in with a party, a bottle of champagne was opened and there was laughter all round. Looking at my plate of nuts he said, "Ah! I see you have found something for supper." I was too slow to think of a clever response. Back at the house *madame* was still out, but her son took pity on a famished walker, making me a ham omelette and producing a wilting banana.

Kristell at St.-Jacut-de-la-Mer painted a picture of a community transformed by tourism. She explained that about 800 people lived in St.-Jacut but 10,000 during the summer holidays. Many of the houses were second homes and prices had risen so much that young Bretons were finding it difficult to get on the property ladder. At least industries like food processing were growing and there was work in Rennes. Many of the people on the north coast commuted considerable distances to work. Kristell continued, "Of course there are a lot of old people around here, but I think the elderly are often more isolated in the large towns than in the countryside. You know we have the *commerces ambulants*, travelling shops selling everything from bread and meat to clothing. The old folks can buy all they need without a journey. The salesman is someone to talk to. On the down side, if they need hospital treatment for anything serious they have to make a long journey, probably to Rennes, Brest or even Nantes one hundred and twenty miles away."

Kristell was a district nurse herself who visited the sick and elderly in their homes. She had to rush off in the morning and left me to make my own breakfast.

The France Télécom research station was moved out to Pleumeur-Bodou to diversify the local economy away from agriculture and this brought several other telecommunications firms to the hinterland of Lannion, which has attracted its share of new industries in recent years. Now, however, some of this new employment is under threat from rationalisation. France Télécom had just announced redundancies when I arrived and fearful employees had been demonstrating in the streets. It was a quiet Saturday afternoon and young people were hanging around on street corners, smoking and eating crisps. I dropped into a café, avoiding two louche-looking drunks who were pestering the customers. As elsewhere in France there is fear about the future. I got into conversation with a local man who became very excited when I asked about the redundancies. "Things are getting really bad," he said. He admitted that he had been working all night and maybe that had affected his temper.

While tourism has emptied some of the north coast communities of life, the picture was different the nearer I got to Rennes. Antrain, with a population of 1,100, had an abattoir and a food factory which drew employees from some way around. At Vieux-Vy-sur-Couesnon Frédéric described the slaughter of 6,000 pigs a day and the preparation of cuts of meat packaged ready for the supermarkets. "There are few second homes, unlike on the coast. We are only twenty-five miles from Rennes. There's a secondary *collège* six miles away. A bus comes every morning to pick up the pupils. You only have to travel further if you enter the *lycée*."

Rennes is one of the fastest growing cities in France. As I approached, apartment blocks straddled the skyline and run-down factories and warehouses lined the canal bank, with plenty of concrete surfaces for the local graffiti artists to display their talents. The gallery of masterpieces included a workman in overalls and a cap raising a glass to Sarko and the glitzy face of a female star with the caption, "Carla the slag".

After the Second World War there was a massive exodus from the land and many Bretons ended up settling in Rennes, while new industries like Peugeot-Citroën arrived. I passed their car plant at Janais south of the centre. Yet a shadow hangs over all this success and a Citroën worker told me that his employers had cut the work force from 11,000 a few years ago to 9,000 today. Rennes' affluence has produced a lively street life, a modern driverless metro system and fine new buildings. Most of the old streets on the north bank of the Vilaine have been pedestrianised and provide a good excuse for a stroll. On the second evening of my visit I found twenty restaurants in the Rue St.-Georges. The Café des Bains was full of young people and the food more imaginative and better value than some of the traditional cooking in the countryside.

During three weeks on the north Breton coast before Easter I saw very few fellow walkers. I stayed mainly in hotels and *chambres d'hôtes* and missed the comradeship of walkers' hostels. Most of the accommodation was comfortable and the reception friendly, but some of the hotels were family establishments which had seen better days. The hotel building at Trebeurden had chipped paint, strips of wallpaper hanging off the wall, a curtain rail about to fall down, plastic tables and chairs in the dining room and long light pendants.

Not infrequently the *chambres d'hôtes* offered a higher standard of accommodation, with prices to match. Near Pleumeur-Bodou I was ushered into a large stone Breton farmhouse. When Virginie and her husband first found these buildings they were totally run-down, but no expense had been spared on the restoration: exposed stonework and old beams. Inside I found a very cosy atmosphere with a roaring log fire and plenty of books on Brittany. Virginie was a business woman who had to have a project to keep her occupied. She had worked for General Electric in Paris for twenty years. I asked her why she had moved to Brittany. "Well, it's more typically French than living in Paris," she said. She did not seem to see the irony of moving to an area with a non-French history to find the real France

Sometimes I received the Gallic brush-off. I left my anorak by the counter in a shop in Binic. When I went back for it a few minutes later the owner feigned ignorance. On another occasion I was walking through the Forêt de Rennes to my hotel at Liffré. As thunder rumbled overhead I stepped up my pace. Reaching the bridge over the main road just as the heavens opened I sprinted for the front door, arriving in a smart reception area looking thoroughly dishevelled.

The hotel was a modern purpose-built Logis de France. It looked comfortable enough, but when I enquired about the possibility of a packed lunch for the next day the conversation went something like this.

"Can you provide me with a picnic lunch for tomorrow?"

"No, I am afraid not; we don't do that sort of thing."

"Really? You couldn't find just a scrap of bread and cheese and maybe a piece of fruit."

"Well no, because that would mean we would have to have ordered the bread (half a baguette) and the apple in advance. It would really be much more convenient if you went to the local shops to get what you want."

"You mean you have absolutely nothing left over after breakfast?"

"No, we know exactly how much bread we will need in the morning and there will be nothing left over."

"You obviously don't understand that I am walking long distances each day. I don't want to walk four miles in the wrong direction. As a large hotel you ought to be able to provide something to keep me going."

"I cannot help that. Picnics are not something we normally provide."

"So you are not prepared to help me out."

"Well I suppose I could go and ask the chef."

"Please do that."

"What time do you want this picnic?"

"At 9.30 a.m. when I leave."

"Oh well, in that case we can probably provide something, but it won't be very special."

"I don't need anything special; just something to keep me alive!"

Although I missed the company of walkers in Brittany I enjoyed plenty of interesting encounters with local people. My lodging after Mont-St.-Michel was a cheap boarding house built of concrete. There was no furniture in my room apart from the bed, and electric wires stuck out of the walls. A large tank of goldfish occupied the entrance area. The thermometer had reached 30°C. *Monsieur* and *madame* were lazing around a table in the garden, which was covered with the debris of a previous meal. The owner was an enormous man with a large stomach, dressed in a singlet and shorts. I made the mistake of asking him what was happening locally, to which the answer was "nothing." This opened the floodgates for a tirade about the state of affairs in his country while I was dying to disappear and have a shower.

The owner loved to speak really fast and show off his repartee. It was perhaps not surprising that his wife was quiet. He complained about being chained to the place, but it was she who had to go out and keep the money coming in. He liked to tease her about how good a house husband he was, getting the guests their breakfast and looking after their every need.

"What do *monsieur* and *madame* want?" he said in a mockingly obsequious voice. I ate my evening meal with them on the terrace: pâté, barbecued lamb and chips and dessert from the local supermarket. At least it was washed down with Ricard and plenty of wine. Two dogs begged for food and various guests wandered past the terrace on their way out. They were a mixed group, typical perhaps of the racial diversity in some large towns: an Algerian in running shorts who had done the Nantes marathon in three hours; a large African with a Chinese wife and three children; an older couple who had only been together for three weeks, according to my host. She was probably in her mid-forties and minced around in a long tight-fitting denim dress. Her hair had been dyed platinum blond and her skin roasted a leathery brown.

I was on the receiving end of many acts of kindness during my walk around France, but nowhere more so that at Plouézec. Although my hosts did not normally offer evening meals, they invited me to share a four-course feast, including a succulent *blanquette de veau,* and refused to accept payment. The living room was very tidy. A clumsy walker, I felt that I might break some priceless ornament of which there were many. Cherubs smiled on me from all directions and Louis XV-style chairs added to the air of formality. However, the couple put me at my ease and I enjoyed a fascinating tour d'horizon of local life. He told me that when he retired he stood for the office of mayor, serving for thirteen years, and then gave me a baffling résumé of the structure of French local government. The former mayor's pride and joy was a beautifully restored old windmill on a ridge overlooking the sea and he took me to see it the following morning. Unfortunately one night the previous year a terrible storm had battered the coast and the sails were wrecked. He had to make an insurance claim for over €40,000. Now the Moulin de Craca is complete once again, and the locals make two hundred and twenty pounds of flour a year just for fun; *folklorique*, to quote his words.

*

On my last day in Brittany I received another call from an unknown voice like the one in Alsace.

"Is that Mr. Terence Cudebird?"

"Yes. Cudbird."

"Sorry, Mr. Cupboard. I am a doctor at Warwick Hospital. Your mother fell in her flat and she has broken two bones in her foot. We are keeping her in for a few days."

"How long will it be before she can go home?"

"I'm afraid I can't say yet when she might be released. She is acting very strangely. We wanted to carry out a blood test but she refused to cooperate. She has been abusive to the staff and gets very upset. Has she had mental problems?"

I breathed a long sigh and explained her medical history as best I could. "In my view she has the beginnings of dementia and I think her GP would share this view."

"I understand you are abroad, Mr. Cupboard. When are you coming home?"

"In two days' time."

"Is there any possibility you could come home a day earlier? If you could come to the hospital and calm your mother down it would help us a lot."

Once again I jumped on a high speed train to Paris and begged Eurostar to waive the penalty for travelling on a different train from that shown on my ticket. Once again they obliged. The next day I was standing by my mother's bed in Warwick Hospital. The doctor said her bones were mending, but that was not his main concern. She was very immobile and clearly mentally disturbed. They could not release her until they were satisfied she could be cared for safely at home.

"This is a terrible place, Terence. I can't sleep because the nurses talk all night. There are funny things going on here. They're up to something. I don't know what, but I'm frightened."

My mother's paranoia seemed to be taking over.

"They're just trying to help you get better so that you can go back home. Please accept the treatment."

An assistant came up to her bed to ask what she wanted for lunch tomorrow. "Go away. Leave me alone. Stop interfering with me," she bawled. Then turning to me she shouted "Take me home. I can't stay a minute longer."

Something boiled over inside me. I had promised years before that I would always look after her, but this was too much. "If you behave like this they will keep you here. Just snap out of it and cooperate with the hospital."

This was followed by more crying. It was no good. I couldn't win either way.

After much cajoling and long discussions with the occupational therapist, psycho-geriatrician and social worker I managed to get her released a week later. I instituted a tighter care regime in her flat. Cleaners came every week. The District Nurse looked in to change the boot on her foot. Even once the bones healed she could no longer move freely around her flat on her own. I started doing all her shopping and generally running her life. After a succession of unsatisfactory carers we found a real gem, a local woman called Beccy whom my mother adored. Beccy could handle her when I found it increasingly difficult. Her mood swings got worse, but Beccy seemed to be able to jolly her along. She loved her visits but always told me, "Stop ordering me about. I am perfectly capable of looking after myself."

My father was also gradually losing his independence. He had given up driving his car and eventually I persuaded him to sell it. A kind neighbour did his shopping and washing up. Social Services fitted stair rails but he refused a personal alarm. Meals on wheels called every day. I took him for a consultation at Romford Hospital because of concerns about his heart. The foyer was as busy as a mainline railway station and I pushed my father up to the cardiology department to a waiting room packed with patients. After some time he asked, "How long do I have to wait?"

"As long as it takes."

"Could I avoid all this?"

"Well you could always go privately, Dad, but you're a socialist. I thought you believed in the National Health Service. This is what it's like. They're very busy."

He grimaced and sat quietly until his turn came. Apparently his condition was not serious. There was no need to panic.

*

While at home I plotted the next stage of my journey. I had crossed the Loire at St.-Nazaire to reach what used to be called the borders of Brittany near Pornic, that is before Petain's government decided that the Loire-Atlantique *département* belonged to the Loire region. The map of the Vendée to the south did not show an obvious route from the coast to the Poitevin marshes, which I had to cross to reach the Gironde and Bordeaux. I relished the adventure ahead.

13

THE VENDÉE AND THE SAINTONGE
MARSHES AND LAZY RIVERS

NOT LONG AFTER entering the Vendée I emerged from a pine forest behind the dunes to find campsites crammed with caravans and mobile homes. "Fast food-Moules Frites; La Sirène-Laverie Automatique-Burgers-Camping Caravanning Sol a Gogo" read the signs, the latter with a drawing of a Mexican hat and a clump of cacti. White bodies crowded around the swimming pools, one of which was overlooked by a miniature lighthouse. A line of stark white apartment blocks stood on top of the Corniche Vendéenne, low cliffs flaky like an oyster shell. South of Sables d'Olonne neat seaside villas spread as far as the eye could see. At St.-Vincent-sur-Jard the tide of identical cottages, with apricot coloured plaster, white shutters and red tiled roofs, had almost submerged the few old buildings, including the Tiger's Lair, retirement home of Georges Clemenceau, Prime Minister and Father of Victory for the troops of the First World War. After fifty years in politics he craved isolation to write about Asian religions and stare at his garden, designed with Monet's help overlooking the ocean. Determined to lead the simple life he told one lady visitor, who asked where the bathroom was, to use sea water. Clemenceau would not find much seclusion today.

French weather forecasters often promise better weather south of the Loire. The Vendée enjoys as much sun as the Côte d'Azur and for many British as well as French it has become the ideal spot for a family holiday. And yet it has a lot more to offer than sea and sand. There are four very different types of landscape: the coast, the marshes, the *bocage* and the plains. From the border with the Loire-Atlantique I wound my way south across the first two, then turned inland south of Sables d'Olonne to cross the *bocage*. Here muddy lanes provided welcome relief from the ubiquitous tarmac of farm roads. Near Chantonnay I joined the Chemin de St.-Jacques coming from Mont-St.-Michel and skirted the plain, before leaving the Vendée along the canals of the southern marsh.

Roads are level and the walking is easy. Ten miles can pass very quickly, and feeling your leg muscles stretch up a steep slope is a rare sensation. But walking for long distances on hard surfaces puts constant pressure on knees and hips. At one point hobbling in pain spoilt the pleasure of being in the open air. I collected six blisters on my feet in a new pair of boots, with ankles, heels and toes covered in weeping sores. My discomfort was compounded by eating a suspect fish stew and going down with food poisoning. I could hardly put one foot in

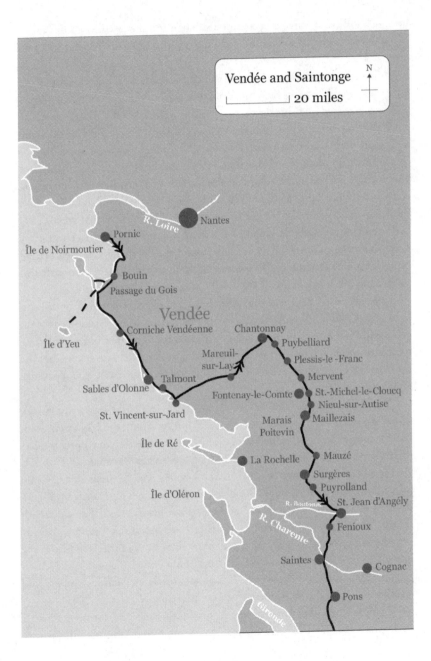

Vendée and Saintonge

N

20 miles

R. Loire
Nantes
Pornic
Île de Noirmoutier
Bouin
Passage du Gois
Vendée
Corniche Vendéenne
Chantonnay
Puybelliard
Plessis-le-Franc
Île d'Yeu
Mareuil-sur-Lay
Mervent
Talmont
St.-Michel-le-Cloucq
Sables d'Olonne
Fontenay-le-Comte
Nieul-sur-Autise
St. Vincent-sur-Jard
Maillezais
Marais Poitevin
Île de Ré
Mauzé
La Rochelle
Surgères
Puyrolland
Île d'Oléron
St. Jean d'Angély
R. Boutonne
Fenioux
R. Charente
Saintes
Cognac
Gironde
Pons

front of another, retreated to a comfortable hotel and collapsed. Later I swapped my boots for a pair of well-cushioned trainers. This did the trick and I had no more trouble.

Most of the coast consists of sand dunes, a case of one step forward and half a step back. Clemenceau sketched his native *pays* in a number of short pieces collected together after his death as *Figures de Vendée* (1930). He refers to the wind blowing the sand into hills and valleys, and the umbrellas of pine throwing their shade over wild flowers and animals alike. Sometimes rocks appear by the sea, in one case producing a coastline as wild and beautiful as any in Brittany. The cottage gardens on the Île d'Yeu are a riot of vegetation, not surprising considering that the climate here is milder than on the mainland. The south coast, however, looks like part of the Armorican peninsula, which geologically it is, consisting mainly of granite with small amounts of quartz. During my visit the ocean pounded the rocky cliffs around the Pointe du Châtelet, driving clouds of spume into the sky. Development seems to have been restricted on this coast, so that it is a paradise of nature all too rare in the south-west.

Opposite the island low tide exposes a ridge of rocks pointing out to sea, known as the Pont d'Yeu. According to local legend, St. Martin made a pact with the Devil. Satan had to build a bridge to the island before the cock crowed. If he succeeded the first Christian to cross the bridge would fall into his hands. The cock crowed in the middle of the night, Satan forfeited his reward and the bridge remained unfinished.

Behind the dunes of the Vendée are two great areas of reclaimed marshland, one north of Sables d'Olonne and the other further south, the Marais Poitevin. In the former straight paths follow drainage ditches through open polders of crops protected by a high sea wall, and the isolated farmhouses look like converted cowsheds. Near Bouin a maze of ponds and channels laps right up to the farmyards and provides a suitable habitat for many birds such as avocets. Bouin and its church spire stand out across the marsh. Until the nineteenth century the village was an island. Clemenceau described this landscape exactly as it is today: "Nothing interrupts your view right to the furthest limits of the horizon. A thin willow tree, a farm and a bell tower provide the few landmarks in the infinity of the sky." There were, he said, a few scattered farmers' cabins, and strangers despised the marsh people as "dwellers in huts".

I approached the great southern marsh through the former monastic settlements of Nieul-sur-l'Autise and Maillezais. From the twelfth century onwards the abbots drained the malarial swamps and created networks of canals. The marsh is divided into two distinct areas, the damp marsh to the east and the dry marsh stretching westwards to the sea. The former is lush and green, its meadows surrounded by willows and poplars. Beyond Maillezais I found the wet marsh on my left and the dry marsh on my right: parched grey fields with fewer hedges and canals. To the untutored eye the stretches of water are motionless and serve no particular purpose, other than to drain the surrounding fields. In fact, they have been designed to encourage the flow of water from the dry marsh into the wetter area, and from there to the major arteries and back to the ocean.

The tracks of the inland *bocage* wind between sprouting hedgerows and through unkempt coppices. Intimate rivers funnel between gentle folds in the earth and occasionally deeper chasms like the *cirque* of the River Vendée at Mervent, which gave the *département* its name. Small enclosures of padded grass provide rich food for cattle. The *bocage* lies higher than the surrounding plains and marshes, a last outcrop of the Armorican peninsula. Despite consolidation of agricultural holdings many of the hedges have survived. There are few villages of any size in this well-settled landscape; rather a succession of scattered hamlets along twisting lanes. Clemenceau enjoyed hunting among "the brambles, broom and gorse, on rocky slopes overlooking the slow curves of the River Lay as it twists between banks of alder and damp meadows."

The Lay provided a connecting thread for a couple of days. At Mareuil-sur-Lay it meanders gracefully past a Romanesque church on a hill, to slide over a weir. The next day I crossed it again on the way to Chantonnay, a slender juvenile stream in a narrow shady valley. One might have imagined that with the surrounding profusion of greenery water supply would not be a problem in the Vendée. Yet the local authorities are lobbying for another reservoir to be constructed by damming one of the rivers. According to a farmer I stayed with in the *bocage*, the extra demand has been created by all the holiday homes on the coast. He complained that property owners there had no incentive to reduce water consumption for the two months a year they were in residence because they were charged a flat fee regardless of usage.

Patrick was very concerned about environmental issues. He had converted his farm to organic methods several years ago, raising cattle for meat but also growing vegetables, and was passionate about the need to stop poisoning the soil by using pesticides and nitrates. When I told him you could buy vegetables in English supermarkets flown in from all over the world, he was full of scorn.

"What about the environmental cost?" he said. Two of his teenage children were starting to study organic farming, but his wife had to work for a firm selling conventional fertilisers to make ends meet. Later on I stayed with a lady who was enthusiastic about buying organic and fair trade products. She apologised that the brioche on the table was not "bio".

"Why is the President always encouraging us to consume more? It has got to stop. We must save the planet."

These green opinions complemented her concern to protect the countryside from cuts in local services. She complained that village schools and local post offices were closing, just to save money and make things more efficient.

The Vendée produces a diverse range of agricultural products apart from meat and dairy in the *bocage* and cereals on the plain. One woman showed me her 6,000 ducks in a shed which would probably end up as *confit de canard*. Small vineyards can be found dotted around the Vendée, but most of them only produce wine for local consumption. I saw orchards of apples, rows of artichokes and tobacco. For the second time on my journey I met a local man gathering dandelions, *pissenlit*. The French add the leaves to salads, believing them to have many beneficial properties, not least the alleviation of a *crise de foie* (liver crisis) brought on by excessive eating and drinking. They are also a diuretic, hence the popular name "piss in the bed".

THE WILD WEST NO LONGER

The main area of open agricultural plain is in the south of the Vendée, although there is also an isolated strip around Chantonnay. I could have been anywhere in northern France: open fields, few trees, concrete water towers and electricity pylons. The Vendée does not have any large conurbations, but a number of small towns have developed some sophisticated modern industries in recent years. The transformation of the *département* from rural backwater to diversified industrial economy is one of the success stories of post-war France, and there was plenty of evidence of such change around Chantonnay. Here I despatched the blister producing boots and then set off around the ring road to find my lodging for the night in a neighbouring village. Walking along the hard shoulder while forty-ton trucks shatter your eardrums is not most people's idea of a pleasant stroll. I was right in the middle of a large industrial estate and the factories did not look more than a few years old. I could have been anywhere in Le Grand Ouest.

The main clients of the café with rooms were the industrial workers nearby.

Monday was normally a rest day, but the young *patron* decided to take pity on me and provide a bed. The shutters were kept down on the windows, which made eating inside a claustrophobic experience. The climax of a meagre meal was a burnt lasagne, which even the rough local wine could not disguise. A number of men in anoraks and trainers, their hair tied in ponytails, were playing bar billiards next door. One man could not tear himself away from the fruit machine. Later on the *patron* disappeared for the night, leaving me locked in a dingy room overlooking a courtyard. I made the mistake of putting things under the bed, only to disturb months of dust. Were the sheets clean? It was difficult to tell. I turned off a hideous orange table light and went to sleep.

One of the popular images of France is the rural idyll; a haven of peace full of crumbling châteaux and old stone cottages, an escape from the modern world. The Vendée is far from such an idyll these days. At one time Parisians would have seen it as an undeveloped place, fiercely Catholic and conservative, where the peasants often lived no better than their animals. These were the people who fought the Republican troops in a bitter guerrilla war after 1793, using the *bocage* as ideal cover for daring ambushes. Every time I ventured into a boggy lane I imagined wild-looking Chouans jumping out to slit my throat. The marshes also offered them protection, their strongholds including those level polders surrounding the island of Bouin. Here they used to evade their pursuers by vaulting across the ditches using a long pole. Clemenceau described the technique over a hundred years later as an art which needed practice. They relied on their knowledge of this difficult terrain, but sometimes their self-confidence led them into danger.

A shallow stretch of water cut the Île de Noirmoutier off from the mainland until the modern bridge was built. Twice a day the tide recedes to uncover a narrow ridge of sand which provides a safe passage for a few hours. Today there is a causeway for vehicles and towers for people to climb in case the incoming tide traps them. I plodded across in the wake of 4 by 4s throwing up spray and armies of locals armed with buckets to gather shell fish on the sands. In the 1790s the crossing was much more perilous. A ragged army of rebels ended up to their waists in water and had to beat a retreat.

While you can still walk in the Vendée for a day and see very few people, the countryside is densely populated and many of the main roads are busy during the rush hours. Autoroutes now cross the *département* and there is a new TGV service all the way to Sables d'Olonne. To get a true picture of the Vendée today you must focus not only on the old buildings around the parish church of each village, but also on the rows of neat villas on the outskirts where builders have created a pastiche of the traditional Vendée farmhouse. South of the Loire curved red tiles replace slate roofs, and most Vendée farmhouses are single storey, as if huddled up against the Atlantic gales. Whitewashed walls and brightly coloured shutters are dazzling in the sunlight.

This is not countryside full of grand houses. Before the Revolution there were few wealthy aristocrats to build them. At Le Plessis-le-Franc I would much rather have lived in the quirky *pigeonnier*, a pepper pot tower of rough stone and tiles capped with a lantern of black slate the shape of a bell. Standing in the middle of a field it looked like the perfect retreat. The towers and high pitched roof of the main house suggested that the original owner was a rustic squire who wanted to impress. Most of the churches, meanwhile, are simple monuments to faith, unless a wealthy patron had a particular reason to pay for something grander. The images which stick in my mind are the honest simplicity of the church at Puybelliard, with its rough stonework and Gothic choir, and the naive carvings of sheep around the west door at St.-Michel-Le-Cloucq. This imagery seemed appropriate because this is where I rejoined the Chemin de St. Jacques

Nieul-sur-l'Autise

232

from Mont-St.-Michel; simple church architecture to put me in a contemplative frame of mind.

The Chemin led me on to the great abbeys at Nieul-sur-l'Autise and Maillezais. Nieul boasts the most complete Romanesque cloister in western France, its stout columns overshadowed by the arcaded tower of the large church. Inside the virgin stone of the nave is austere, stripped down to the bare essentials of massive columns leading the eye upwards to the barrel vaulting. The Abbaye de Maillezais must once have been larger than Nieul. Now its ruined remains stand out on a knoll overlooking marshes on one side and five miles of empty plain on the other. No wonder in the Middle Ages these great abbeys dominated the minds of peasants raised in small hovels.

ANGELS AND A MAGICIAN

When my legs begged for a rest I had to accept whatever food and lodging were available as I could not drive a few miles down the road to find something more suitable. Ten miles south of Sables d'Olonne I stayed in some converted farm buildings restored with great care. Bernard the owner kept three hundred sheep and his wife taught at a primary school. The one snag was that they did not provide an evening meal so I had to foot it up a dark country road into the village and, despite having a torch, managed to stumble into some unlit roadworks. Out of season Talmont-St.-Hilaire was a ghost town. The houses straggled down a main road and had few redeeming features, despite the existence of a ruined castle to add a touch of the picturesque. All I could find open was a pizza parlour. Two women from my bed and breakfast were also eating there. "Why are you walking around France on your own?" they asked. "The French wouldn't walk alone. They're far too sociable."

As I washed the slices of cheese and salami pizza down with a sickly orange drink I could see that this insight was correct. It explained the puzzled reactions my appearance frequently provoked.

Yet being alone has its advantages if you want to get close to people. On at least three occasions in the Vendée I was asked to dine with the owners of a *chambres d'hôte*, because it seemed rather pointless to eat separately. On my first night on the Chemin de St. Jacques a widow called Odette offered me free hospitality. She had thrown herself into the local community and told me about the choral group to which she belonged. Taking out a book of Christmas carols familiar to English ears she asked if I could sing them for her, so I duly found

233

myself tackling "Angels in the Realms of Glory" in the middle of France and completely out of season. Then she said that she had to drive twenty miles to look after some grandchildren for two days and offered me the run of her house. Lucie, her daughter-in-law who lived next door, would feed me. "She is always doing this," said Lucie, "and she has nothing worth stealing."

I accepted gratefully and made a contribution.

My next meal with my hosts turned out quite differently. Fabienne, fashionably dressed with streaked blond hair, was a chatterbox. She ran her *chambres d'hôte* as a business, having previously owned a pizza restaurant which burnt down. Resilient and resourceful would be appropriate words to describe her. During our meal together the phone never stopped ringing. She had signed up with Smart Box, an organisation which offers customers vouchers for a night at an exclusive *chambres d'hôte*, which they can give to a friend. She was taking thirty calls a night and was booked up to Christmas. Every five minutes I heard her repeating, "I am sorry *madame*, but I have no weekends free for the rest of the year and no space in the high season." Her husband commented, "These people drive half way across France just to get a free night. It's incredible!"

Thierry was a magician. "I saw bodies in half," he said, "and one day I will saw Fabienne's tongue in half too." Fabienne seemed to find such carping comments rather irksome. "I'm very busy changing sheets and cooking for all these people. Next week I have a party of fifty for dinner. I am only a woman." At one time she used to be Thierry's assistant, no doubt in a sequined dress doing a twirl while he pulled rabbits out of hats.

Sometimes finding something to eat was a struggle. In Maillezais everywhere was shut, except for one restaurant which did not serve dinner on Thursdays. I appealed to the owner's better nature, explaining that I was famished after a long day walking. Miraculously a four-course meal appeared at a very reasonable price: tuna salad, pork chop, cheese and tart. If I had been taking a French *dictée* I would have made a complete hash of it. I thought the waiter said *poire ou pruneaux*, pear or prunes, but in fact he said *far aux pruneaux*. Why was he offering me a lighthouse, *un phare*? His tart was like what is known in Brittany as a *far breton*: a gelatinous yellow pudding with squashed prunes at the bottom, and in any case it was filling. Several men with pot bellies were drinking at the bar, occasionally dashing outside for a smoke. They stared at me with curiosity when they were not exercising their Gallic charm on the only woman in the establishment. Although she was of a certain age, it is amazing what a jumper off the shoulder and long hair can do…

The people of the Vendée must be determined and resilient. In a previously backward area of France they have created a modern prosperous community which is attractive to outsiders. Clemenceau said the Vendéens were sturdy and tenacious people and he was no exception. His well-used duelling pistols lie at the bottom of his bed, next to a tiger's head and a pair of African spears. On the Vendée coast he created a garden in the most unsuitable spot imaginable: a bed of sand buffeted by the salt-laden winds.

THE SAINTONGE: GRAPES AND GARGOYLES

Once I had passed Mauzé on the Canal du Mignon the landscape changed. I lost the Chemin de St. Jacques near a flyover on the edge of town and only retrieved the situation by scrambling over some crash barriers. Mauzé's favourite son is René Caillé, who crossed the Sahara to discover Timbuktu in 1828. No doubt he lost his way a few times in much wilder country. I strode across the open plain once more all the way to Surgères. The next day there was more of the same, except for a swell on the ocean of ploughed earth the further south I went. I even had to climb a hill at Puyrolland, so called because Roland, the hero of the eponymous *chanson*, is supposed to have flung his axe down here, causing an upheaval in the process. That day was a test of endurance on the tarmac and I had to stay focussed. After fifteen miles I reached the Boutonne. The sight of this indolent river wandering between grassy banks and lines of poplars filled me with confidence that the end was in sight. The path took me all the way into St.-Jean-d'Angély, twenty-two miles from Surgères, but as always there was a sting in the tail. I lost my way on the outskirts of the town and wandered around in circles looking for my lodging. Eventually completing the walk in less than seven hours, I collapsed into bed without bothering to eat.

After St.-Jean I found several isolated churches which had probably been surrounded by houses until the Black Death. The countryside was taking on something of the character of the *bocage*. Later I learnt that farmers have deliberately put back the hedges for environmental reasons and to please tourists. There were several steep-sided valleys before I reached the River Charente at Saintes. One was reserved for use by the local archery society, and I half expected a French Robin Hood to appear from behind a tree, but apparently Red Indian costumes are much more popular.

In the Middle Ages pilgrims followed the Roman road south from Saintes.

Now lorries thunder between two rows of trees stretching into the distance, not a very attractive prospect for a walker. The Compostela trail meanders across a gently undulating plain, never far from the traffic. Builders' merchants' sheds and car showrooms mar the fringes of towns. The predominant crop is grapes, interspersed with perfectly drilled rows of wheat, tobacco, apple orchards and the occasional patch of woodland. One ponderous château deep in a park looked like the perfect escape from modern life, shutters closed and a grove of cow parsley lapping around the immense stone barn and tall Romanesque church. Some of the substantial grey stone farm houses had been decaying gently for years, with rusting balconies and peeling oak doors.

I asked a local man what happened at Saintes and he replied that, apart from tourism, it was a staging post on the road to Bordeaux. This has been its raison d'être for centuries since it lies on a main pilgrimage route. St.-Eutrope was built as a pilgrimage church on a grand scale. At Pons I passed under the arch of the hospital where pilgrims had to sleep on rough stone ledges, assuaging their hunger on bread passed out by the monks. Compared with this a modern walkers' hostel seems like the Hilton. Today simple country churches, as well as abbeys and cathedrals, are open to more than 100,000 people who make the pilgrimage every year. Many of them are retired, although some are young. They come from all over Europe. The Chemins de St. Jacques have been adopted by the EU as European cultural itineraries. St. James' cockle shell can be found everywhere.

Their motivations are various. Some embark on this pilgrimage for spiritual reasons. They are believers. Putting up with the difficulties on the trail is a way of getting closer to God. Some have just experienced an upheaval in their lives. Perhaps they have lost their job. They want some peace to think about what they will do next. Others have had a mental breakdown. They are looking for a way out. For many the St. Jacques provides a cultural journey across attractive countryside where they can visit historic sites and to some extent experience the life of a medieval pilgrim.

The Saintonge was a separate province of the old French Kingdom. It has a distinct character, two aspects of which I particularly noticed: the cultural heritage of Rome and the local Romanesque style of the High Middle Ages, and the vineyards producing grapes for cognac.

Saintes was a Roman town, Mediolanum, complete with aqueduct, arena and triumphal arch. Medieval builders in the Saintonge replicated such Roman arches many times on the west fronts of churches and abbeys, but transformed them into wonderful galleries of sculpture. The figures are often naive and touching in their humanity, while teaching the faithful about God at work on earth. Minstrels, grotesque faces and fabulous beasts come alive alongside angels and apostles. The signs of the zodiac are a common theme as well as friezes of intricate foliage. On the church front at Fenioux devils with tails push wrongdoers into the flames of hell, while in Saintes at the Abbaye de Ste.-Marie des Dames we can see the gruesome sufferings of the early Christian martyrs. Belfries with arcades of classical columns rise above these sanctuaries, often surmounted by a roof of interlocking stone tiles like a pine cone. The architects were constantly inventing new forms: the huge crypt at St.-Eutrope in Saintes only half underground, the false domes in the aisles at Ste.-Marie and the Lanterne des Morts at Fenioux. The latter is an extraordinary structure, a slim tower on the site of a former cemetery, decorated with eleven columns and an arcade on the top. It looks like a bundle of sticks of dynamite about to explode into flame. The faithful used to light a fire at the top to mark a funeral or a religious festival.

In the Saintonge I admired not only Romanesque sculpture but also the immaculate rows of vines which proliferate south of Surgères. Before St.-Jean-d'Angély they sweep down open slopes scattered with flints. South of the Boutonne vines look like any other agricultural crop; enclosed in level fields of chalky soil in the *bocage*. I arrived when vigorous pruning was in progress and a pungent smell of smoke hung over some of the vineyards. One couple rested from their labours to explain that most of their grapes went to make cognac. They pruned the vines back to two shoots with about seven buds each. They also produced a *vin de pays* using the chardonnay grape and, in this case, they left only one shoot on the stump of the vine.

Apart from fine Romanesque churches, the small towns of the Saintonge contain many secular buildings of great charm and character from previous centuries: the walled enclosure at Surgères; the carved Renaissance fountain, gate tower and wooden-beamed houses at St.-Jean; the hanging gardens by the quay, meandering medieval streets and eighteenth-century houses in Saintes. Full of fascinating corners, they tempted me to stop walking and linger for a few days. The pace of life seemed pleasantly unhurried, especially in St.-Jean-d'Angély, and these towns had sufficient run-down buildings to convince me they were not museums. Inevitably I found a second-hand bookshop full of buried treasure

Lanterne des Morts, Fenioux

next to the cathedral at Saintes, and a bearded owner who was suspicious of the modern world. When I handed him my credit card he launched into a speech about our obsession with security. "I'm not worried about it," he said. "What we have to ask is, who is watching whom and why?"

From this he made an easy transition to materialism. "Human beings always want more. They hurry about with no time to stop and think. It must be marvellous to walk long distances and have the time to look at things. I prefer studying nature. Last weekend I watched two ibises mating in a marsh near here. They are descended from the sacred ibises of ancient Egypt. It's a rare sight. I will never forget it. I don't agree with the Judeo-Christian belief that man should lord it over other animals and control the planet. There are too many human beings anyway. Eventually we will die out."

Pons provided a picturesque setting for a relaxing evening: medieval walls and a gaunt fortress, now the *mairie*, surging out of a rocky escarpment crisscrossed by narrow alleys. At the bottom of the hill another sluggish river meandered between small islands, its surface reflecting the iridescent green of ash and willow. My hosts Ingrid and Jacques had followed a familiar migration path from the cold winters of Lorraine, via Paris, to the milder Atlantic climate of the south-west. They had found their perfect haven, a restored house with high ceilings by the water, their garden as lush as the surrounding vegetation. They enjoyed canoeing up and down the stream, looking for kingfishers and the yellow oriole from Africa. The town was small enough to be calm in the summer rush to the coast, but large enough to provide good schools and everything they needed.

*

A call from Lizzie interrupted this idyll in the garden.

"I'm afraid your mother felt faint the other day and pushed her wrist alarm. The ambulance men thought her heart ought to be checked out by a cardiologist. She has been taken back to hospital. What was the name of the specialist she saw a couple of years ago?"

Immediately I thought about the problems the doctors had experienced last time she was admitted.

"Will I have to come home?"

"Absolutely not. I don't think it's that serious."

"How is my father?"

"He's suffering from another infection. The doctor has given him some strong antibiotics. Mike will make sure he takes them. What would we do without him? We can't be there everyday. If someone doesn't give him the pills he won't take them. Is he cussed or genuinely forgetful?"

"He doesn't believe in medicines. There are lots of unused boxes of pills in his house. I am sure his memory is going too."

*

Wandering through the Saintonge I seemed well within my comfort zone. The walking was easy, with points of interest and warm hospitality. A retired butcher and his wife fussed over me as if I was undertaking some epic feat. The quietly spoken owner of a stone manor house produced a delicious supper when he did not usually offer meals, just because I was a walker. But the sight of someone begging on the footbridge into Saintes brought me up with a jolt. He was a young Romanian living in a squat, *sans papiers* as the French would say and therefore having difficulty finding work. A Catholic charity had taken pity on him and given him a new set of clothes.

"I can't go back to Romania," he said, "there is no work there. It is hopeless."

I reflected that superficially at least my way ahead was clear, whereas his was not. As we talked, the Charente flowed slowly beneath us. The next river to cross on my trail would be the Gironde. Yet my sense of direction was an illusion. I was trying to find some respite from reality. I had no idea how I could come to terms with it.

14

AQUITAINE
PILGRIMS AND PINES

I STAYED IN A hostel at Mirambeau where the owner complained about Santiago pilgrims who expected board and lodging for nothing. "I try to practise my faith," he said, "but I think they should be prepared to make a contribution." "The pilgrims who expect everything for nothing stuff themselves at dinner," his wife said sarcastically. From the garden I could just make out the pale ribbon of the Gironde estuary in the dusk. I was only three days from Bordeaux and well on my way to the Pyrenees to complete my circuit around France.

It was at the hostel in Mirambeau that I met Bruno. He walked with me until we reached a village where I wanted to look at some irreverent gargoyles on a Romanesque church. Bruno was not the slightest bit interested. He explained that he did not bother with photos and never stopped. He had to cover twenty-two miles a day. Bruno was slim and moved fast.

"I am a runner," he said. "I've never done a major walk before."

When we started off in the morning I was amazed to see that he did not heave his rucksack onto his back, but proposed to drag it along behind him. "I've hurt my shoulder," he said, "so I have designed this trolley with three wheels each side. It's made to roll the sack over rocks."

He proceeded to attach his trolley to a belt around his waist. The whole contraption looked very uncomfortable. "How do you manage on a grassy track?" I asked.

"It's a bit of a problem if the grass is too long. It gets stuck in the wheels. So I walk mainly on the roads."

Bruno said he was not a practising Catholic but was doing the walk for spiritual reasons. A man of few words, he wanted to be on his own, although he said he enjoyed impromptu encounters with different people. He was fifty years old, had worked for France Télécom since the age of sixteen and still had eight years to wait before he could retire on full pension, seventy per cent of his normal pay. He planned to spend May walking the Compostela trail, taking a whole month off while hardly using up any of his five weeks' annual leave. This could probably only work in France. May has four public holidays and, in addition, he could take time off for hours worked in excess of the statutory thirty-five, and also to compensate for overtime at weekends.

I crossed a small river by the former abbey church of Pleine-Selves. A sign announced the start of the Gironde *département* and, more important, the first

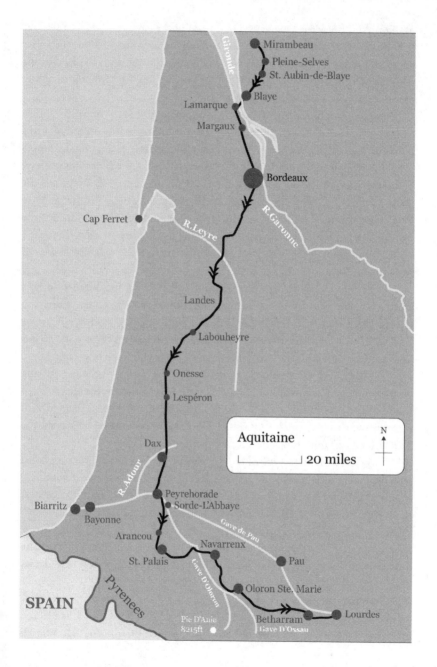

of the famous Bordeaux vineyards. For the rest of the day I saw little but straight lines of vines stretching in immaculate rows to the horizon. This was the Côtes de Blaye producing quality wines, if not the finest in the region. Blaye is one of those place names which trap the unsuspecting English visitor into wrong pronunciations—it sounds like "Bligh".

Near St.-Aubin-de-Blaye I found accommodation in a nineteenth-century version of a classical house, full of bourgeois self-importance. Covered in heavy mouldings it was far too high for its width and looked as if it might topple over. The mahogany furniture, gilded mirrors, faded floral wallpaper and china figurines added to the oppressive atmosphere. In the courtyard the proprietor made a wine of the Premières Côtes de Blaye. The website describes the property as a *gentilhommière*, a house suitable for a gentleman. When Mireille, the manageress, ran me down the main road to the local transport café I thought I would be roughing it. How wrong I was! The car park at the *Le Relais Roubisque* was full of forty-ton trucks and their drivers packed the restaurant inside. Large men in singlets and shorts with shaven heads were tucking into a generous hors d'oeuvres buffet. No fry ups here but plates full of raw vegetables, beans and melon. Once they had demolished this healthy food they tackled veal steaks with haricots, cheese and another table loaded with desserts. I could not help but join in. The cost, with wine and coffee, was €12; just about the best value I have ever had in France. I did wonder, however, how the drivers at the bar gulping back Ricard could stay within the alcohol limit. Maybe they were going to sleep it off in their cabs. While we were inside a cracking thunderstorm erupted with hailstones the size of small footballs. Later I discovered these had ripped the young shoots off the vines, a disaster for the *vignerons*.

A very different scene greeted me at breakfast. Across the antique table laden with delicate porcelain cups and six varieties of jam I blinked at an extraordinary apparition. A portly *monsieur* in a white linen suit and pink floral shirt sat next to his wife, whose dyed hair was almost as bright as her husband's attire. Between them a white poodle, with immaculate coiffure and a pink bow, stared at me from a carry cot. *Monsieur* was an artist from Marseille, selling oils of the Côte d'Azur in the Impressionist style, very different from the court scene with ladies in crinolines which covered one wall of the salon.

Once past the inevitable sprawl of villas and discount stores outside Blaye I came face to face with Vauban's mighty fortress, the fourteenth I had ticked off on my journey. Vauban did not actually supervise the construction himself but turned up in his carriage one day in 1685 and made a few alterations to a plan prepared by a local man called Ferry. In any case there was already a fort here when he arrived; it simply needed updating. Vauban must have been a man of amazing energy, rushing back and forth across France and up to Versailles to keep the king informed.

Blaye is a good example of his art with its massive ditches, triple ramparts and hallmark triangular bastions. Hundreds of poor people's houses were demolished to make way for all this stonework (they would have had good reason to shout "Merde à Vauban", to quote the refrain from Léo Ferré's song). When I stood on the terrace overlooking the Gironde, some two miles wide at this point, I understood the reason for all this effort. Vauban built a second fort on one of the gravel banks which dot the estuary and a third on the far bank. With the latest cannon he could be sure that enemy ships would be sent to the bottom before they reached Bordeaux.

The ferry chugged across the smooth surface of the Gironde, tracing a parabola against the incoming tide. No other ships ruffled the flow of the river. Before 1914 the quayside at Blaye would have been crowded with merchant vessels. Now it seemed to have lost its purpose. The back streets looked shabby and one in five of the population is out of a job. After the oil shock of 1973 new container terminals were built nearer the sea and now this waterway is almost deserted.

I stepped off the quayside at Lamarque straight into the most famous vineyards in the world, the classed growths of the Médoc. The landscape is bleak and unremarkable; flat stretches of sandy gravel and on the surface enough pebbles to make me think I was walking on a beach. Do not be deceived: this soil is eminently suitable for vines. Water drains through easily and the roots have to dig deep into the ground to extract the nutrients which help give Bordeaux its unique flavour. Elegant château courtyards behind iron railings speak of discreet wealth. Château Malescasse stands within sight of the ridiculous church tower at Lamarque, which looks like a cross between a lighthouse and a three-tiered wedding cake. At the end of each row of vines a bush rose adds a touch of crimson and provides a useful warning of pests. Malescasse is a modest Cru Bourgeois Supérieur. My route avoided the grandest classed growths.

The main road through the Médoc was full of traffic. This is not an idyllic rural sanctuary, but a vast market garden throbbing with the sounds of commerce. As I jumped constantly onto a grassy bank to avoid being mown down, I noticed that the vines had been replaced by a waterlogged marsh of tangled vegetation. This is typical of the low-lying areas between the gravel banks. It was my first taste of a landscape which stretches all the way past Bordeaux to the foothills of the Pyrenees.

I turned off onto a quieter side road just north of the famous Château Margaux. For the next fifteen miles into Bordeaux I hardly saw any vines, just a sprawl of suburban villas with small patches of heath in between. All the same I was given the friendliest possible reception by passers by. They assumed I must be going all the way to Santiago and jumped out of their cars to shower me with gifts and greetings. At first I was completely taken aback. Outside a row of bungalows near Margaux a small car halted behind me and suddenly I felt a firm arm on my shoulder. An enormous hulk of a man held me in his grasp, while his wife thrust a dubious bottle of wine without a label into my hand.

"You must take this," he said. "It will make you strong for the pilgrimage."

I feared drinking a whole bottle of rosé for lunch would ensure I never reached Bordeaux. Then he rummaged in his pocket, pulled out €8 and thrust them into my palm. "You will need this too to help you on your journey."

I protested in vain in my English way. "Look, it is very kind of you but I am sure there are others more deserving…"

He would not take no for an answer, so I put the coins in my pocket and thanked him profusely. He introduced himself.

"I came from Poland many years ago and settled here, working as a mechanic. My wife is from Belgium. Now I'm retired, but I have had a good life here. Would you like to come to lunch?"

He beckoned towards the garden of one of the bungalows.

With some regrets I declined. "I must reach Bordeaux tonight."

"Then I will drive you there after we have eaten."

"Yes but I prefer to walk. That's what I am here to do."

Somehow I extracted myself from his warm embrace and plodded on clutching my bottle of wine and €8, which I later gave to charity. There is a Catholic tradition of giving alms to pilgrims going back to the Middle Ages. Pilgrims were poor and suffered many hardships to strengthen their faith. They deserved help. I did not ask my new friend if he was Catholic but, as a Pole, it was more than likely.

BORDEAUX

Eighteenth-century Bordeaux wore its wealth on its sleeve. Everywhere I strolled the pre-revolutionary city flaunted its commercial success: the self-confident façade of the Palais de la Bourse with its opulent stonework and imposing windows looking down on the Garonne; the high arched doors of the merchants' houses on the Quai des Chartrons watched over by contorted faces sculpted in stone, the *mascarons*. I stood on the opposite bank and tried to imagine the majestic sweep of the river, *la lune,* the moon, as the Bordelais call it, full of shipping. Now this waterway is practically deserted.

Traders came from all over Europe to do business here: Dutch, Portuguese, and English among others. Of course there was a large Jewish community. The Bordelais took slaves from West Africa to Martinique, Guadeloupe and St.-Domingue (modern Haiti), but made far more money selling products from the plantations there, particularly sugar. Then, as now, it was the French state that took a guiding role in creating a magnificent city which would attract people from far and wide. The Intendant Tourny, for which today read prefect or even mayor, laid out the stately *allée* bearing his name. It leads to the colonnades of the classical theatre which looks imposing enough for a European capital. On the Esplanade des Quinconces, the largest public square in Europe, the citizens could wander by the river in the shade. Now it is the central bus terminus and a site for fairs, during my visit a Foire aux Jambons. (Only in France could you find a fair whose sole purpose was to seduce customers with different types of ham.)

The ambition of all this planning on a grand scale took my breath away. After a while I wanted to escape from the dead straight lines to the more intimate medieval city which lies alongside with its narrow winding streets, small squares and turreted gates. I lounged in the shade of the great flowering chestnut in the Place du Parlement, stared up at the stand-alone clock towers by the cathedral and the Eglise St.-Martin, giggled at the pastiche of devils with pitchforks pushing wrongdoers into hell on the west front of Ste.-Croix, and mingled with Muslims leaving prayers near the market, a quarter also popular with students. I had lunch, not in a large *brasserie* on one of the wide avenues, but in a vegetarian restaurant where a sallow-faced lady told me with fervour in her eyes that she had been "bio" for forty years.

Bordeaux had its golden age, but in the nineteenth century buildings with grandeur and delicacy gave way to bourgeois solidity; witness the inner-city streets I sped through on my way out of the city. Now young couples are refurbishing the single-storey dwellings of this era. Since 1945, moreover, the state has intervened to rejuvenate Bordeaux once again, and in the last thirty years two powerful mayors and a regional authority with clout have used public money to create an attractive urban environment. The esplanade along *la lune*, with its gardens and *miroir d'eau*, and the new law courts designed by Richard Rogers are admirable examples of how a city can be transformed. Some people hate the Rogers building, but I was stunned by the way he had blended the old and the new, the beehive courtrooms echoing the tower of the castle alongside. The entrance is via a grand staircase over a moat which laps against the medieval walls. Despite more new development the old industrial right bank feels divorced from the main part of the city. The river is wide and there is only one bridge in the centre, the old Pont de Pierre built on the orders of Napoleon. The joke in Bordeaux is that the right (bank) votes left and the left right, to underline the difference between the two halves.

As in the eighteenth century a prosperous and diversified economy has encouraged outsiders to work and retire near the Gironde. I came across several examples in the space of forty-eight hours: a man who had grown up in a military family in Gabon in West Africa; another born in Algeria who had worked throughout Africa but arranged his final posting to Bordeaux so he could retire here; another who had worked for a public utility all over France before coming to rest in the city; yet others from Lille who enjoyed good days at Cap Ferret on the coast, a paradise for swimming, cycling and tasting oysters. I wished I could have stayed longer.

The centre of Bordeaux contained plenty of reminders that I was still on the trail to Compostela. The basilicas of St.-Seurin and St.-Michel, as well as the cathedral itself, are pilgrimage churches with chapels built for the Jacquaires to say their prayers. I plodded out through the southern suburbs where more local people wanted to stop and say hello. One man jumped out of his car with a broad grin on his face. He told me he had been to Compostela four times, as well as trekking to the shrine of our lady of Fatima, which he found much more moving. He was not impressed when I said I would prefer not to cover twenty-five miles in one day's walk in the Landes.

"I have had a stent fitted in my heart and I have done it!" he exclaimed.

South of Bordeaux I was accosted by Michel, the president of the local association of Jacquaires. He had walked to Compostela ten times and met his wife in the process. He looked slim and athletic and radiated an inner contentment. He had enjoyed the opportunity for spiritual reflection and living a simple life. Clearly the experience had changed him.

*

As I left Bordeaux I received a text from Beccy, my mother's carer: "Muriel bck aftr hrt check. Poss infctn like be4. District nurses 2 call."

*

LES LANDES

I now had to cross the Landes to reach Dax one hundred miles away, which took seven days. The Landes form one of the largest forests in Europe at around two and a half million acres. The author François Mauriac created the classic image of the region in his 1927 novel *Thérèse Desqueyroux*, describing how the wind moaning in the trees drove the heroine mad and made her try to poison her husband. I approached the Landes with some trepidation. Would I be marching for eternity down straight forest roads enclosed by dense rows of dark pines?

Fortunately the reality was quite different.

Today's forest is an entirely artificial landscape. Until the middle of the nineteenth century the Landes was a vast heath with few trees. The vegetation consisted mainly of gorse, broom, heather and moor grass, all of which thrived on the sandy soil stretching along the Atlantic Coast and many miles inland. Much of the Landes was badly drained and so there were extensive marshes. On a clear day inhabitants could see the Pyrenees, and most were shepherds who wore long sheepskin cloaks in winter and who got around on eight-foot stilts which helped them jump ditches and see a long way. It was Napoleon III (French Emperor 1852-70) who started the programme to drain the Landes and plant pine trees, which provided a more solid basis for the economy of the region. In places I discovered the wide horizons of the original landscape before the pines arrived. Between the plantations smaller woods of deciduous trees and tangled masses of vegetation grow in waterlogged black peat. Rivers like the Leyre and myriad smaller streams flow between trees dappled in sunlight, while water-loving plants such as flag irises and orchids line their banks. Sometimes the colour of the water is peaty brown, but if it flows over sand it is as clear as crystal. The Landes are not entirely flat. The water courses usually lie in shallow depressions in the pine plateau. Outside Lespéron a gorge two hundred feet deep echoed to the sound of croaking frogs. Dunes covered in trees can rise to around one hundred feet and in the south there are hills foreshadowing the Pyrenees to come.

Plenty of conventional agricultural crops grow in the Landes on enormous fields carved out of the forest: maize, asparagus, peas, lettuces and carrots. The sandy soil here needs constant fertilisation and irrigation. Large pumps draw water from less than three feet below the surface of this former bog and spray it out of giant gantries like metallic spiders. I also saw orderly rows of huts for raising chickens, some of which were allowed to roam free on the fallen trees outside. White ducks sat in large compounds of sun-baked earth. Though *magret de canard* and *confit de canard* are very popular dishes in France, visitors may find the taste for them palls after too much repetition on local menus. "No more fucking duck," as an Australian said after eating it for a whole week.

Large settlements are few and far between in the Landes. The largest village I visited in a week was Labouheyre, with a population of around 4,000 but on a hot afternoon looking like the set for a Clint Eastwood movie. Outside the *Café des Sports* a few local workers were having a smoke when they were not inside downing another 1664. One of them eyed the square for the slightest sign of movement. There was nothing to look at, except an electronic display flashing details of rubbish collections and the artistic trellis of plane trees covering the grass. Every few miles on the path I crossed a clearing containing a number of traditional single-storey dwellings; vertical wooden beams separated by brick or plaster, barns with weathered wooden slats occasionally topped with lattice work. Many of these cottages built for humble forest dwellers are now highly desirable second homes.

Everywhere large trees lay uprooted or leant over at a crazy angle, top-heavy poles of gnarled grey bark with a sprig of green on top. Enormous stacks of logs lined all the forest paths. In one spot I saw twenty, each at least twelve logs high. Further on a maze of fallen trees blocked the path and I had to climb around them to get through. On 24 January 2009 a cataclysmic event altered the face of the Landes, possibly for ever. Cyclone Klaus ripped through a very precise corridor in the centre of the forest, felling almost every tree in sight. Now parts of the Landes look like a wood on the Western Front destroyed by heavy shell fire: branches ripped from the main trunk like limbs hacked off in battle; trees split in half like matchsticks. Some estimates suggest that over half the forest was destroyed. Now there is a vast surplus of felled wood and owners do not have the capital to replace damaged trees. Estonians and Poles have been brought in to help with the process of clearing up, their voices conspicuous in some of the villages. Pine can only be kept for two years because it lacks the resistance to decay and insect attack of other woods, and even then it has to be sprayed constantly with water. The European Union has voted funds to help with clearance and replanting, but they have been slow to arrive and may not be sufficient. One proprietor of a small patch of forest talked bitterly about the current situation. "The Parisian bankers who own the big house opposite have a large tract of forest. No doubt they can take the hit but I am suffering."

Some of the forest paths stretched to a vanishing point in a monotonous straight line. Objects by the side of the white sandy track hovered in the heat haze like a mirage. There was no escape from the sun and dust. Other paths were sinuous and shady but a lot of the walking was on tarmac, which caused blisters to reappear. Sometimes I had to walk along busy highways where long straight stretches tempted motorists to drive fast. All was quiet among the pines, but I slept in a series of rooms on roads where lorries rumbled past all night. On one occasion a cramped bedroom with a lumpy mattress stood next to the main

TGV line to Bordeaux.

I followed the Compostela trail through the Landes and was greeted like a pilgrim. Alongside a motorway motorbikers peeped, motorists waved and lorry drivers honked their horns. I was also offered gifts of food. And then in the *auberge* in Onesse-et-Laharie I met Eric with Esther. Eric came from Domfront in the Orne and religious practice clearly meant something to him. Strong and fit, he had decided to take two months off between jobs and walk all the way to Compostela from his native Normandy.

"I do not think we should ask each other what we do at home," he said. "We should accept people as they are and not prejudge them on the basis of occupation, race or class. I want to avoid the stress of the work place. I love meeting people in an unstructured way. You learn to weigh the effect of your words on others and not to be judgemental. Every day is an adventure. Now I've got a chance to reflect and change my life. "

I agree with Eric. It is always an adventure to meet people outside the circle of friends you see every week.

Eric had picked up a strapping Spanish girl called Esther, who had tattoos on her legs and feet. She spoke a few words of French, mixing them liberally with her native language. Before every remark she exclaimed "OK!" and waved her arms in the air. "OK, when I reach Cape Finisterre," she said, "OK, I will throw my rucksack away and all the rubbish in my life and OK, start again."

Esther was a vegetarian and did not eat dairy products because she said they caused excess levels of mucus. Eating meat resulted in impurities in the blood. She wanted to rid her body of all these toxic substances. She had a small rucksack, but it weighed a ton because she was carrying all sorts of healthy food: a litre of olive oil, lettuce, tomatoes, avocado, mushrooms, chick peas, quinoa and bread. Eric may have been dying for a steak, but Esther had trained him to eat salad sandwiches, although I noticed at lunch that he sneaked some dried sausage into his meal. She developed several blisters, some of which were bleeding, and slumped on the roadside applying bandages to every toe. Eric was very attentive. He might have to be tough and leave her, I thought, if he was to get to Compostela on time.

I entered Dax in a thunderstorm, trudging down a long road of warehouses and through suburban housing estates. The dry River Adour looked like a drain full of sludge, and monolithic concrete blocks lined its banks, including the 1930s-style Splendid Hôtel, rust staining its white façade. I had been shut away

252

in the Landes for a week, but now re-entered the busy world. Beyond the river I could see the first hills worth climbing since Alsace.

I did not find much to detain me in Dax. Old streets surround the cathedral, a grandiose baroque edifice which took two hundred and seventy-five years to complete. Inside is a fine portal from the old Gothic west front transported to the north transept. It contains lifelike sculptures of the apostles including St. James with his cockle shell. The old baths steam at a temperature of 64°C, for this is a spa town where people come for the cure at fifteen thermal establishments. Groups of middle-aged ladies with white permed hair and anaemic skin gossiped about their day trying to restore their health. My hotel on the ring road won a prize for the noisiest in France. I pulled the shutters down at night and stuffed wax plugs in my ears, but still it was difficult to sleep. The lorries rumbled right through my room, or so it seemed. I could not wait to escape.

THE BÉARN

According to the guidebooks the Béarn is an ancient province, close to the Pyrenees and popular with British owning second homes. I was looking forward to a pleasant stroll through an English landscape: peaceful grassy paths between bristling hedgerows; leafy woods; rolling hills with distant views of the mountains. Unfortunately on the first day out of Dax it rained as I escaped from a ribbon of builders' yards to stumble along the verge of a busy main road. Then as the grass strip disappeared I jumped over a traffic barrier on a steep bend to escape the oncoming lorries—out of the frying pan into the fire, I clung to the metal rails to avoid tumbling down a steep bank into a stream below while the rain fell even harder. Vaulting back onto a bridge I dashed into a nearby café on the far side. It was a relief to escape the noise of motors changing gear over a *grand crème*. The *patron* was on the phone selling his business, but had time to tell me that there was a large quarry just down the road, which explained the succession of tipper trucks pounding the small bridge every few seconds. I awarded this section a five-star rating for danger and noise.

In Peyrehorade a lady running the bread stall in the market took pity on a poor pilgrim and gave me free pastries. Now I had to cross the valley of the Gave de Pau and a motorway, before reaching my rural paradise. It seems that in this part of France the rivers draining the Pyrenees are called *gaves*. They are full of opaque ice-green water flowing very fast and totally unsuitable for navigation, let alone swimming. The term derives from an ancient pre-Celtic word *gaba*, meaning a river hemmed in by its banks, certainly appropriate in this case. The flat fertile land watered by these rivers is entirely different from the surrounding hill country. Near Sorde-l'Abbaye most of the fields seemed to be full of kiwi fruit, their creamy blossoms hanging from wires which supported the trees espalier-style. Large pebbles lay scattered on the ground, no doubt washed down by the *gaves*. Some of them had been used to build the old farmhouses.

In the hill country at Arancou I received a warm welcome from Jean-Pierre and Colette who were taking a holiday from their native Normandy to look after the hostel. The local *commune* had decided to continue the ancient tradition of providing hospitality to pilgrims and had converted an old stone house dating from 1265 into the most lavish accommodation imaginable, with every detail beautifully finished. Jean-Pierre was broad-set with a large bushy beard and expressive eyes which twinkled with delight at anything which interested him. "If you are going to Lourdes, pray for me to lose weight!" he said.

Jean-Pierre had huge hands. He was a sculptor and came from a long line of craftsmen. He had completed the pilgrimage from Le Puy to Santiago de Compostela some years ago and, when he heard about this venture, just had to help. He had produced a lively relief sculpture to fix on an outside wall, recording the fact that Arancou is almost exactly halfway between Paris and Santiago; five hundred and sixteen miles each way.

Over supper outside I discovered that Jean-Pierre was something of an Anglophile. "I love fish and chips," he said, "but why have you let so many foreigners into your country?" He was also passionate about history and paid tribute to the British soldiers who risked their lives to train the *maquis* in the Second World War. Going back to the First World War he said, "France has never recovered psychologically from the losses sustained between 1914 and 1918." No doubt this explained his opposition to the war in Afghanistan.

Jean-Pierre insisted that I look carefully at the work of the master masons who built the churches at Arancou and nearby Villenave-sur-Bidouze. The former has all the reverent simplicity of early Gothic with a high choir in flecked brown and white stone, while the sister church Villenave still has Romanesque features. On the west doorway I found a typical Basque emblem, the marguerite flower, also replicated on the arches of the old bridge. Jean-Pierre thought the sculptures were done by the same mason. Here I crossed the River Bidouze and entered the Pays Basque.

The sound of barking guard dogs had followed me right round France.

In the Landes I became so infuriated with the noise that I decided to strike back. Outside a farm house an odd assortment of dogs started howling: hunting beagles, a mongrel, a spaniel and a fox terrier. I responded by rushing at them with raised stick, whipping them into a frenzy. Fortunately in most cases dogs are shut in behind wire fences, which must make the manufacturers a fortune since they are universal. In the Basque Country, however, gates are often left open and the unwary walker risks a bite or two. On one occasion three dogs rushed at me with evil intent until the call of their master in the local patois persuaded them otherwise. Wandering down one lane I was alarmed when a large white Pyrenean *patou* came out of a garden. These dogs weigh in at up to one hundred and forty pounds and have been known to take on wolves. I had come across them in the Alps near flocks of sheep and had learnt to be careful. This one looked like a small lion, but I soon realised I need not have worried. He was as docile as could be and sauntered after me for a walk until his mistress arrived to collect him in a car.

After Arancou the Pyrenees suddenly seemed much nearer. On top of the hills I was above the world of ordinary mortals, staring straight at the snow-capped mountains to the east. The distinctive point of the Pic d'Anie (8,215 feet) rose up in the middle of a dark ridge among couloirs streaked with white. Nearer the coast overlapping cones like green volcanoes died away to the sea. Grassy tracks and woodland alternated with hot tarmac for the rest of the day. Blisters troubled me once again and I had to stop twice for roadside repairs. By the time I reached St.-Palais I was desperate for a drink and François' garden was a welcome oasis of calm.

François was lean with a mop of wavy hair falling over his forehead and a strong nose. He had something of the artist about him and I could see he was a man of taste from the way he had restored his house. My guess was right: he had run a landscape gardening business in Bordeaux before deciding to settle permanently in St.-Palais. Courteous and attentive, his words could also be as sharp as a rapier's point. I said my aim was to get to Lourdes. "*C'est le comble de l'horreur de l'église catholique,*" was his indignant reply, meaning that it was about as frightful—and as Catholic—as it gets. The combination of the sarcasm in his voice, a wave of the arm and the dismissive look in his eyes was devastating. He summed up in one sentence the antipathy that many educated Frenchmen have felt towards Rome since the days of Voltaire, who talked about crushing the infamy of Catholicism.

François loved his *coin* which he never left. "The French don't travel as much as the Anglo-Saxons. I expect you know France better than I do." He had, however, made a real study of Basque history and we continued our discussion of this subject over dinner.

There are seven Basque provinces, four in Spain and three in France. I had just entered the middle of the three French ones, known as Basse Navarre. Beyond St.-Palais my path lay through the eastern one known as Soule. The third runs along the coast. Navarre used to be a mighty kingdom stretching both sides of the Pyrenees and incorporating the Basque lands. The warlike Basques had a reputation for disliking outsiders and it was probably they who attacked the rearguard of Charlemagne's army causing Roland to sound his horn, even though the *Chanson de Roland* blames the Moors. Jean-Pierre had said that the Basques used to attack pilgrims and on one occasion murdered several near Arancou. In 1521 the Spanish King conquered the provinces of Navarre south of the Pyrenees and the royal house of Navarre fled north. For a time the parliament of Navarre sat in St.-Palais. Another house in François' street had sculptures of Henri d'Albret of Navarre and his wife Jeanne from that period. The Kings of Navarre were closely connected to the French royal family. After half a century of civil war and religious massacres Henri and Jeanne's son became King of France and Navarre was incorporated into the royal province of the Béarn.

In Spain the Basques enjoy autonomous regional government, but not in France where around 250,000 Basques live. While the language is taught in some schools and road signs are duplicated in Basque, only 25 per cent speak it regularly and the language has no official status. François said he was proud to be Basque, but only spoke a few words of the language. It was difficult to learn, he said, although adult classes were available. "Today most Basques in France just want to preserve their culture. They're not interested in political agitation."

While having lunch in a village square on my way to St.-Palais I noticed that there was a Basque party for the European elections. They achieved less than five per cent of the vote in Pyrénées-Atlantiques.

The region enjoys a mild climate and I often saw banana plants and palm trees growing in gardens. Local farmers produce a great variety of fruit and vegetables, the most common crop now being maize, grown predominantly for cattle feed and also as a bio fuel. In the past the vast majority of Basques worked the land. The farmhouse, where an extended family group lived with their animals, was the basis of society and a subsistence economy, an efficient economic unit where tasks could be shared, including looking after the young and old. So it was no surprise that I saw plenty of distinctive architecture in the villages through which I passed. Typically the traditional Basque house looks rather like a Swiss chalet, with a large sloping roof and living rooms on the first floor opening onto a balcony. Often the latter has carved or fretted woodwork and it overhangs the street. A large doorway on the ground floor, often surrounded with carved stones, gives access to the space for animals, hay and farm implements, while the exterior woodwork is usually painted in a special red which is said to be like bulls' blood. Modern builders have imitated this style in recent housing developments, but the ground floors have been designed for human use.

After incorporation into the Kingdom of France and peace with Spain, the Basque Country experienced a period of economic growth. The wealthy built large houses quite unlike the old farms. In the main street at Garris near St.-Palais I saw an elegant sundial on a façade, a balcony supported by carved heads and a large tower indicating a noble owner. The Basques were also sailors and merchants, but many settled permanently overseas, mainly in South America. The eldest son always inherited the family farm, and often the younger sons had no prospects so they left their homeland. As a result a significant proportion of the populations of Argentina, Chile and Uruguay are of Basque origin. François told me the history of his family. His house had been built by his great grandfather's brother. He went off to Chile and made a fortune trading skins, coming back to St.-Palais to spend his retirement. François' house was magnificent. The front of solid grey stone had high arched windows which opened onto a quiet town garden where climbing roses cascaded down onto the gravel terrace. Inside the high ceilings provided plenty of space for old furniture lovingly polished: a dresser decorated with marguerites, solid cupboards with carved doors and marble fireplaces.

The Basques also seem to be attached to symbols of their culture. Everywhere I saw the Basque cross, which looks like four joined-up apostrophes, and in churchyards the gravestones are often discoid in shape. The Basques also enjoy traditional games of which the best known is *pelote*, an outdoor version of real tennis played against a wall, with a basket attached to the arm serving as a racquet. Every village has its court from which the Basque flag flutters, two diagonal crosses green and red on the Basque red background. The last symbol which many men wear is the black beret. Plump-faced farmers wearing berets smiled at me from their tractors. Older men wore them in bars.

Back on the trail a notice deep in hazel thickets commanded: "SILENCE PALOMBIÈRES." Here licensed hunters have hides to shoot migrating pigeons in the autumn, sometimes frightening the birds by imitating the call of a larger predator and driving them into nets where they are trapped. It is an old tradition in these parts, but to outsiders massacring hundreds of birds on the move south seems particularly distasteful. Human migrants were also on the move in the shape of Santiago pilgrims. To reach Navarrenx I had to walk along the St.-Jacques trail that originates in Le-Puy-en-Velay but in the wrong direction. It was Sunday and soon the trickle of early risers turned into a flood. As I struggled up one hill a lady raised her eyebrows and asked the obvious question, "Why are you climbing?" As I was obviously out of step with the true pilgrims I felt I had to justify myself. First of all, I explained, I was doing a trip around the circumference of France *à pied*, but this just resulted in puzzlement. "I am walking to Lourdes," seemed like a better line to silence further questions. The average age of these walkers was high and I met two sprightly ladies in their seventies who were fit enough to cover over 200 miles finishing at Roncesvaux. They spoke in a Midi accent and came from Nîmes. "*Bons pieds, bons yeux pour l'instant*" (feet OK, eyes alright for the time being), one of them joked.

A man standing by a side altar in the church in Navarrenx boomed "*pèlerins ici*" in a heavy Béarnais accent. Every word he spoke seemed to end in "a" and sounded more like Italian than the machine gun French of the north. Having given a dramatic account of the history of Navarrenx he led us across to the parish rooms for a glass or two of chilled dessert wine. Swiss and German pilgrims mixed with French, but I was the lone Englishman. Only four per cent of those attending the weekly receptions come from Great Britain. Our host sang a song in Béarnais, a variation on the Occitan language of the south. Later I heard the same local twang as two ladies led prayers at the pilgrims' mass. The priest judging from his voice was not a local.

Over a delicious supper four guests at the *Relais Jacquet* entertained me with a stream of banter. They were a group of male friends from the Champagne region and all in different ways involved in making fizz. One was a grower, another bought grapes for the big houses, a third printed labels and a fourth was a salesman. They were walking the Compostela trail, but one of them had sprained his ankle and had to drive the backup vehicle. We all laughed about the problems of sleeping in big refuges with other people snoring. The grower said, "My friend here is a great guy, but when he snores he sounds like the engines of the *Titanic* before it sank. I throw rucksacks at him to make him shut up but nothing works." Their departure next morning was equally noisy as they went off down the street playing whistles and a trumpet.

The Béarnais farmhouses in the valley of the Gave d'Oloron were quite different from those only a few miles behind me in the Basque Country. Tall and rectangular, their slate roofs soared towards the sky at a dizzying angle. Solid mullioned windows, towers and stone arched gateways suggested a prosperous agriculture in centuries gone by. Navarrenx had its old houses too, but their purpose was quite different. In the sixteenth century the Kings of Navarre turned the town into a royal fortress, hiring an Italian military architect familiar with the latest techniques. The massive walls tower above the river and when Vauban visited a century later he only had to make a few minor adjustments to the defences. The Navarrese finished the work just in time. In 1563 the Queen of Navarre became a Protestant and turned the recently completed church into a Protestant *temple*. The walls were strong enough to defeat Catholic adversaries for sixty years. In 1620 the Protestant governor left his elegant house on the Place d'Armes to present the city's keys and the treasure of the Kings of Navarre to Louis XIII.

Roads of nondescript villas spread across the plain around Oloron-Ste.-Marie. Ste.-Marie grew up as a pilgrimage town and the entrance to the cathedral shows Romanesque sculpture at its finest: the twenty-four Elders of the Apocalypse playing all sorts of medieval instruments, scenes from everyday life in the Béarn including a boar hunt and fishing for salmon. The eyes of the figures may look a little alarming, but that is because they were filled with glass in the nineteenth century.

In Oloron on the other side of the river I met Patrick and Corinne. His father came from Almeria in southern Spain but his mother was Norman and they had gone to seek their fortune in French Morocco where Patrick grew up. Over supper on the terrace they told me about life in the valley. The population had grown in recent years and was now about 24,000. There was quite a lot of industry in the valley including Lindt, the chocolate firm. Communications were good. Bordeaux and Toulouse were only two and a half hours away by road. Everyone wanted a house with a garden and farmers were selling their land and developers building new estates. I had noticed this all over western France. Since the financial crisis property prices had slumped. Young people were struggling to find work and lived longer with their parents. "Messier-Dowty makes undercarriages for the Airbus and is setting up a factory in Mexico. The union is worried that the Oloron factory will shut down and all the work will move abroad. This has happened in so many other places. Threatening strikes and offering financial incentives won't affect the outcome. If they want to leave they will."

A thick canopy of oak and beech covered the turbulent Gave d'Ossau. Then suddenly I emerged from the woods to find the mountains right in front of me, steep tree-covered slopes leading to rocky pastures and in the distance gullies filled with snow. For a few miles I trekked across a ridge of heather and bracken, with scarcely a house in sight in the deep valley below. The outer buttresses of the Pyrenees stretched in a straight line to Bétharram. Once there I would only have a short distance to walk to reach Lourdes, the end of the journey. It was difficult to believe a path 4,000 miles long stretched behind me, yet I felt only the slightest sense of anticipation.

In a gloomy dining room a young Italian with long hair and dreamy eyes looked like a prince from one of Botticelli's paintings. His French and English were minimal, but I gathered he was covering 25 miles a day on the Compostela trail having started in Venice. Another five hundred miles to go, twenty days, no problem! Not long after I met another of his compatriots. On a blazing white track a pilgrim suddenly shouted out to me from a few yards away.

"I am lost! Where am I? Italia! Italia!"

I found it difficult to understand his confusion because we were only a short distance from a village. Surely he did not think he was in Italy. He looked distracted and there was a strange glow in his eyes. He carried a long wooden staff with an amethyst and a crystal ball on top. A large gold cross hung around his neck.

"I am walking to Fatima in Portugal," he said, "and then back to Compostela."

Benoît and Paulette's farmhouse stood on a col. The late afternoon sun was still bouncing off the road outside, but Paulette's shuttered kitchen was like an ice box. The marble table top, stone walls and cherry wood furniture, with its deep brown patina, looked as if they had been there for generations. Benoît and Paulette's welcome was simple and from the heart. They were clearly devoted to each other and had run the farm together all their lives. Benoît was born here and the land had been in his family for several generations. Now his children had departed for the large towns and none of their eight grandchildren was interested in farming. They did not visit often, preferring beach holidays. Benoît and Paulette knew that one day they would have to sell up and move into a retirement home. They accepted this stoically but I felt a pang of sorrow for them. Another element of the old world of hill farming in the Béarn would disappear.

For the moment they were still active enough to maintain a fine vegetable garden. Over a delicious farm supper of tomato soup, home-made sausages and Paulette's apple tart we talked about the changes in their world. Both had strong local accents. Benoît spoke Béarnais when he was young, as did most of his school friends, but the teacher used to encourage them to talk only in French. Now the local language is being reintroduced into the school curriculum, yet even so Benoît was not very tolerant of regional minorities demanding special rights. "The Basques always want something extra they can keep for themselves," he said.

Benoît and Paulette grew up in a very different environment, but easily accepted many features of modern life. They were aware of the economic crisis and how it threatened employment in their region. Being old they worried about local services they needed and believed that in France there were not enough doctors willing to work in the countryside. If you were taken ill at home you either had to call someone from Pau twenty miles away or phone the fire brigade.

I told Paulette about the strange pilgrim I had met on the trail. She said, "You meet a lot of people like that on the trail to Santiago. *Un peu illuminé.*" She meant, with more than a touch of irony, that a heavenly light surrounded them.

Paulette and Benoît liked to receive pilgrims. Offering hospitality brought the world to their doorstep and they enjoyed getting cards and letters from the USA, Canada, Australia, Germany and elsewhere. "Pilgrims often turn up with no money," he said "but we let them sleep in the field opposite and give them breakfast. We've had Russians sleeping there recently. Most of the pilgrims are educated people. They know how to behave."

"Some of them are troubled," Paulette added. "They're not necessarily religious, but they come away to sort their heads out."

At ten that evening a dreamy young man arrived leading a white horse. He looked like a portrait of a Romantic poet. He said he had ridden all the way from the Camargue and seemed to think he would have no trouble finding hay for the horse and somewhere to sleep. He did not have the money for stabling. The eyes of the horse stared blankly at us betraying exhaustion, hunger and thirst. Benoît

said, "None of the farmers around here have any hay left. Most of the grass has been eaten by cattle. I've got maize pellets for my chickens, but I can only spare a couple of handfuls."

Opposite the house Benoît owned a steep field which plunged downhill to a thicket. "You can put your horse in there," he told the young man. "He won't get out easily. You can sleep on the veranda of the bungalow we are building."

Paulette wondered what he would do on the journey through the mountains if his horse lost a shoe. We left him to settle down for the night under the stars. Maybe he was right not to worry about such practical matters as food and water.

I woke up in the middle of the night and stared out of the window above my bed. The full moon shed a bright pearlescent light over the mountains, its glare softened by wisps of mist in the valleys. The sweet smell of fresh grass wafted in from the fields. I tried to retain every contour in my memory. Next morning Paulette was keen that I should take the best possible path to Lourdes. She wrote out detailed instructions and repeated several times, "the Gave must always be on your left." I was approaching the end of my escape around France on foot.

LOURDES

After leaving Benoît and Paulette I went to the top of the hill above Bétharram to find the cemetery of the Catholic fathers who had gone out from the abbey below to save the world, but returned here for their final rest. Beneath three large *calvaires* and amidst straggling roses I found the graves of priests who had travelled all over South America, Morocco and China. The Way of the Cross zigzagged downhill through fine beech woods to Notre-Dame de Bétharram below. At each turn a neo-Romanesque chapel sheltered a relief portraying an episode in Jesus' last hours

Bétharram means *beau rameau*, beautiful branch in Gascon. According to an old story a young girl was drowning in the river, but was saved when the Virgin held out a branch on which she could pull herself to safety. The interior of Notre-Dame de Bétharram has a unity of style not to be found in every baroque church of the seventeenth century. Moreover, the walls are decorated in bright colours, gold, blue and red, rather than the sombre grey of natural stone. Gold stars cover the blue ceiling like the sky at night; crystal chandeliers sparkle over the nave; a golden angel with a trumpet proclaims the Good News from the top of the pulpit; rich paintings of biblical scenes in heavy gilt frames adorn the walls; medallions surrounded in red and gold depict the prophets of the Old

Testament. This is a religion of the senses rather than the intellect. Next door are the massive white walls of the Notre-Dame seminary, the headquarters of the Congregation of Priests of the Sacred Heart founded in 1837.

The sun flashed on the rippling river, producing an effect like a constantly changing electronic display. As I entered the last gorge before Lourdes the midday angelus floated on the breeze. Little light reached the forest floor and an invisible ghostly train rattled past on the other side of the river. Gradually the branches parted to reveal blue sky above, but the contours of the surrounding mountains were swamped in a sea of leaves. I tried to imagine how wild this country might have been in 1858 when Bernadette Soubirous first saw her visions of the Virgin.

Unexpectedly houses appeared and the journey, which took three years to

Bernadette and her lambs

plan and execute, was almost over. I came into the blinding light of the esplanade by the river, with the faithful filing past the grotto to signify their trust in God. I lit a candle for a friend at home with cancer and then came face to face with suffering. I had walked many miles on my own two feet and here in front of me was a man in a wheelchair, paralysed from the neck down. He was from County Cork. His nurse asked if I had walked here as a pilgrimage. He had suffered a double blow in that his son had died recently in an accident. I spent some time talking to him and posed for photographs.

A long procession wound its way from the grotto, where the Virgin Mary is said to have appeared to Bernadette, to the vast square in front of the Basilica of the Rosary. Pilgrims from all over Europe carried banners and candles: from Poland, Spain, Italy, Germany, Croatia, Ireland and Great Britain. Their chants were warm and reflective, unlike the marching tunes of our Protestant culture. Repeatedly they raised their candles in praise of Mary, the Immaculate Conception, and eventually She appeared borne under a canopy. Young people in uniforms and nurses with starched aprons pushed the sick in wheelchairs. There were crippled children pushed by parents, adults afflicted by every imaginable ailment, a tide of human suffering borne patiently at least for a night. The scene was reminiscent of the crowds of sick people desperate to see Jesus in the Gospels. The lights of the faithful glowed on the staircases rising above the Rosary dome and spotlights played on the golden crown. Many casual bystanders may have felt a lump in their throats. Over five million believers come here every year. If you are a postmodern sceptic and you think popular faith is dead, you had better think again at Lourdes.

The small Pyrenean town of 4,000, which Lourdes once was, has been submerged by the pilgrimage industry. From the castle gardens I surveyed the religious site which has tamed the natural wildness of a river running through a Pyrenean valley. Whether you are a non-believer or a Protestant like me, there is much at Lourdes which seems downright vulgar and kitsch: the shops full of cheap souvenirs, the bottles of holy water. Religious tourism at Lourdes is on an industrial scale. The cafés with their neon signs and the shops and package tours seem to have overwhelmed the place. The still, small voice heard by Elijah would be drowned out here. The hotel where I stayed was huge, the service impersonal and the food poor.

The Virgin told Bernadette, "Go, tell the priests to come in procession and build a chapel here." Since 1858 they have certainly done that. There is the Basilica of the Immaculate Conception built on top of the rock in Gothic style, the neo-Byzantine Rosary Basilica with its rich mosaics and the Basilica of Pius X, a vast underground public car park. Linking them together is a square which can accommodate 100,000 people. And then there is the belief in cures; that somehow a pilgrimage to Lourdes might result in a miraculous release from disease. This sort of belief linked to a saint and a spring goes back a long way, as we have seen in Brittany. But what place does it have in the twenty-first century?

There is another way of looking at this outpouring of faith. If sitting in silence by the grotto, or being pushed forward by a young person, makes a sufferer from cancer better able to face what is to come, makes him or her feel supported by the love of other humans and ultimately by Christ, then it has some value. There are also plenty of Catholic youth groups in Lourdes and the laughter of young people fills the streets, another comfort perhaps to the old and sick. The story of Bernadette at the grotto is rich in symbolism: the rock of faith, the water which washes mankind clean of sin, the candle symbolising the light of Christ coming into the world. It is possible to feel the power of this symbolism while remaining agnostic on miracles. This sort of experience still meets a deep-seated human need.

It is worth recalling that the hierarchy greeted news of Bernadette's apparitions with scepticism one hundred and fifty years ago. It was four years before the Bishop of Tarbes declared them to be genuine and he had to be nudged along by the French Emperor Napoleon III, whose wife was a devout Catholic and whose son was a sickly child. The Church was simply confirming what many Catholics believed, in the same way that in 1854 the doctrine of the Immaculate Conception set the seal on many centuries of popular devotion to the Virgin.

Lourdes might seem a strange place to have finished my journey. On the surface it is hardly characteristic of modern France; the land of the Enlightenment and thought by most Anglo-Saxons to be the most secular state in Europe. In the town square at Pons in the Saintonge I had passed a statue of its favourite son, Émile Combes, who helped ensure that the French Republic and its institutions are secular. Surely France is the country where the wearing of all religious symbols has been banned in schools. Yet what Lourdes shows is that all such generalisations about a country are flawed. Although traditional Catholic worship is in decline in France, the legacy of nineteenth-century mysticism, emphasizing love and forgiveness rather than judgement, still lives on.

POSTSCRIPT

LOURDES BROUGHT ME back to the question of suffering in a personal way. My mother is now confined to a wheelchair in a care home. The last act in the story of her decline was played out on my mobile in the forests of the Landes. She caught another infection which affected her mind and made her fight like a wild animal. She went to hospital for treatment and then the doctors would not release her back to her flat without twenty-four hour care, which was impractical. For several days I made frenzied calls to social workers, nurses and a care home manager, while walking down forest tracks. Eventually I arranged for her to be admitted to Cedar Lawn, without coming home myself until I reached the end of my walk. I knew she would be well looked after but still felt guilty. I comforted myself that if she had been well, she would have urged me to finish the job.

My mother hated the home and resented her dependence on the staff. "I'll get the buggers," she used to say. When she was frightened she would lash out. For a period the doctor authorised sedative drugs. Now she has good days and bad days. Sometimes we chat about the past but her talk is a struggle for forgotten words. Frequently it degenerates into verbiage addressed to her soft toys. When she smears a chocolate ice cream across her face she has the impish grin of a naughty child. In high spirits she puts on her stage voice, reminiscent of the Noel Coward plays in which she once acted: "how awfully kind of you darling!" Then she downs a glass of sherry with a flourish. Unfortunately these antics don't keep the dark shadows at bay for long. Insecurity comes back to haunt her like a nightmare. Then she sobs, cries out for her mother or shouts, "God is the key to all unknown."

Shortly after I returned to the UK my father forgot to turn off the gas on an old fire and it leaked into the house while he was asleep upstairs. Neighbours alerted the emergency services. He had no idea what was going on. He did not like carers coming in but it was obvious he needed constant help. Previously a lawyer who used to handle large property deals, he now panicked about the simplest things. He repeated every question endlessly. Even the smallest rearrangement of the furniture in his room disturbed him. His poor memory made reading books difficult. He was also humiliated by his prostate problems.

Now he is settled in a residential home near me he looks in better health and has put on weight. His library of books remains unread in the arts and crafts oak bookcase that belonged to my grandfather. His extensive collection of classical CDs is gathering dust on a shelf. The TV is never switched on and the radio stays silent. He is polite and courteous to the other residents but can't be bothered with small talk. He dips into the *New Statesman* magazine and I can still reprise the discussions on politics I enjoyed as a boy. The routine of the institution fills most of each day: breakfast, coffee, lunch, tea, supper, with the added irritation of an enforced bath three times a week. He often hangs his head in his hands and says, "I'm sorry. I feel very lost. I can't remember what I have to do next."

For both my parents time has lost all meaning and the past is slipping from their grasp. More and more I see how memory defines what it is to be human. Often we try to recreate the past to give ourselves comfort. Describing a landscape we have travelled through is just such an exercise. Sometimes, on the other hand, we try to escape memory's clutches and it comes back to plague us. Whatever our experience memory is an essential prop. Gradually Muriel and Peter are leaving the stage behind a curtain of confusion, their unique personalities disappearing in a vacuum.

I have been through the difficulties many children are experiencing with their elderly parents in our ageing society. The challenge is emotional as well as physical. When should you intervene? What help should you offer? How do you take over the things they cannot do without making them feel powerless and humiliated? How do you accept their behaviour as just an illness? How can you hold on to all the good things they did for you in the past?

It did not take long to discover the limits of my compassion. I resented the demands of the present and the burdens of the past. From time to time I became angry and then felt guilty. I tried to cope by putting my parents' condition out of my mind, to be in denial. I soon discovered this was a useless tactic. The memories of how they used to be would always come flooding back more powerfully than ever: my father jumping down the scree on Great Gable; my mother executing high kicks on the stage. With my limited understanding of old age dementia I made the critical mistake of challenging irrational behaviour and causing needless distress. It was only later that I discovered a better way: treating the fantasy world of confusion as entirely normal and getting on with what needed to be done without a confrontation. Acceptance of the situation took a long time.

Through all these upheavals my escape around France on foot helped to keep me sane. It opened up new experiences, new perspectives. The slow rhythm of walking was like a silent meditation, through which I gradually became reconciled to the past and its loss.

ACKNOWLEDGEMENTS

I WOULD LIKE TO acknowledge the help of many people who made this journey possible. Without the ability to converse in French I would have had nothing to write about. I am indebted to Norman Isaacs who taught me at KCS Wimbledon many years ago, and more recently to the staff of the Oxford University Continuing Education Department and to many friends in France who gave me the opportunity to practise. I studied French History at length in my youth and again I must thank the staff at KCS, and particularly Robin Reeve, and also my teachers at Peterhouse, Cambridge and University College, London. Mr. Christopher Dodd and the physiotherapists at the Nuffield Orthopaedic Centre in Oxford put my right knee back together. It hardly troubled me throughout my journey—a tribute to their skill. A number of friends, French and British, kept me going by joining me from time to time: Hugh and Sheina Macmillan, John and Etelka Davey, Alan Jordan, Charles Cunningham, Anne and Mike Page, Anthony Bryceson, Jacques Prouff, Annette and Alain Desaulty, Jean Remondeau and Raymond Foucher. I want to thank the carers who looked after my mother in my absence and in particular Beccy Garside. I am also grateful to Mike and Molly Sullivan, who did so much for my father while he was in his own home. Above all I thank my wife Lizzie, who accompanied me forty per cent of the way and who has lived with the mood swings of a first-time author.

INDEX

text